The Longman Companion to
Germany since 1945

Longman Companions to History

General Editors: Chris Cook and John Stevenson

Now available

The Longman Companion to

Germany since 1945

Adrian Webb

ONGMAN
·ndon and New York

Addison Wesley Longman Limited
Edinburgh Gate,
Harlow, Essex CM20 2JE, United Kingdom
and Associated Companies throughout the world.

Published in the United States of America by Addison Wesley Longman, New York.

First published 1998

ISBN 0–582–30736–8 CSD
ISBN 0–582–30737–6 PPR

British Library Cataloguing in Publication Data

A catalogue entry for this title is available from the British Library

Library of Congress Cataloging-in-Publication Data

Webb, Adrian, 1938–
   The Longman companion to Germany since 1945 / Adrian Webb.
      p.   cm. — (Longman companions to history)
   Includes bibliographical references and index.
   ISBN 0–582–30736–8. — ISBN 0–582–30737–6 (pbk.)
   1. Germany—History—1945–1990—Handbooks, manuals, etc.
   2. Germany—History—1945–1990—Chronology. I. Title. II. Series.
DD257.W39   1998
943.087—dc21   98–20576
                                                                    CIP

Set by 35 in 9½/12pt New Baskerville
Produced by Addison Wesley Longman Singapore (Pte) Ltd.,
Printed in Singapore

Dem Täubchen gewidmet

Contents

Acknowledgements

It is a welcome but demanding challenge to single out all those who have contributed to the realisation of this book, but I owe a particular debt to the late Dr Martin Warschauer who first introduced me to German language, life and letters. I must also express special appreciation to Professor John Röhl of the University of Sussex, under whom I first studied contemporary Germany, to Professor Bruce Graham, also at Sussex, who encouraged me to write this book, and to Dr Chris Cook and Dr John Stevenson, the series editors, for their advice and constant support.

I am indebted to the staffs and resources of the libraries of the University of Sussex, the West Sussex County Council, Chichester, and the German Historical Institute, London, and also to the German political parties and public bodies which responded to my queries so effectively. I am also grateful to Brian Hunter for his comments on the text. Needless to say such errors of fact or interpretation as remain are strictly mine.

Not least, I am grateful to the staff of Addison Wesley Longman for their invaluable role in turning a concept into a reality. My greatest thanks, however, must be reserved for my wife, Valerie, who gave hours of invaluable advice and comment on the manuscript as well as leading me through the detail of word processing.

Introductory note on German equivalents and usage

Those interested in Germany are not necessarily familiar either with its language or its institutions and the following brief notes are included here for their guidance in using the book.

The German federal system is appreciably different from the unitary British and French systems, and different again from the American federal system The German terms *Ministerpräsident*, with its plural *Ministerpräsidenten*, and *Land*, with its plural *Länder*, have therefore normally been preferred to the potentially misleading equivalents of 'prime minister' and 'state', which are commonly used. *Bundestag* or *Volkskammer* and *Bundesrat* or *Länderkammer* have similarly been preferred to the slightly ambiguous 'parliament'.

The political parties in Germany are normally known by their initials and that practice has been followed in this book, which has the added advantage of saving space. They are explained in the text, principally in section 2.4, but they are set out here also for easy reference:

BFD	*Bund Freies Deutschland*	Free Germany Association
BHE	*Block der Heimatvertriebenen und Entrechteten*	Refugee Party
CDU	*Christlich Demokratische Union Deutschlands*	Christian Democratic Union of Germany
CSU	*Christlich-Soziale Union*	Christian Social Union
DBD	*Demokratische Bauernpartei Deutschlands*	Democratic Farmers' Party of Germany
DKP	*Deutsche Kommunistische Partei*	German Communist Party
DP	*Deutsche Partei*	German Party
DRP	*Deutsche Reichspartei*	German Reich Party
DSU	*Deutsche Soziale Union*	German Social Union
DVU	*Deutsche Volksunion*	German People's Union
FDP	*Freie Demokratische Partei*	Free Democratic Party
FVP	*Freie Volkspartei*	Free People's Party
KPD	*Kommunistische Partei Deutschlands*	Communist Party of Germany
LDPD	*Liberal-Demokratische Partei Deutschlands*	Liberal-democratic Party of Germany

NDPD	*Nationaldemokratische Partei Deutschlands*	National Democratic Party of Germany
NPD	*Nationaldemokratische Partei Deutschlands*	National-democratic Party of Germany
PDS	*Partei des Demokratischen Sozialismus*	Party of Democratic Socialism
SED	*Sozialistische Einheitspartei Deutschlands*	Socialist Unity Party of Germany
SPD	*Sozialdemokratische Partei Deutschlands*	Social-democratic Party of Germany
SRP	*Sozialistische Reichspartei*	Socialist Reich Party
ZP	*Zentrum*	Centre Party

Most German cities are known by their German names in the English-speaking world, with a handful of exceptions such as Cologne (*Köln*) and Munich (*München*). Normal practice has been followed, but readers of older texts may find Aix-la-Chapelle for Aachen, Coblence or Coblenz for Koblenz, Francfort for Frankfurt, Mayence for Mainz, and others. Similarly, the eastern European names of cities in what was Germany or within the German cultural area have been adopted except in cases of particular relevance where both forms have been given, with the most appropriate name first, e.g. Gdansk (*Danzig*), Szczecin (*Stettin*), and Wroclaw (*Breslau*). The neutral descriptions East and West Germany have normally been preferred to the formal German Democratic Republic and Federal Republic of Germany.

Both some foreign countries, and cities and streets in East Germany, changed their names between 1945 and publication and have sometimes changed them back again. The names quoted in the text are those applicable at the time in question.

SECTION ONE

Historical chronology

1.1 The inheritance of May 1945

Although this Companion opens with the death of Hitler on 30 April 1945, history is a continuum and the attitudes and perceptions which were to help shape German history over the next 50 years were clearly discernible well before the War had drawn to its close. The distrust between the Soviet Union and the west dated back to the 1917 Russian revolution itself, when Churchill had famously urged that 'bolshevism be smothered in its cradle'. Many in 1939 and after would have much preferred to fight the Soviet Union in alliance with Germany rather than the other way round, a fact of which Stalin was very well aware. He was equally aware that as recently as 3 January 1945 the Americans had rejected his request for emergency credit of US$6,000 million at 2.25 per cent interest. Roosevelt's successor as American president, Truman, was, moreover, known to be highly antipathetic to the Soviet Union.

It can, though, easily be forgotten that in 1945 the tensions between America and France over Germany were often as great as those between America and the Soviet Union, if not greater. France in general, and General de Gaulle in particular, deeply resented the French exclusion from the conferences first at Yalta in February and then Potsdam, where the map of Europe was effectively redrawn. The Americans and the Soviets, and perhaps the British most of all, who felt they had been left in the lurch in 1940, tended to see such French protests as a distracting nuisance for the powers who had actually done most of the fighting. Even before the War was over, General de Gaulle and the American military government in Germany were locked in acrimonious dispute over who should occupy Stuttgart. De Gaulle's resolve, when he returned to power in 1958, to take France out of NATO's command structure could already be foreseen.

The underlying reality was that the impact of the War on the various victors had been utterly different and that fact shaped their attitudes and policies towards Germany throughout the postwar period. The damage to France was primarily psychological. Although Normandy had suffered severely, most of France had remained physically untouched and the largest human losses had been suffered by the deportees. The real wounds were the collapse of will in 1940 and the subsequent tacit acceptance of the Vichy regime. Moreover, after three wars with Germany in less than a century, the very concept of victory seemed to have lost much of its point.

The British saw things quite differently. It was they who had first declared war on Nazi expansionism, they who had stood alone against Hitler after the collapse of France and before the entry into the War of either the United States or the Soviet Union, and they who had created a total war economy without sacrificing democracy. The War had boosted their self-confidence after all the disappointments of the twenties and thirties. Human losses were moderate, and were shared by servicemen and civilians and between age groups in a way quite different from the concentrated killing of a male generation in the First World War. The British felt they had earned and deserved their victory. The real cost was financial. Britain had fought a war it literally could not afford, and was effectively bankrupt. Its last significant and truly independent act as a global power was arguably to come in 1947 when Bevin as Foreign Secretary persuaded an initially reluctant America to take over the anti-Communist role in Greece, which it could no longer afford to play.

The Americans were on the other hand in a positively benign situation. The War had never touched the American mainland, human losses were modest for the country's size, and were in any event attributable as much to the War against Japan as that against Germany, and American industry had profited from the stimulus of wartime production. Not least, Britain's debt was America's credit.

The impact of the War on the Soviet Union could hardly have been more different. Immense swathes of its most productive territory had been devastated by ferocious fighting since 1942 and human losses at perhaps 25 million were proportionately higher even than Germany's. Many citizens of the city of Minsk were reputedly still living in holes in the ground as late as 1952. All the Soviet Union had left was the prestige of the Red Army which had engaged perhaps 90 per cent of the German Army and won, and the associated prestige of the Communist system which had crushed Hitler's crusade to free Europe from bolshevism. Moscow in May 1945 totally shared London's delirious sense of victory over the forces of evil.

It is hardly surprising against this background that the postwar approach of the Allies to Germany was so different. France from the very beginning was thinking in terms of integration and internationalisation, if not quite in the sense in which they were later to be realised in the European Union. Britain's attention, however, was absorbed by its priorities of reform at home and reform of the Empire and the urgency of improving the dire financial situation. Germany, once defeated, very rapidly became almost a distraction from these pressing problems. America's immediate instinct was a return to isolationism, and the arguments used to persuade it to retain its involvement in Europe acquired an anti-Soviet slant almost by default. The Soviet Union, mindful that it had suffered from two unprovoked German assaults in fewer than 30 years and that in the last the declared German aim had been to eliminate Slav populations to clear the land for German settlement, was determined to ensure at all costs that Germany never had the ability to attack it again.

These very real differences of experience were both reinforced and confused by equally real ideological differences. Left-wing thinking argued that German Nazism was the direct consequence of capitalism. This point of view was strongest in the Soviet Union, whose Marxist-Leninist philosophy taught that capitalism was by definition aggressive and oppressive, but it was a view widely held also in the British Labour Party and on the French Left. The logic of this view was that Germany would have to be economically and socially restructured if it were not to rise again as an aggressive power, and that approach can be clearly discerned in the earlier Allied pronouncements on Germany. It was not, however, a view shared by the Americans, for whom capitalism was a liberating force, promoted by and itself promoting democracy. Whereas, therefore, the Soviet Union designedly sought to remould Germany from top to bottom in its own image, the Americans instinctively accepted the German status quo as soon as its specifically Nazi features had been removed. The British, for whom leading industrialists such as Krupp had been amongst the worst war criminals, made scant protest as the Americans, on whom they were all too financially dependent, promoted their reintegration in German society.

These conflicting interests, perceptions and ideological viewpoints were inevitably reflected amongst the Germans themselves. They knew very well that the Eastern Front had seen by far the worst Nazi excesses, and were afraid well before the War ended of what might be meted out on them once the situation was reversed. The western Allies, however great the bitterness they had incurred through their ruthless pursuit of saturation bombing – and that should never be underestimated – were almost always seen as the lesser evil. On the other hand, the interwar period in Germany had had many of the features of an intermittent civil war and many on the Left felt genuine gratitude to, and confidence in, the Soviet Union as the guardian not only of their personal interests but of scientifically demonstrable economic and political truths. Their sense of disgust when the western Allies and the Americans in particular proved willing to deal with the likes of General Gehlen when the War was barely over, was intense and the high proportion of former Nazis in such influential places as the foreign ministry in Adenauer's Germany was to prove a significant factor in East Germany's ability to retain a measure of public acceptance in its highly vulnerable early years.

There is a sense, though, in which all these considerations are barely relevant. Virtually all Germans were faced in May 1945 with the challenge of literal survival and in many important respects the real history of Germany in the first eighteen months after defeat is not what did happen but what did not happen. Mass starvation and mass epidemics of cholera and typhoid did not in fact occur, despite unparalleled devastation and population displacement on a scale, as others have pointed out, not seen in Europe since the barbarian invasions which marked the end of the Roman Empire. In part this was sheer good fortune but in part also it was the reflection of a measure of generosity on the part of the Allies who, in the case of Britain and the Soviet Union at least, were in desperate need themselves, which could not have been foreseen.

Such considerations no doubt encouraged those Germans who had any choice in the matter to make a fresh start. It may also be that the ordinary German had become more afraid of the Nazi state in its last years than he had consciously realised and felt a certain personal liberation even in total defeat. Certainly the fears of the Allies that the Nazi regime would continue underground, in such forms as the werewolf resistance organisation, proved totally unfounded whatever continuing sympathies the Nazi period may have enjoyed. Perhaps the fact that defeat was so absolute and in certain respects so rapid helped to draw a line under the past. The last year of the War had seen as many German deaths as the rest of the War combined. Perhaps again all sides were sobered by the inescapable evidence of their own destructiveness. The past was simply no longer an option.

1.2 Chronology of key events up to unification

1945

30 April. Hitler commits suicide in the State Chancellery in Berlin. The Soviet hammer and sickle is hoisted over the Reichstag.

1 May. Dönitz broadcasts from Hamburg that Hitler 'has fallen . . . at his command post . . . fighting to the last breath against Bolshevism and for Germany'. He, Grand-Admiral Dönitz, is his appointed successor as Führer.

2 May. Count Lutz von Schwerin-Krosigk, finance minister since 1932 and without strong party ties, broadcasts that he has been appointed by Dönitz as foreign minister.

7 May. End of the war in Europe with Germany's unconditional surrender to the three major Allies in Rheims, France. The terms are signed by Col.-Gen. Jodl representing both the German High Command and Grand-Admiral Dönitz as head of state. Soviet troops find charred bodies, believed to include that of Hitler, in the ruins of the Chancellery. They also find the bodies of Josef Goebbels, Nazi minister for propaganda, his wife and seven children in an air raid shelter nearby. All nine had taken poison.

8 May. V.E.Day. Germany surrenders formally in Berlin, with Field Marshal Keitel, General-Admiral von Friedeburg and Col.-Gen. Stumpf of the Luftwaffe signing for Germany.

11 May. Henry Stimson, American war secretary, announces that America, Britain, France and the Soviet Union have completed plans for a 'stern military government' for the whole of Germany pursuant to the Yalta Agreement. Each victor is to have its own zone of occupation, the boundaries of which are currently being drawn and to be represented on an Allied Control Council. General Eisenhower is to be the American representative on that Council and also the military governor of the American Zone of Occupation, with Lt-Col. Lucius Clay as his deputy.

14 May. Austria, united with Germany since the *Anschluss* of 1938, is given a separate government by the occupying Allies.

19 May. America takes over occupation of its provisional sector.

22 May. Field-Marshal Sir Bernard Montgomery is appointed Commander-in-Chief of the British Forces of Occupation in Germany and the British member of the Allied Control Council for Germany.

23 May. Heinrich Himmler, former chief of the German police, head of the SS and the Gestapo, and interior minister, commits suicide following his arrest by British troops at Bremervörde. He is buried in an unmarked grave with no religious service on 26 May.

Arrest of Grand-Admiral Dönitz, his 'Flensburg Government', the German High Command and many other leading Nazis. General-Admiral von Friedeburg, Commander-in-Chief of the German Navy, and a signatory of the capitulation in Rheims and Berlin, commits suicide.

30 May. Marshal Georgi Zhukov is appointed as the Soviet representative on the Allied Control Council. (General de Lattre de Tassigny had earlier been appointed by France.)

The first batch of 300,000 German soldiers to be demobilised in the British Zone is allocated under 'Operation Barleycorn' to harvesting previously carried out by slave labour.

5 June. The 'Allied Representatives' (Montgomery, Eisenhower, de Lattre de Tassigny and Zhukov) acting by authority of their respective governments and in the interests of the UN formally declare:

> The Governments of the United Kingdom, the United States of America and the USSR and the Provisional Government of the French Republic, hereby assume supreme authority with respect to Germany, including all the powers possessed by the German Government, the High Command, and any State, municipal or local government or authority . . . The Governments of the United Kingdom, the USA, and the USSR, and the French Provisional Government, will hereafter determine the boundaries of Germany or any part thereof, and the status of Germany or of any area at present being part of German territory.

The following joint statement was issued on the zones of occupation in Germany:

> 1. Germany, within her frontiers as they were on Dec 31, 1937, will for the purposes of occupation, be divided into four zones, one to be allotted to each power as follows:
> An Eastern zone to the Union of Soviet Socialist Republics;
> A North-Western zone to the United Kingdom;
> A South-Western zone to the United States of America;
> A Western zone to France.
> The occupying forces in each zone will be under a Commander-in-Chief, designated by the responsible power . . .
> (It was stated at the same time that there would be a permanent co-ordinating committee under the Control Council.)
> 2. The area of Greater Berlin will be occupied by forces of each of the Four Powers. An inter-Allied governing authority [in Russian, *komendatura*] consisting of four commandants, appointed by their

respective Commanders-in-Chief, will be established to direct jointly its administration.

[*Source*: Keesing's Contemporary Archives, pp. 7227–8]

11 June. The British start to replace the Americans as occupiers of the Northern Rhineland and Cologne following delimitation of the zones of occupation.

14 June. The British capture Joachim von Ribbentrop, the last of the Nazi leaders, other than Martin Bormann, to be accounted for. Bormann's body was finally identified in Berlin in 1998.

21 June. American forces withdraw from parts of eastern Germany in favour of Soviet forces, following delimitation of the Soviet Zone. They order many key German personnel to accompany them.

23 June. Final delimitation of the French Zone which is carved almost exclusively out of the area under American occupation.

1 July. The British withdraw from Magdeburg and from parts of Mecklenburg, including Wismar and Schwerin, now in the Soviet Zone.

14 July. The 'non-fraternisation' order in the American and British Zones is relaxed to allow troops to talk with Germans in streets and public places, but not to enter private houses.

17 July. The Big Three Summit between Truman, Churchill (replaced by Attlee following his appointment as prime minister on 26 July) and Stalin opens at the Cecilienhof, Potsdam, just outside Berlin.

2 August. Potsdam Conference ends with agreement on the decartelisation, demilitarisation, denazification and democratisation of Germany. The arms industry and the monopolies are to be dismantled and an economy devoted to peaceful purposes built up. Support is pledged for the German people in establishing a unitary, democratic state and a living standard at the level of Europe excluding Great Britain and the Soviet Union. The Oder-Neisse line is accepted pending a peace settlement as Germany's eastern boundary and the northern part of East Prussia including Königsberg (now Kaliningrad) is to be transferred to the Soviet Union (see map 2, p. 318). Germans living in Poland, Czechoslovakia and Hungary are to be transferred to Germany in an orderly manner. Germany is placed under an obligation to pay reparations, and to be treated as an economic whole.

8 August. The agreement is signed in London between the representatives of the four Allies, establishing the International Military Tribunal for the trial of war crimes, including crimes against peace and crimes against humanity. The initial trials are to be held in Nuremberg.

13 August. Sir Hartley Shawcross, the Attorney-General, is nominated as chief prosecutor for Great Britain.

29 August. Publication in London of the names of the first accused to be tried at Nuremberg. (See 'War crimes' in *Glossary* for fuller particulars.)

3 September. The provincial administration of Saxony-Anhalt decrees a land reform which acts as a model throughout the Soviet Zone. All holdings of more than 100 hectares are expropriated without compensation, as is all land owned by Nazi activists and war criminals. Some 2.2 million hectares are parcelled out among 120,000 farm labourers, 165,000 smallholders, 91,000 expellees and others. The proportion of agricultural land confiscated is at its highest in Mecklenburg at 54 per cent.

11 September. M. François de Menthon, the former minister of justice, is nominated as chief prosecutor for France.

11 September–2 October. The London Conference of foreign ministers of the Allies, including China and France, established at Potsdam to draft peace treaties with the former enemy states, meets but collapses in disagreement.

The French urge reconsideration of the proposed appointment of state secretaries for German administrations to prepare for the envisaged central German government, arguing that Germany is being refashioned on centralised lines before it is known whether any parts of it wish to draw away from Prussia. They also seek full consideration of their plans for the permanent administration of the Rhineland and the Ruhr by America, Belgium, Britain, France, Luxembourg, the Netherlands and the Soviet Union.

25 September. The Allied Control Council in Berlin announces 'certain additional requirements arising from the complete defeat and unconditional surrender of Germany, with which Germany must comply' in pursuance of the decisions reached at Potsdam. They include the termination of all diplomatic and commercial relations, the complete and final abolition of the General Staff and of the Nazi Party, and the payment of reparations and occupation costs.

29 September. General Eisenhower, American Commander-in-Chief, reports that average German food consumption is about one third below the recognised subsistence level of 2000 calories daily. He argues also that the presence of zonal boundaries is disrupting economic activity and notes that the American Zone includes only a small part of Germany's industry and none of its coal.

30 September. The 'non-fraternisation' order is further relaxed to allow American and British troops to enter private homes. Mixed marriages, however, remain banned until 31 July 1946 in the British Zone and 11 December 1946 in the American Zone. 'Non-fraternisation' orders had not been promulgated in the Soviet Zone.

A levy of clothing, blankets and footwear is imposed on Germans in the British Zone for distribution to those in particular need, including Allied displaced persons, concentration camp victims, and former prisoners of war.

2 October. Field-Marshal Montgomery warns of a West German famine and economic collapse. His target food ration of 1,500 calories daily compares with the British civilian ration of 2,800 calories, but is still not being achieved everywhere.

12 October. The Allied Control Council seizes and confiscates I. G. Farbenindustrie, then the world's largest chemical conglomerate. Much of the plant is to be dismantled and sent abroad as reparations.

16 October. Preliminary estimates of food import requirements in the three western zones for 1945–46 amount to some 4 million tons of grain, if a daily ration of 2,000 calories for the non-farm population is to be sustained. The estimates omit the needs of the up to ten million expellees from the east.

21 October. The British blow up the U-boat pens at Hamburg.

11 November. Britain announces that it is sending 112,500 tons of wheat, 50,000 tons of potatoes and thousands of army ration packs to its zone to ward off mass hunger.

16 November. The Allied Military Government confiscates all undertakings of Krupp of Essen.

20 November. An Allied Control Council law bans all sports clubs whose activities might be turned to military use. They range from boxing to cycling, rowing and skiing.

30 November. An Allied Control Council law aims to eliminate all forms of militarism by banning such organisations as ex-servicemen's associations and parades of any description, whether military or civil.

22 December. The British take over direct control of all coal mines in their zone. The French do likewise in their zone, including the Saar, three days later.

1946

9 January. The Allied Control Council decides to restrict German steel production capacity to 7.5 million tons annually, not more than 5.8 million in any one year to be produced without prior approval.

27 February. Food rations are significantly reduced throughout the British Zone, with a new rate of 1,014 calories for ordinary consumers compared with 1,500 calories in the American Zone. The British cabinet had decided in the context of a world food crisis that Germany should enjoy the lowest priority. Food riots follow, particularly in Hamburg and the Ruhr, in the ensuing months.

26 March. The Allied Control Council approves a plan on the level of postwar German industry. It divides industries into four categories and envisages a reduction in output to about 50 per cent of 1938 levels, equivalent to a reduction of some 30 per cent in the prewar standard of living.

1 April. Postal communications reopen between Germany and the rest of the world, excluding Japan and Spain, but censorship remains in force.

8 April. The CDU, KPD, LDPD and SPD jointly appeal to the Allied Control Council not to separate the Rhineland and the Ruhr from Germany. They argue that it cannot survive without the resources of those areas.

3 May. General Lucius Clay, the American deputy governor in Germany, suspends reparations from the American Zone and charges both France and the Soviet Union with being responsible for the failure of the Allies to agree over Germany.

22 May. The British blow up the Blohm and Voss naval shipyards in Hamburg. They had been among the largest in Germany.

30 June. The Soviet authorities prevent further movement out of their zone to the three other zones.

16 August. The Americans and the British reject the alternative French proposals to the American plan for the economic fusion of the zones on the grounds that the Potsdam Agreements envisage a central German administration. The Soviet Union concurs on 30 August.

6 September. James Byrnes, American secretary of state, speaking in Stuttgart, presages a more sympathetic stance by America towards Germany. He advocates a federal political structure and promises that American forces will remain until a lasting peace has been achieved. His speech is strongly attacked in France and Poland.

16 October. Ten of the eleven leading Nazis sentenced to death by the International Military Tribunal in Nuremberg are hanged in the gymnasium of Nuremberg prison. The eleventh, Hermann Göring, commits suicide in his cell the night before. (See 'War Crimes' in *Glossary* for fuller particulars.)

21 October. Some thousands of East German managerial and technical staff and their families are moved with their industrial plant to the Soviet Union under Operation Ossavakim.

1947

1 January. The American and British Zones are fused under a 'bizone' agreement. Formal responsibility for the administration of economic affairs in the American and British Zones is largely transferred to the German-run Administrative Office for Economic Affairs at Minden.

10 February. Peace treaties are signed by the Allies in Paris with Bulgaria, Finland, Hungary, Italy and Romania, but not with Germany.

1 March. The state of Prussia is formally liquidated by the Allied Control Council.

4 March. Britain and France sign the Treaty of Dunkirk as a defence against the possibility of future German aggression.

10 March–24 April. The American, British, French and Soviet foreign ministers, meeting in Moscow, again fail to agree on a German peace treaty. Mr Molotov seeks reparations of US$10 billion at 1938 prices, internationalisation of the Ruhr, recognition of the Oder-Neisse line as the German border, and a provisional all-German government based on the mass organisations as well as the political parties.

28 March–2 April. Hunger marches are held in Düsseldorf and throughout the Ruhr.

9 May. More than 150,000 people demonstrate in Hamburg against the shortage of food, which is alleged to have fallen to 800 calories per person. The British authorities blame the severe winter and the reluctance of farmers to deliver quotas.

23 May. America and Britain agree that there shall be German political representation in an 'Economic Council' in their bizone.

29 August. America and Britain agree a revised plan for the level of German industry based on an increase in the permitted output of steel. The French have major reservations lest the prewar disequilibrium between French and German heavy industry should be restored. The Soviet Union protests that the plan violates the Potsdam Agreement because it has been negotiated bilaterally.

5 October. The Saar elects its first Landtag. It returns a large majority for ratifying a constitution which makes the Saar autonomous within an economic union with France.

16 October. The Americans and the British decide to fix the final number of factories to be dismantled in their zones at 682, of which 496 are in the British Zone, as against an earlier total of 1,636. The decision provokes German resentment and unrest.

28 October. The American military government launches a campaign against communism throughout its zone. It is allegedly in response to an inflammatory address by Colonel Tulpanov, a Soviet political official, to a SED conference in Berlin.

1948

7 January. The Frankfurt Declaration by the American and British military governors proposes increased power and status for the German Economic Council. Both France and the Soviet Union dispute the governors' allegations that the changes are of a purely economic nature and without political significance.

16–29 January. Some 2.5 million people are involved in a number of protest strikes against food shortages in the American and British Zones. Maldistribution and the black market are primarily blamed for the shortages.

1 June. The Six-Power London Conference between America, Belgium, Britain, France, Luxembourg and the Netherlands agrees to establish a federal (West) German state.

18–26 June. A currency reform is introduced in the American, British and French Zones which replaces the *Reichsmark* (RM) with the *Deutsche Mark* (DM). In the Soviet Zone the *Reichsmark* is replaced by the *Mark der deutschen Notenbank* (MDN). The Soviet Union cites the reform as justification for the ensuing Berlin blockade.

24 June. The Soviet Union blockades all land routes across its zone into West Berlin. The Berlin airlift is launched two days later. (See section 5.2 for fuller particulars.)

28 December. A Six-Power agreement is reached on the statute of an International Authority for the Ruhr. It is bitterly opposed by the whole spectrum of West German politicians from Dr Adenauer of the CDU to Max Reimann of the KPD.

1949

8 April. The foreign ministers of the western Allies reach agreement in Washington on the terms of the Occupation Statute defining the powers to be reserved to them on the declaration of a West German state. They also agree on prior trizonal fusion.

4 May. The Soviet Union agrees to lift the Berlin blockade in return for Four-Power talks on Germany.

12 May. The Berlin blockade is raised.

10 August. Dr Adenauer, leader of the CDU, attacks Britain in a speech at Essen during the first Bundestag election campaign. He maintains that Ernest Bevin, the British foreign secretary, is alone in opposing German entry to the Council of Europe, that 'European unity with the inclusion of Germany would become a reality despite England' and that Britain through her dismantling policy is the 'main obstacle' to a 'reasonable solution' of the German problem.

11 August. Dr Schumacher, leader of the SPD, also attacks the dismantling programme and maintains that it is 'inadmissable to repair previously committed injustices by new injustices'. He also alleges that the 'persistent arrogance' and the 'incapacity to learn' of the Allies are the 'heaviest mortgages' on the establishment of German democracy.

14 August. The CDU/CSU with 139 seats emerges as the strongest party in the first Bundestag elections, followed by the SPD with 131.

7 September. The West German Bundestag (lower house) and Bundesrat (upper house) meet for the first time in Bonn.

12 September. The Federal Assembly, meeting in Bonn, elects Professor Theodor Heuss as West Germany's first president.

14 September. Dr Konrad Adenauer is elected as West Germany's first Chancellor by 202 votes to 142 with 44 abstentions and one spoilt paper. 202 votes were the absolute minimum for appointment on the first ballot.

21 September. The Federal Republic of Germany (West Germany) comes formally into existence. (See section 2.2 for fuller particulars.)

30 September. The Occupation Statute comes into force limiting the responsibilities of the occupation authorities in West Germany.

7 October. The German Democratic Republic (East Germany) is proclaimed in East Berlin. Unlike West Germany it has the power to conduct its own foreign relations and Rudolf Appelt becomes its first ambassador to the Soviet Union on 15 October. The western Allies refuse to recognise the new state and other non-Communist countries follow suit. (See section 2.3 for fuller particulars.)

12 October. The first East German government is announced under Otto Grotewohl of the SED, which has a clear majority in the government of ten to eight. (See section 2.3 for fuller particulars.)

15 November. Chancellor Adenauer announces that the western Allies are prepared to slow down the rate of dismantling.

22 November. The Petersberg Agreement, concluded at the Petersberg Hotel outside Bonn, eases many of the economic restrictions on West Germany in the Occupation Statute.

1950

22 January. Dr Thomas Dehler, West German FDP minister of justice, maintains in a speech in Hamburg that France was more responsible for the outbreak of the First World War than Germany and that Hitler was a 'product of Versailles'. The French high commissioner in Bonn protests the next day that 'such words in the mouth of a minister are of an extremely shocking character'. Chancellor Adenauer and his government dissociate themselves from Dr Dehler's remarks.

1 March. Food rationing other than for sugar ends in West Germany.

29 March. The West German refugee ministry reports that 1,148,000 German soldiers and 190,000 civilians are still missing after the Second World War. They are additional to an estimated 3 million killed and 3.4 million 'permanently wounded' as of 1945, many of whom had died prematurely.

9 May. West Germany accepts an invitation from the Council of Europe to become an associate member.

13 May. The western Allies issue a declaration on Germany in Paris, announcing that they are to relax controls over Germany progressively and restore its sovereignty to the maximum extent possible under an occupation regime. Chancellor Adenauer describes it the next day as an extraordinary step forward compared with the attitude of the western Allies hitherto.

23 May. The western Allies protest to the Soviet Union at the creation of the East German *Bereitschaften*, a militarised police force of some 50,000 men. They maintain that it is contrary to the Potsdam declaration outlawing German military organisations.

12 July. East Germany and Czechoslovakia sign an agreement for mutual assistance against the Colorado beetle. Both countries had accused America of dropping large numbers of the beetle, which destroys potato crops, since 22 May. America describes the charges as 'patently absurd'.

12–14 September. The foreign ministers of the western Allies, meeting in New York, agree to end the state of war with Germany, to permit the establishment of mobile police formations on a *Land* basis, to revise the Occupation Statute and to review the Prohibited and Limited Industries Agreement of 1949. The foreign ministers of Britain and France, Ernest Bevin and Robert Schuman, remain opposed to the principle of German rearmament in any form whatever.

15–18 September. America first seriously proposes West German rearmament at a meeting in New York of the NATO foreign ministers.

1 October. East Germany becomes a member of COMECON. (See section 3.3 for fuller particulars.)

24 October. René Pleven, French prime minister, launches the Pleven Plan for German rearmament within the structure of a federal European Army.

26 November. The new coalition government of Schleswig-Holstein has for the first time at *Land* level a *Ministerpräsident* and deputy, who had both been members of the Nazi Party. The new *Land* minister of reconstruction and transport had been a member of the SS.

19 December. The NATO council in Brussels agrees to West German rearmament in principle, but accepts that France may pursue it in the context of a federal European Army.

1951

31 January. The Americans release Dr Alfred Krupp von Bohlen und Halbach, former head of the Krupp arms works and imprisoned for war crimes. His property is restored to him on the grounds that the confiscation order was the only one to arise from the trials, was not a normal part of the American judicial system and was generally repugnant to American concepts of justice. (See 'War crimes' in *Glossary* for fuller particulars.)

6 March. The Allied High Commission conducts the first revision of the Occupation Statute. The revision permits the creation of a West German foreign ministry and gives West Germany the conditional right to conduct its own foreign relations.

15 March. Chancellor Adenauer becomes acting foreign minister.

3 April. The Allied High Commission in West Germany repeals the Prohibited and Limited Industries Agreement of 1949. The successor agreement is appreciably more limited in scope.

2 May. West Germany becomes a full member of the Council of Europe.

6 May. The neo-Nazi SRP obtains 11 per cent of the vote and sixteen seats in the Lower Saxony *Land* elections. The SRP had called for the restoration of the Third Reich including the *Anschluss* with Austria, and for a neutral Germany as a third force between America and the Soviet Union.

9 July. Britain formally ends its state of war with Germany. Australia, New Zealand and South Africa issue comparable proclamations.

Israel declares that:

> six years after the end of hostilities the German people have not made any expiation or reparation for the crimes committed by the Nazis. To this day the Germans continue to enjoy the possession of property stolen from their Jewish victims before they sent them to the death chambers. As long as this state of affairs continues,

Germany's war against the Jewish people cannot be regarded as having come to an end.

13 July. Cuba, Denmark, France and Norway formally end their state of war with Germany.

24 October. America formally ends its state of war with Germany.

21–22 November. The foreign ministers and high commissioners in Germany of the western Allies, together with Chancellor Adenauer, approve a draft agreement in Paris on the main principles of future relations between the western Allies and West Germany.

1952

8 February. The Bundestag approves West German participation in the Pleven-inspired European Defence Community (EDC) by 204 votes to 156, with six abstentions.

1 March. Heligoland is returned to West German control by the British, who had used the island as a bombing range since the War. The cost of reconstruction is estimated at some DM54 million.

10 March. The Soviet Union in the 'Stalin note' proposes a peace treaty to create a neutral, democratic and united Germany with its own defence forces.

25 March. The western Allies respond cautiously to the 'Stalin note'.

9 April. The Soviet Union submits a further note on a possible peace treaty.

29 April. A French airliner flying between Frankfurt and Berlin is attacked by Soviet fighters, injuring three on board. The Soviet Union maintains that it was flying outside the corridor.

1 May. Referring to the impending signing of the Treaties of Bonn and Paris by West Germany and the western Allies, President Pieck declares that East Germany will have to organise its armed defence if the West German people do not prevent 'the conscription of youth for the service of American imperialism'.

11 May. Some 30,000 West German Communists demonstrate in Essen against the 'Western war treaties', despite a police ban. One demonstrator is killed by the police in alleged self-defence.

13 May. The western Allies respond cautiously to the further Soviet note.

16 May. The SPD's executive committee rejects the proposed contractual agreements with the western Allies and demands new negotiations on a basis of 'genuine equality'. The SPD is exercised in particular by the question of the Saar and believes that reunification should take precedence over integration with the west.

21 May. The national committee of the East German National Front approves the establishment of military forces (*Streitkräfte*). Many former frontier and transport police are organised as the People's Police in Barracks (KVP).

26 May. Chancellor Adenauer and the foreign ministers of America, Dean Acheson, Britain, Antony Eden, and France, Robert Schuman, sign in Bonn the contractual arrangements formally ending the occupation of West Germany and restoring sovereignty to it. The key constituent convention on relations between West Germany and the western Allies revokes the Occupation Statute, abolishes the Allied High Commission and the *Land* commissioners, and converts the high commissioners into ambassadors. Under Article 2 of the convention, however, the western Allies retain their rights to station armed forces in West Germany, and their rights in Berlin and Germany as a whole, pending unification and a peace settlement.

The Treaty of Bonn is subject to the entry into force of the next day's Treaty of Paris.

27 May. Belgium, France, Italy, Luxembourg, the Netherlands and West Germany sign the Treaty of Paris, aiming to create the European Defence Community (EDC), whereby West German forces would be placed under common integrated control. (The Treaty fails to achieve ratification by France and therefore never comes into formal force.)

2 June. Dr Schumacher expresses the view of the SPD that the contractual agreements and the EDC treaty may provoke the full militarisation of East Germany.

9 July. Ulbricht announces that the Central Committee of the SED has decided that 'the planned construction of socialism should begin' in East Germany. He adds in accordance with Stalinist orthodoxy that 'the intensification of the class struggle is inevitable'.

14 July. An eight-month inquiry by a Bundestag committee into press allegations that leading officials of the West German ministry of foreign affairs were former Nazis or members of the ministry under the Nazi regime results in the dismissal of four, including the head of the personnel department. Seventeen others are exonerated, but three of them are considered inappropriate for foreign postings, including the former secretary of Ribbentrop's 'European Committee' established to work out Hitler's 'New Order'.

19 July. East Germany enforces its requirement that the churches sever connections with the west by refusing clergymen visas to attend congresses in West Germany.

24 July. East Germany establishes the 'Service for Germany' labour corps in which boys and girls of seventeen will serve, normally voluntarily, for six months. Members will be educated in Stalinism-Leninism and motivated with the ideal of the armed defence of their homeland.

26 July. East Germany imposes strict travel restrictions on its citizens. Those leaving their homes for three days or more will need prior police permission and those away from their homes for 24 hours will be required to register with the local police. The property of those fleeing, or preparing to flee, to the west will be confiscated as will second homes and branch businesses in West German ownership.

23 August. The Soviet Union again submits a note on a German peace treaty.

10 September. West Germany and Israel sign a reparations agreement whereby West Germany agrees to pay DM3.5 billion to Israel in goods and services over a twelve-year period. The agreement is strongly resented in the Arab world, which alleges that it will raise Israel's war potential.

23 September. The western Allies respond to the Soviet note of 23 August.

23 October. The West German Constitutional Court declares the SRP unconstitutional. (See sections 2.4 and 2.8 and under 'Remer' in *Biographies* for fuller particulars.)

2 December. At the request of Chancellor Adenauer the western Allies table a draft resolution at the UN recommending the establishment of a UN Commission to determine whether 'genuinely free and secret' elections could be organised throughout Germany. The draft resolution is opposed by the Soviet bloc and by Israel, with the latter insisting that very extensive 'moral guarantees' are required from Germany before its full sovereignty can be considered.

1953

15 January. Georg Dertinger, East German foreign minister (CDU), is arrested for spying.

The British high commissioner, acting under powers reserved in the revised Occupation Statute, arrests a group of seven former leading Nazis led by Dr Werner Naumann, nominated in Hitler's will to succeed Dr Goebbels as minister for propaganda. A second member, Dr Gustav Scheel, had been nominated in the will as minister of culture. No charges are brought and particular resentment is expressed by the BHE, the DP and the FDP at the suggestion that they might have been infiltrated by the Naumann Group.

3 March. Col.-General Alfred Jodl is posthumously exonerated by a denazification court in Munich of the war crimes for which he had been executed in 1946. (See 'War Crimes' in *Glossary* for fuller particulars.)

10 March. America maintains that two Czechoslovak fighters have attacked two American fighters over the American Zone of Germany and shot down one of them. Czechoslovakia maintains they had penetrated 25 miles inside its airspace and refused orders to land.

12 March. Soviet fighters shoot down a British bomber in the Hamburg–Berlin air corridor, killing the crew of seven. The Soviet Union maintains that it had intruded 75 miles inside East Germany and refused orders to land. The British admit that the bomber might have made a navigational error, but insist that it was unarmed and over the western Allied zone when shot down.

18 March. The Israeli reparations agreement is ratified by the Bundestag by 239 votes to 35 with 86 abstentions. Opponents include the DP and the KPD, together with individual members of the Bavarian Party, the CSU and the FDP. Those abstaining include the rest of the Bavarian Party, the Centre Party, the greater part of the FDP, and Dr Schäffer, West German finance minister.

19 March. The West German Bundestag ratifies the EDC Treaty.

1 April. The Naumann group is handed over to the West German authorities. Five are accused by them of conspiracy endangering the state.

East Germany introduces new work norms requiring an extra 10 per cent increase in output for no increase in wages and the forfeiture of 10 per cent of wages by workers who do not achieve the new norm.

6 April. Chancellor Adenauer begins the first ever visit of a German head of government to America. He lays a wreath at the monument of the unknown soldier at the national cemetery at Arlington.

1 May. East Germany withdraws ration cards from a large proportion of the middle class, including independent farmers, on the grounds that it is 'non-productive'. Some two million people are affected, a number of whom leave for the west.

11 May. Winston Churchill, British prime minister since 1951, annoys America, France and West Germany by calling for a summit meeting with the new post-Stalin Soviet leadership. Chancellor Adenauer fears a new 'Yalta'.

28 May. The Soviet Union follows western precedent by separating the military functions of its Commander-in-Chief from the diplomatic functions of the new post of high commissioner, which enjoys ambassadorial status.

9 June. The death of Stalin on 5 March is reflected in the announcement of the 'New Course' by the East German Politbüro. It admits to Party and governmental mistakes and promises an end to discrimination against non-conforming social groups. Teachers will no longer have to declare their loyalty to Marxism-Leninism. Amongst the specific measures announced two days later are the restoration of ration cards to all citizens, the return of small businesses and farms to their owners on application, and a review of judicial sentences.

14 June. East Germany announces the release of 4,000 political prisoners serving sentences of up to three years and the early release of another 1,500.

15 June. Some building workers strike in East Berlin.

16 June. 300 workers on building site 40 on Stalinallee (later Karl-Marx-Allee) initiate a demonstration through Berlin in favour of lower work norms. They are joined by thousands of fellow workers, but fail to be received at either official trade union or government level.

17 June. Between 300,000 and 372,000 workers, or some 5 per cent of the work-force, strike at more than 270 sites across East Germany. Some West Berliners participate in the demonstrations in East Berlin. The Soviet army and the 'People's Police in Barracks' suppress the demonstrations, killing 21 and injuring many more. An academic assessment of 1957 was to find that more than 1,000 East Germans had subsequently been imprisoned and seven sentenced to death.

The demonstrations nevertheless succeed in their economic if not their political objectives.

18 June. The Soviet military authorities announce that they have executed a West Berliner, Willy Goettling, for organising disturbances in the Soviet sector on the orders of a foreign power. The western Allies deny that they had employed him as an 'agent provocateur', although they accept that some of the killed and injured were from the western sectors.

22 June. East Germany responds to the demonstrations by withdrawing the new work norms introduced in April. It also increases pensions by 15–20 per cent, restores workers' cheap fares, diverts East Mark (MDN) 70 million from heavy industry to social housing, and ceases to deduct sickness leave from paid holidays.

1 July. Chancellor Adenauer claims in the Bundestag that, although definite figures are not available, there is reason to believe that 62 people have been sentenced to death and 25,000 imprisoned in East Germany subsequent to the demonstrations.

10 July. President Eisenhower of America offers Chancellor Adenauer US$15 million worth of foodstuffs to relieve the shortages in East Germany, and simultaneously asks the Soviet government to help with its distribution. The Soviet and East German governments indignantly reject the offer two days later.

15 July. East Germany calls for discussion of the German problem with West Germany under the slogan of 'Germans round one table'.

The foreign ministers of the western Allies gathered in Washington invite the Soviet minister to a meeting to discuss free all-German elections and the establishment of an all-German government.

27 July. America launches its food distribution programme from centres in West Berlin. Five million food parcels are distributed over the eleven-week programme period, with some 34 per cent of the recipients coming from East Berlin and the balance from East Germany.

4 August. The Soviet Union responds to the western invitation in the post-Korean War climate by seeking Chinese representation at a Five-Power conference to discuss international problems including Germany.

15 August. The Soviet Union suggests the creation of an all-German government elected by the East German Volkskammer and the West

German Bundestag. That government would then enact a democratic electoral law.

23 August. The Soviet Union announces that it will require no reparations from East Germany after 1 January 1954, and will relinquish the seized German companies functioning as Soviet concerns. (See section 3.3 for fuller particulars.)

24 August. Poland announces that it also will require no further reparations from East Germany.

The Soviet bloc promotes its legations in East Berlin to full embassies.

3 September. The SPD objects to the allegation by the American secretary of state that an electoral defeat for Dr Adenauer would be 'disastrous to Germany and the possibility of German unity'. It describes his allegation as 'a malicious attempt by the American government to interfere in the German elections' and an 'unbelievable attempt by the United States to deceive German voters by perverting the facts'.

6 September. The CDU/CSU wins the 2nd Bundestag elections, but remains dependent on coalition partners to form a government.

1954

25 January–18 February. The American, British, French and Soviet foreign ministers meeting in Berlin fail to agree on Germany. Molotov, for the Soviet Union, requires any future united Germany to be neutral.

12 March. Finland formally ends its state of war with Germany.

25 March. The Soviet Union recognises East Germany as a sovereign and independent state conducting its own internal and external affairs, but the former Soviet occupation forces remain in East Germany.

8 April. The western Allies state that they will continue to recognise the Soviet Union as the power responsible for its zone, and decline to recognise or deal with East Germany.

8 June. East Germany announces that Georg Dertinger has been sentenced to fifteen years' imprisonment with hard labour for espionage on behalf of America and Britain.

14 June. Four West Berliners, who appeared to have been kidnapped, are sentenced to terms of fifteen years, fifteen years, ten years and five years, all with hard labour, by the East German Supreme Court. They are accused of having been 'the main organisers of the fascist putsch of 17 June 1953' and of acting on the orders of 'espionage organisations' in West Berlin.

14 July. East Germany announces that Dr Karl Hamann, formerly minister of supply (LDPD), has been sentenced to ten years' imprisonment with hard labour for having 'sabotaged the nation's food supply'. He had been dismissed and arrested in December 1952. His LDPD co-chairman till that time, Dr Hans Loch, had accused him of responsibility for the deteriorating food situation.

20 July. The head of the West German security service, Otto John, apparently defects to East Berlin where he attacks Chancellor Adenauer as a neo-Nazi revanchist. (See *Biographies* for fuller particulars.)

6 August. Otto Grotewohl, East German prime minister, accepts American flood distress aid 'with thanks'. *Neues Deutschland* on 1 August had described the American offer as 'infamous' and a cloak for the infiltration of American spies.

The Soviet government annuls all decrees and ordinances issued by its military authorities in East Germany between 1945 and 1953.

30 August. The French Assembly votes against ratifying the EDC Treaty, and thus undermines the whole project. German rearmament is put in limbo as a result.

28 September–3 October. The London Conference of America, Belgium, Britain, Canada, France, Italy, Luxembourg, the Netherlands and West Germany agrees to rearm West Germany within NATO, to restore West German sovereignty and to found the Western European Union (WEU).

23 October. Chancellor Adenauer signs the Paris Agreements at the NATO Conference there, embodying the decisions reached at the preceding London Conference. (See *Glossary* for fuller particulars.)

20 December. The Soviet Union threatens to annul its alliance treaties against Germany of 1942 with Britain and 1944 with France if West Germany is rearmed.

30 December. The French Assembly ratifies October's Paris Agreements on German rearmament.

1955

15 January. A Soviet declaration considers it possible to come to an understanding on the establishment of appropriate international supervision of all-German elections.

25 January. The Soviet Union terminates its state of war with Germany. Czechoslovakia follows on 3 February, Poland on 18 February, Bulgaria on 1 March, Hungary on 22 March and China on 8 April.

3 March. The Allied High Commission permits the resumption of Lufthansa passenger flights starting from 1 April.

21 March. The Soviet Union announces that, following consultation between itself, East Germany, Albania, Bulgaria, Czechoslovakia, Hungary, Poland and Romania, there is unanimous agreement on the principles of a treaty of mutual defence and on the organisation of a unified command, in the event of ratification of the Paris Conference Agreements.

24 March. West Germany completes the ratification of the Paris Agreements on entry into the WEU and NATO, and the 1954 Franco-German agreement on the Saar. (See section 3.2 for fuller particulars.) The former had been bitterly opposed by the SPD, the latter by the SPD and the FDP.

5 May. The Paris Agreements of October 1954 come into formal effect. The western Allies thereby formally terminate their occupation of West Germany (but not of Berlin), leading the Soviet Union to annul its alliance treaties with Britain and France two days later. The Occupation Statute is revoked, and the High Commission and the *Land* commissioners abolished. West Germany is now fully sovereign and independent.

8 May. West Germany formally becomes a member of NATO and the WEU.

Otto Grotewohl announces that, in the light of the Paris Agreements, the *Volkspolizei* is to be 'developed into an effective instrument of defence'.

14 May. Following the ratification of the Paris Conference Agreements, East Germany and the countries of the Soviet bloc sign the Warsaw Pact.

15 May. The foreign ministers of America, Britain, France and the Soviet Union sign the Austrian State Treaty (Peace Treaty) on the basis of Austria's permanent neutrality. The Treaty specifically prohibits union (*Anschluss*) with Germany.

1–3 June. West Germany participates in the Messina Conference, which leads to the establishment of the European Economic Community (the Common Market) two years later. (See section 3.2 for fuller particulars.)

7 June. The Soviet Union invites Chancellor Adenauer to Moscow. He accepts.

24 July. The Geneva Summit of Eisenhower, Eden, Faure and Khrushchev ends with all Four Powers accepting 'their common responsibility for the settlement of the German question and the reunification of Germany . . . by means of free elections'.

26 July. Khrushchev claims in East Berlin that 'the mechanical re-unification of both parts of Germany which were developing in different directions' would be pointless. He makes no reference to free elections and claims that the East German workers would not accept the loss of their political and social achievements. Reunification was dependent on the establishment of a European collective security system.

8 August. The espionage agency under the former Lt-General Reinhard Gehlen is transferred from American to West German control. Lt-General Gehlen had directed the Wehrmacht's counter-intelligence on the eastern front, 1942–45, and his organisation of some 3–4,000 agents had been funded by the Americans since 1947.

12 August. Otto Grotewohl, the East German prime minister, calls for convergence and co-operation between East and West Germany.

8–13 September. Diplomatic relations are established between West Germany and the Soviet Union during Adenauer's visit there. Thousands of East German prisoners are released after his visit, but West Germany recognises neither East Germany nor the Oder-Neisse line as Germany's frontier with Poland.

20 September. An East German–Soviet treaty formally restores East German sovereignty. The Soviet High Commission is abolished and the

Soviet ambassador to East Berlin is charged with relations with the western Allies on all-German questions. Soviet forces remain with the approval of the East German government.

23 October. The Saar rejects in a plebiscite a statute proposing Europeanisation, and endorses reunion with West Germany.

27 October–16 November. The American, British, French and Soviet foreign ministers meeting in Geneva fail to agree on Germany and European security.

8 November. East Germany and Poland sign the Görlitz agreement. (See section 3.3 for fuller particulars.)

12 November. The first West German troops are commissioned.

9 December. Proclamation of the 'Hallstein Doctrine' by West Germany. (See section 3.1 and *Glossary* for fuller particulars.)

12 December. Otto John returns to West Germany claiming that he had been been kidnapped and that his attacks on Adenauer had been made under duress. (See *Biographies* for fuller particulars.)

15 December. West Germany is admitted to the UN Economic Commission for Europe, with Czechoslovakia and the Soviet Union dissenting.

1956

16 January. The Soviet Union effectively completes the return of the last 9,626 German prisoners, including 3,890 former prisoners of war, still held on war crimes charges. Their release had been a major objective of Chancellor Adenauer in his 1955 Moscow talks.

18 January. The Volkskammer approves the establishment of a National People's Army (*Nationale Volksarmee – NVA*).

27 January. East Germany conducts the first trial under the new political crime of 'incitement to flee the republic' (*Republikflucht*), introduced in December 1955.

22 April. The Soviet military in Berlin expose a 1-km American spy tunnel running from the American sector to the East German central telephone exchange. It had permitted the CIA, at a cost of $4 million, to eavesdrop on all East German and Soviet telephone conversations through East Berlin for more than nine months. The East German and Soviet authorities present it as a political tourist attraction for six weeks.

21 June. An SED investigatory committee into the administration of justice, established following Khrushchev's denunciation of Stalin at the 20th Congress of the Soviet Communist Party, rebukes the ministries of justice and state security and their ministers for malpractices, including the inappropriate introduction of ideology, and the arbitrary dispensation of justice. Ulbricht announces on the same day that almost 20,000 people have been released since the amnesty of April that year.

21 July. Legislation is approved introducing conscription to West Germany.

17 August. The KPD (West German Communist Party) is declared illegal by the West German Constitutional Court. (See section 2.8 for fuller particulars.)

6 October. The four FVP members of the cabinet resign over alleged CDU leaks of confidential discussions. The Chancellor reorganises his cabinet accordingly ten days later.

16 October. East Germany pardons Dr Hamann and releases him from prison.

31 December. The Saar is incorporated in West Germany at midnight as its tenth *Land*.

1957

10 February. Marshal Bulganin states in a letter to Chancellor Adenauer that the Soviet government is 'not satisfied' with the development of relations between the two countries since the Chancellor's visit to Moscow in 1955. The letter alleges that the organisers of NATO wish to use West Germany for an aggressive war against the interests of the German people. It continues that discussions should be held urgently on extended trade relations, on greater scientific and cultural co-operation, and on concluding a consular convention.

28 February. Chancellor Adenauer responds by agreeing that early talks be held on the questions raised by the Soviet Union. He also calls for the repatriation of German citizens allegedly held in the Soviet Union against their will, with particular reference to scientists at the nuclear research laboratory at Sukhumi on the Black Sea.

12 March. East Germany and the Soviet Union sign a treaty regulating the stationing of Soviet troops in East Germany. Soviet interests are pre-eminent.

25 March. West Germany signs the Treaty of Rome establishing the European Economic Community and the European Atomic Energy Authority. (See section 3.2 for fuller particulars.)

4 April. Chancellor Adenauer indicates that the *Bundeswehr* will have to be equipped with tactical nuclear weapons in view of developments in other countries' forces.

9 April. The Saarland government bans the Saar Communist Party on the instructions of the West German Constitutional Court. The two Communist members of the Landtag lose their seats accordingly.

12 April. Eighteen of West Germany's leading nuclear physicists, including the four Nobel prizewinners: Professors Otto Hahn, Werner Heisenberg, Max Born and Carl-Friedrich von Weizsäcker, issue a joint declaration from the Max Planck Institute in Göttingen that they will refuse to co-operate in any respect in the production, use or testing of nuclear weapons.

20 April. A letter from Marshal Bulganin, the Soviet prime minister, to Harold Macmillan, the British prime minister, shows renewed interest in the 'Eden Plan' of 1955 for a limited disarmament zone in central Europe.

27 April. The Soviet government accuses West Germany of becoming 'the main European springboard and chief NATO shock-force for atomic war in Europe'.

29 April. Dr Heinrich von Brentano, West German foreign minister, rebuts the Soviet accusation as grotesque and notes that West Germany is the only state in the world to have voluntarily renounced the right to produce atomic weapons. It will, however, provide for its own security with such weapons.

7–9 May. Harold Macmillan becomes the first British prime minister to visit West Germany since its establishment as a state.

10 June. West Germany makes the opening of talks on the topics agreed on 28 February conditional on parallel talks on repatriation.

5 July. The first three West German divisions are formally placed under NATO command at Marburg.

23 July. The West German–Soviet talks open, and last for nine months with numerous interruptions.

27 July. East Germany issues a proposal for a confederation between East and West Germany. It is subject to the preconditions that they withdraw from the Warsaw Pact and NATO respectively, that German armed forces be strictly limited and that the Four Powers reach agreement on the phased withdrawal of their forces, and that no nuclear weapons be held anywhere in Germany.

28 July. Chancellor Adenauer and the western Allies reject the East German proposal.

29 July. The western Allies and West Germany issue a twelve-point declaration of common policy on German reunification. It maintains that the reunification of Germany remains the joint responsibility of the Four Powers and that only a freely elected all-German government can undertake the consequent obligations.

7–14 August. Nikita Khrushchev, First Secretary of the Soviet Communist Party, pays a seven-day visit to East Germany.

8 August. Khrushchev, addressing a special session of the Volkskammer, supports the East German proposal for a confederation.

24 August. The first Luftwaffe squadron to become operational is placed under NATO.

15 September. The CDU/CSU under Adenauer wins the 3rd Bundestag elections, enjoying for the first time a majority of votes cast as well as seats.

2 October. The 'Rapacki Plan', named after its originator, the Polish foreign minister, is submitted to the UN General Assembly. The plan envisages a nuclear armaments-free zone in central Europe including the whole of Germany.

13 October. East Germany announces that all its paper currency in circulation is being withdrawn with immediate effect, and that exchange for new notes will be at par. Otto Grotewohl claims that the reform is necessary to prevent manipulation by elements in West Germany, where holdings of East Marks had been accumulating. Shoppers in West Berlin and refugees had been exchanging East Marks (MDN) for West Marks (DM) at the rate of four to one.

19 October. In accordance with the Hallstein Doctrine, West Germany severs relations with Yugoslavia for recognising East Germany the previous month. (See also section 3.3.)

11 December. The Volkskammer approves legislation whereby any person leaving East Germany without official authority will be subject to up to three years' imprisonment with hard labour and heavy fines.

1958

20 January. The Soviet Union agrees to repatriate to West Germany 21 scientists and rocket experts detained since 1945, latterly at Sukhumi. They had been offered repatriation to East Germany in 1956.

5 March. Franz-Josef Strauss, West German defence minister, announces in Washington that his government would accept an American offer of *Matador* pilotless bombers for its forces. The *Matador* could carry both conventional and nuclear weapons, but any nuclear warheads would remain under American control.

20–25 March. The Bundestag holds an impassioned four-day debate on foreign affairs and defence, the longest debate in its history to date. SPD and FDP speakers are sympathetic to the Rapacki Plan, but the concluding resolution, approved by 270 votes to 165, argues that West Germany must be equipped with the most modern weapons (in practice nuclear weapons) until a general disarmament agreement has been reached.

27 March. The SPD calls on the West German people to demand that the government reverse its decision to equip the *Bundeswehr* with nuclear weapons.

28 March. The executive of the German Trade Union Federation decides to organise demonstrations against the decision throughout the country.

Yugoslavia expresses its concern and considers referring the issue to the United Nations.

28–29 March. Extensive protest demonstrations are held in many major West German cities and universities.

2 April. The number of West German divisions under NATO command reaches seven.

10–12 April. The foreign ministers of East Germany, Czechoslovakia and Poland denounce the Bundestag resolution as a revival of German imperialism and militarism. They repeat their support for the Rapacki Plan.

25 April. The West German–Soviet talks opened in July 1957 result in the signature in Bonn by Dr von Brentano and Anastas Mikoyan, first vice-chairman of the Soviet Council of Ministers, of Soviet–German trade agreements and a consular convention.

3 May. America formally rejects the Rapacki Plan.

31 May. The western Allies put forward an agenda for a Summit meeting with the Soviet Union which includes German reunification.

2 July. The Bundestag unanimously approves a resolution calling on the Four Powers to appoint a working group to prepare joint proposals for the solution of the German question.

11 July. Khrushchev announces to the SED Congress that East Germany will not have to pay the East Mark (MDN) 600 million annual support costs of Soviet troops there after 1 January 1959.

5 September. The East German government proposes talks on a German peace treaty. It criticises the Bundestag resolution, maintaining that a decision on the unification of East and West Germany 'is the innate right of the German people themselves'. The western Allies decline to respond as it would imply recognition of East Germany.

9 September. The West German government refers July's Bundestag resolution to the Four Powers.

18 September. The Soviet Union endorses the East German proposals of an immediate peace treaty and a unification commission of representatives of the two Germanys.

East Germany, concerned at the heavy flow of doctors to the west, relaxes its campaign against independent doctors. They will be allowed to continue their private practices and to travel abroad, and their children will have the same rights of university entrance as those of workers and farmers.

30 September. The western Allies advise the Soviet Union that they are willing to discuss German unification in a Four-Power working group but reiterate their view that unification by free elections and the establishment of an all-German government must precede any peace treaty.

10 November. A Soviet note threatens a second Berlin crisis. (See section 5.2 for fuller particulars.)

1959

4–23 January. Anastas Mikoyan, a member of the Soviet Politbüro, travels to America informally with a view to reducing tensions over Berlin.

10 January. The Soviet Union proposes to all countries at war with Germany between 1939 and 1945 and to East and West Germany that a conference be held within two months, either in Prague or in Warsaw, to conclude a German peace treaty. It circulates its own draft text.

The Soviet Union also seeks to refute the arguments incorporated in western notes of 31 December 1958. (See section 5.2 for fuller particulars.) It maintains in particular that:

The quadripartite agreements on Berlin, as well as on Germany as a whole, are of a provisional nature, valid only for the period of the occupation of Germany. The occupation, however, is over. The Soviet Union, the United States, the United Kingdom, France, and other states have announced the ending of the state of war with Germany. In view of this, the contentions of the [notes] about certain rights to continue the occupation are obviously without foundation . . . the question of the unification of Germany has become an internal German problem which can be solved only through rapprochement and agreement between those states.

[*Source*: Keesing's Contemporary Archives, pp. 16709–10]

The Soviet draft text accordingly envisages unification on the basis of such rapprochement and agreement, and additionally requires Germany not to participate in any military alliance which does not also include America, Britain, France and the Soviet Union. West Berlin is to have the status of a demilitarised free city pending unification. These principles apart, the text is undogmatic.

26 January. The East German Chamber of Foreign Trade and the British Federation of British Industries conclude a trade agreement valued at some £7 million in each direction. The British Foreign Office insists that the agreement, which is not the first such between East Germany and a western European state, does not imply recognition of East Germany.

16 February. The western Allies respond to the Soviet Union with the counter-proposal of a Four-Power foreign ministers' conference, to discuss 'the problem of Germany in all its aspects and implications', with the participation of East and West German advisers.

1 March. The Soviet Union continues to urge a Summit in either Geneva or Vienna at the end of April, but accepts the foreign ministers' conference as an interim measure. It suggests that invitations also be extended to the Czechoslovak and Polish ministers.

9 March. Erich Ollenhauer, the leader of the West German SPD, meets Khrushchev in East Berlin at the latter's invitation. Ollenhauer reports subsequently that they were agreed that all problems should be solved by peaceful means and that acceptable solutions were available if goodwill was shown by both sides.

18 March. The SPD publishes its '*Deutschlandplan*', envisaging the progressive rapprochement of East and West Germany by means of an all-German Conference.

20 March. The West German government promises to give the plan its careful consideration, but criticises in particular the implied recognition of East Germany and possible constitutional developments prior to all-German elections.

26 March. The western Allies suggest that the foreign ministers meet in Geneva on 11 May. The Soviet Union agrees on 30 March.

3 April. The Central Committee of the SED writes to the SPD welcoming its proposals and calling for 'normal and comradely relations' between them.

6 April. The SPD executive decides not to respond.

7 April. Chancellor Adenauer agrees to stand for the West German presidency.

21 April. The Soviet Union protests against the stationing of nuclear armaments in West Germany.

11 May–20 June. The American, British, French and Soviet ministers conduct the first session of the Geneva talks on Germany. The East and West German ministers are allowed to attend in an advisory capacity.

5 June. Chancellor Adenauer advises the CDU executive that he is withdrawing his candidature for the forthcoming presidential election. It unsuccessfully asks him to reconsider his decision, which is the subject of strong criticism by the other parties. It is widely considered that the Chancellor's motive is to prevent Professor Erhard from succeeding him as Chancellor.

8–20 June. An East German governmental delegation led by Ulbricht and Grotewohl visits the Soviet Union.

The concluding communiqué reiterates the key points of Soviet policy towards Germany. They are: the conclusion of a peace treaty with 'the two German states now in existence'; the establishment of a confederation between them as a decisive step towards reunification; their conclusion of a treaty renouncing the use of force; and a new status of 'demilitarised free city' for West Berlin.

11 June. Grotewohl proposes a non-aggression pact between all the states on the Baltic coast at a mass meeting in Riga.

19 June. An interview with Chancellor Adenauer published in the *New York Times* reopens the dispute with Professor Erhard. It is formally settled by an exchange of letters four days later.

13 July–5 August. The continued talks on Germany in Geneva fail to achieve progress.

1 October. East Germany replaces the common flag with its own national one, of the same colours but with a hammer, compasses and corn device at the centre.

19–21 December. Eisenhower, Macmillan, de Gaulle and Adenauer, meeting in Paris, invite Khrushchev to a 1960 Summit.

24 December. The Cologne synagogue is daubed with swastikas and the slogan 'Germans demand – Jews get out' by two members of the far-right *Deutsche Reichspartei* (German Reich Party). The synagogue had only just been rebuilt following its destruction in the *Kristallnacht* of

November 1938. It stimulates a wave of swastika daubing throughout West Germany for which some 60 people ultimately receive prison sentences. Many of the incidents are attributable to children.

30 December. Wilhelm Meinberg, leader of the *Deutsche Reichspartei*, denies that it is anti-semitic, and claims that the party as such was not involved in the desecration.

1960

7 January. A. L. Easterman, political director of the European department of the World Jewish Congress, discusses the recent anti-semitic incidents with Dr von Brentano. He makes a number of proposals, including the removal of all former active Nazis from West German political, social and cultural life and a close watch on foreign anti-semitic refugee groups, 'especially Hungarians and Ukrainians'.

16 January. Chancellor Adenauer, broadcasting on all West German radio and television channels, denounces the desecration of the Cologne synagogue and the Cologne memorial to victims of Nazism as a 'disgrace and a crime' which had provoked 'in some other countries a wave of hatred against all Germans, in particular against the Germany of today'.

20 January. The Bundestag unanimously condemns the outbreak of anti-semitic vandalism.

David Ben-Gurion, Israeli prime minister, declares in the Knesset (parliament) that the recent anti-semitic incidents should affect neither Israeli–West German relations, nor Israeli arms sales to West Germany.

27 January. The Rhineland-Palatinate *Land* government bans the *Deutsche Reichspartei*. The leader of the *Land* party, Hans Schikora, had been elected to the Landtag in April 1959.

17 February. The West German government publishes a White Book analysing in detail the 685 anti-semitic incidents between 24 December 1959 and 28 January 1960. It finds no evidence of organised anti-semitism in West Germany, but blames the influence of the *Deutsche Reichspartei* in some cases, and also the impact of East German propaganda alleging anti-semitism and neo-Nazism and drawing attention to the number of former leading Nazis in important legal and political posts.

The German incidents are paralleled by 'copy cat' incidents throughout western Europe and in many other countries.

11 March. East German bishops protest to the East German government over the abuse of basic human rights during the execution of the collectivisation campaign.

14 March. Chancellor Adenauer and David Ben-Gurion, prime minister of Israel, meet for the first time, in New York. Their private meeting is later understood to have resulted in secret West German military aid to Israel of DM320 million, of which 80 per cent had been realised by 1965.

3 April. Bishop Dibelius asks his congregation in East Berlin to pray for their 'despairing brothers and sisters' in agricultural areas.

14 April. East Germany announces that the collectivisation of agriculture has been completed.

4 May. Professor Theodor Oberländer (CDU), West German minister for refugees, resigns following allegations of his involvement in Nazi war crimes in Poland and the Ukraine. (See *Biographies* for fuller particulars.)

16 May. The Summit Conference in Paris is abandoned in the aftermath of the Soviet shooting down of an American U-2 spy plane over Soviet territory.

20 May. Speaking in East Berlin following the breakdown of the Summit Conference, Khrushchev reasserts the Soviet Union's right to conclude a peace treaty with East Germany, but suggests that the situation in Berlin will have to be upheld pending a new Summit in perhaps six to eight months' time.

1961

10 March. Chancellor Adenauer expresses anxiety over the possible impact on world opinion of the Eichmann trial in Israel. He maintains that only a 'relatively small' proportion of Germans had been convinced Nazis and that the 'great majority' had been 'happy to help their Jewish fellow-citizens when they could'.

3–4 June. Khrushchev meets the new American president, John F. Kennedy, at a Summit in Vienna. (See section 5.2 for fuller particulars.)

30 June. Dr Gerstenmaier, president of the Bundestag, presents a declaration, issued with the support of all the parties represented there, appealing 'to the world and before history' for a German peace treaty based on the principle of self-determination by the whole German people.

6 July. The Volkskammer approves a 'German Peace Plan' presented by Ulbricht and closely reflecting Khrushchev's memorandum to Kennedy at the Vienna Summit. It envisages the establishment of a German Peace Commission comprising representatives of the parliaments and governments of the two Germanys.

7 July. Willy Brandt proposes a peace conference to be attended by all the 52 countries which had been at war with Germany. The proposal is strongly criticised by Chancellor Adenauer and Franz-Josef Strauss, the defence minister.

8 July. Khrushchev announces that the Soviet Union is to suspend the partial demobilisation of its armed forces and to increase its 1961 defence expenditure in the light of the growing military budgets in NATO countries, including the arming of West Germany with the latest weapons.

17 July. The western Allies reject any Soviet attempt to alter the position in Berlin unilaterally, and deny Soviet ability to conclude a valid peace treaty with East Germany. The detailed American note is a direct response to the Soviet memorandum presented to Kennedy in Vienna.

25 July. President Kennedy in a broadcast to the American people re-affirms the right of the western Allies to be in Berlin and to enjoy free access to it. He insists that 'we cannot permit the Communists to drive us out of Berlin; either gradually or by force', and adds that the freedom of West Berlin is 'not negotiable'. He announces planned additional defence expenditure of more than $3 billion in the current year and an increase in the size of the defence budget 'to meet a worldwide threat, on a basis which stretches far beyond the present Berlin crisis'. (See section 5.2 for fuller particulars of the crisis.)

3 August. The Soviet Union repeats that it will sign a separate peace treaty with East Germany, but with reluctance, if the western Allies con-tinue to refuse to conclude a German peace treaty with both German states.

5 August. A three-day meeting of the leaders of the member states of the Warsaw Pact is concluded with a declaration of their 'inflexible determina-tion' to conclude a separate peace treaty with East Germany, if necessary.

7 August. Khrushchev announces on Soviet television that the Soviet Union may have to move troops to its western borders in reply to the belligerent measures announced by Kennedy on 25 July. He also notes that America and Britain had earlier concluded a separate peace treaty with Japan.

10 August. Marshal Ivan Koniev, a leading Soviet soldier of the Second World War, is recalled from retirement to become Supreme Commander of the Soviet forces in East Germany.

13 August. The Berlin crisis reaches its climax as East German forces start to seal off East from West Berlin, and the Wall is erected within days.

31 August. The Soviet Union announces that it will resume the testing of nuclear weapons. Ten explosions follow in the next fortnight.

9 September. America announces that it is sending 40,000 troops to Europe in the immediate future, of whom most will go to West Germany.

12 September. West Germany announces that the 36,000 servicemen due to be demobilised at the end of September will be retained for another three months.

17 September. The CDU/CSU under Adenauer wins the 4th Bundestag elections, but loses its absolute majority.

18 September. The Soviet government denounces the 'Bonn–Paris Axis' emerging from the Franco-West German state visits (see section 3.2 for fuller particulars) and maintains that the 'present military collusion between the ruling circles of France and West Germany' emphasises the urgency of concluding a German peace treaty and normalising the situ-ation in West Berlin.

20 September. East Germany adopts the 'Law on the Defence of the German Democratic Republic'. It gives the government power to do whatever it thinks necessary in the political, economic and social fields against the 'increased war preparations of the West German militarists'.

7 November. Dr Adenauer is elected as West German Chancellor by the Bundestag for the fourth time. The FDP, however, only agrees to enter a coalition with the CDU/CSU on the understanding that Dr Adenauer will not serve as Chancellor throughout the term of the new Bundestag.

14 November. For the first time the new coalition cabinet includes a woman, Dr Elisabeth Schwarzhaupt (CDU).

12 December. The Soviet Union requests America to extradite General Adolf Heusinger, chairman of the NATO Military Committee in Permanent Session, to stand trial for war crimes. General Heusinger had been a Lieutenant General and Chief of Operations of the General Staff, land forces, during the war. America rejects the request three days later.

31 December. Ulbricht admits in the Soviet newsaper, *Pravda*, that the movement of East German workers to West Germany since 1949 has lost East Germany East Mark (MDN) 30 billion, equivalent to 40 per cent of national income over the same period.

1962

24 January. East Germany introduces compulsory military service of eighteen months for men aged 18–26.

22 February. West Germany increases the length of conscription by six months to eighteen months. Three of those months had been introduced on an emergency basis in September 1961 in response to the Berlin crisis.

2–8 July. Chancellor Adenauer pays a highly successful state visit to France, which is returned by President de Gaulle in September. They provide ceremonial confirmation of Franco-German reconciliation. (See section 3.2 for fuller particulars.)

26 October. The editorial offices of *Der Spiegel*, a leading West German news magazine, are searched and sealed by the police, following the publication of a purported account of a NATO exercise. (See '*Spiegel* affair' in *Glossary* for fuller particulars.)

1963

14 January. Pursuant to the Hallstein Doctrine, West Germany terminates relations with Cuba for recognising East Germany. (See section 3.3 for fuller particulars.)

22 January. Chancellor Adenauer and President de Gaulle sign the Franco-German treaty of co-operation. (See section 3.2 for fuller particulars.)

2 April. Representatives of all three parties in the Bundestag demand the recall of all German scientists and technicians engaged on rocket development and aircraft production in the United Arab Republic (Egypt), and declare that they will introduce legislation to make it clearly illegal. The Israeli government had earlier called on the West German government to put an end to such activity.

11 October. Chancellor Adenauer tenders his resignation with effect from 15 October, aged 87.

16 October. Professor Ludwig Erhard is elected Chancellor by the Bundestag.

1964

31 January. Dr Hans Krüger (CDU) resigns as minister for expellees, refugees and war victims. The East German government had produced his personal file under the Nazi regime, showing that he had been a judge in a special court at Chojnice (Konitz) which had passed death sentences during the German occupation of Poland. Krüger admitted that he had been the local Nazi leader in Chojnice in 1943 but maintained that he was not aware that he had infringed human or legal rights.

3 February. Ewald Peters, responsible for the security of the Chancellor and his government, commits suicide in Bonn prison, having been charged on 30 January with commanding SS units in southern Russia responsible for mass killings of Jews during the War.

2 April. America, Britain and France, in concert with NATO, again allow East German individuals to travel in western Europe provided they do not indulge in political activity. (Permission had in general been withdrawn consequent to the erection of the Wall.) Any representation of East Germany as a sovereign or national identity will, however, be deemed an undesirable political activity.

17 May. Dr Hans-Christoph Seebohm, West German minister of transport, maintains at a meeting of expellees in Nuremberg that the Sudeten Germans should be given back the territory of which they had been 'robbed'. Chancellor Erhard issues a communiqué five days later emphasising that West Germany has no territorial claims against Czechoslovakia of any kind. (See 'Sudetenland' in *Glossary*.)

23 May. East Germany releases Heinz Brandt, a one-time SED official who had fled to West Germany in 1958 and had been sentenced to thirteen years' imprisonment for spying in 1962. His kidnapping from West Berlin in June 1961 and detention for eleven months without access to a lawyer had inspired worldwide condemnation.

26 May. East Germany releases Georg Dertinger, formerly foreign minister, sentenced to fifteen years' imprisonment for spying in 1954.

18 August. Ulbricht discusses the role of East German Christians with the Evangelical Bishop of Thuringia, D. Moritz Mitzenheim.

7 September. An alternative form of military service in 'building units' is introduced for East German pacifists and is attributed to the August meeting.

6 October. East Germany announces that it is to release some 10,000 people by 20 December under an amnesty. Dr Wolfgang Harich, an intellectual sentenced to ten years' imprisonment in 1957, is amongst the beneficiaries. The amnesty does not extend to those convicted of war crimes, murder or serious spying.

1965

14 February. The West German government confirms that it has assured Egypt that it will end arms supplies to Israel and not supply arms in future to 'areas of tension'.

15 February. Levi Eshkol, Israeli prime minister, strongly criticises the cancellation of German arms deliveries and maintains in the Knesset that 'Germany is not entitled to regard Israel as one of the world's areas of tension'.

17 February. Chancellor Erhard tells the Bundestag that, although West Germany wants good relations with all the Arab states, it has a 'debt of honour' towards Israel and the Jews and that Germany still carries 'the guilt imposed on it by the Third Reich'.

7 March. West Germany announces that it is to seek diplomatic relations with Israel. They are established on 12 May.

16 March. West Germany and Israel sign the final protocol, completing their reparations agreement of 10 September 1952. By the expiry date of the agreement of 31 March 1965, Israel had received equipment and goods valued at US$600 million, and US$262.5 million in credits for oil purchases; a total equivalent to DM3.45 billion.

25 March. Dr Ewald Bucher, FDP minister of justice, resigns over the proposed extension of the Statute of Limitation for war crimes. He argues that it is retroactive legislation and thus contrary to Article 103 of the Basic Law.

21 April. Under heavy international pressure, West Germany extends the Statute of Limitation by making the 20-year period run from 1949. New prosecutions for war crimes are now possible until December 1969.

12 May. Iraq breaks off diplomatic relations with West Germany in protest at its recognition of Israel.

13 May. Algeria, Egypt (UAR), Jordan, Kuwait, Lebanon, Saudia Arabia, Syria and Yemen break off relations likewise.

16 May. Sudan follows suit.

19 September. The CDU/CSU wins the 5th Bundestag elections with Professor Erhard as Chancellor candidate, but does not gain an overall majority.

8 October. The International Olympic Committee decides that East and West Germany will be represented by two separate teams in the 1968 Olympic Games. The East German team will represent 'East Germany' and the West German team 'Germany'. The West German ministry of all-German affairs describes the decision as 'contrary to the Olympic spirit'. Previous Games had featured all-German teams.

1966

31 March. East Germany applies to join the United Nations. It is rejected by America, Britain and France.

12 August. Lt-General Werner Panitzki asks to be relieved of his post as head (Inspector) of the Luftwaffe following 61 crashes by German *Starfighters*, attributed by him to political negligence and inadequate pilot training.

23 August. General Heinz Trettner, Inspector-General of the *Bundeswehr*, resigns in protest at the decision by the ministry of defence on 2 August to allow trade union activity within the armed services.

16 September. Kai-Uwe von Hassel, West German defence minister, announces that fourteen generals and admirals will retire on 1 October.

27 October. The CDU/CSU/FDP coalition government of Chancellor Erhard collapses with the resignation of the four FDP ministers. The FDP had opposed tax increases to balance the federal budget.

6 November. The far-right NPD wins 7.9 per cent of the vote and eight seats in the Hesse *Land* elections.

10 November. Dr Kurt Georg Kiesinger is adopted for the Chancellorship by the CDU/CSU Bundestag majority group.

20 November. The NPD wins 7.4 per cent of the vote and fifteen seats in the Bavarian *Land* elections. Its share of the vote rises to 12.2 per cent in central Franconia, including Nuremberg, and to 19 per cent in the more remote parts.

26 November. The CDU and the SPD announce that 'conditions for a coalition exist'.

29 November. The CDU executive committee approves a grand coalition between the CDU and the SPD by 59 votes to one.

30 November. The SPD Bundestag group votes for the proposed coalition agreement by 126 votes to 53 with eight abstentions. The vote followed strong initial objections from seven of the eleven SPD *Land* organisations and from others, focused on the personalities of Dr Kiesinger and Franz-Josef Strauss and concern over responsibility for policy.

Dr Erhard resigns as Chancellor.

1 December. The grand coalition between the CDU/CSU and the SPD comes into existence with the election of Dr Kiesinger as Chancellor by the Bundestag. His cabinet has eleven CDU/CSU members and nine SPD members.

8 December. The Landtag of North Rhine-Westphalia replaces Dr Franz Meyers (CDU) with Heinz Kühn (SPD) in the first successful constructive vote of no confidence in West German history.

1967

28 January. The Soviet Union issues a statement expressing concern at the alleged rise of neo-Nazism in West Germany and accusing West Germany of 'revanchist aims'.

31 January. West Germany and Romania agree to establish diplomatic relations. Romania thereby becomes the first Communist state other than the Soviet Union to have diplomatic relations with West Germany. *Neues Deutschland*, the East German party newspaper, describes the Romanian decision as 'deplorable'.

7 February. The Soviet ambassador to West Germany submits the draft of a proposed joint statement by the two countries renouncing the use of force.

8–10 February. The venue of the conference of foreign ministers of the Warsaw Pact is moved from East Berlin to Warsaw in the light of Romanian anger at the East German attitude.

27 February. Jordan is the first of the Arab countries which broke off relations in 1965 to resume full diplomatic relations with West Germany.

23 April. The NPD wins 5.8 per cent of the vote and four seats in the Schleswig-Holstein Land elections. It wins 6.9 per cent and four seats in the Rhineland-Palatinate elections on the same day.

2 June. The shooting of Benno Ohnesorg by police in West Berlin on the day gives its name to the '2 June' terrorist movement and heralds a long period of student unrest. (See section 5.2 for fuller particulars.)

4 June. The NPD wins 7 per cent of the vote and ten seats in the Lower Saxony elections.

3 August. West Germany and Czechoslovakia sign a trade agreement which establishes official trade missions in Prague and Frankfurt with the power to issue visas.

25 September. West Germany bans the Croatian Democratic Committee (*Hrvatski Demokratski Odbor*) on the grounds that its activities are contrary to German criminal law and the principles of international understanding.

1 October. The NPD gains 8.8 per cent of the vote and four seats in the Bremen *Land* elections. The DP, which Fritz Thielen, the former NPD chairman, had rejoined, gains only 0.9 per cent.

8 October. Willy Brandt, as foreign minister, calls for 'sincere friendship' with the Soviet Union and offers to conclude a treaty renouncing the use of force.

21 November. The Soviet Union maintains that it has the right under the UN Charter to intervene in West Germany in the case of the 'resumption of aggressive policies by a former enemy state'.

8 December. The Soviet Union demands in a statement to the American, British, French and West German ambassadors in Moscow that West Germany recognise all existing frontiers in Europe, renounce its claim to represent all Germans, abandon the claim that West Berlin is part of West Germany, renounce nuclear defence, and recognise the 1938 Munich Agreement as invalid from its very beginning.

22 December. West Germany rejects the Soviet claims, as do the other ambassadors seven days later.

1968

31 January. Modifying the Hallstein Doctrine, West Germany declares its intention of resuming full diplomatic relations with Yugoslavia.

9 April. West Germany submits proposals to the Soviet ambassador for negotiations with 'every member-state of the Warsaw Pact', including 'the other part of Germany' on an exchange of declarations renouncing the use of force. It is ready to sign a nuclear non-proliferation treaty, to open negotiations with Czechoslovakia over the Munich Agreement, to oppose neo-Nazism and to observe Berlin's Four-Power status. It maintains, however, that Germany's border with Poland can only be determined by a peace treaty concluded with the government of a united Germany. It also rejects the Soviet claim to a right under either the UN Charter or the Potsdam Agreement to intervene in West Germany.

11 April. Rudi Dutschke, the left-wing student leader, is shot and gravely wounded as he leaves the SDS headquarters in West Berlin. (See *Biographies* and 'SDS' in *Glossary* for fuller particulars.)

12 April. Protest demonstrations erupt in a large number of West German cities, but are at their most violent in West Berlin. The Springer building in Munich is attacked, causing much internal damage.

30 June. The Ulbricht personality cult reaches its peak with the official celebrations of his 75th birthday.

5 July. The Soviet government submits an *aide-mémoire* to West Germany largely reiterating the arguments in its statement of 8 December 1967.

20 August. East Germany participates in the invasion of Czechoslovakia. (See section 3.3 for fuller particulars.)

11 September. The Soviet Union reiterates its claim to a legal right to intervene in West Germany.

12 November. Leonid Brezhnev, the First Secretary of the Soviet Communist Party, proclaims the 'Brezhnev Doctrine' of conditional sovereignty for Communist states.

1969

5 March. Gustav Heinemann is elected West German president. He is West Germany's first SPD head of state. The meeting of the Federal Assembly in West Berlin had been preceded by protests from East Germany and the Soviet Union. (See section 5.2 for fuller particulars.)

25 March. The Soviet Union adopts a conciliatory approach towards West Germany and the SPD in particular at a conference celebrating the 50th anniversary of the Communist International. Ulbricht on the same occasion emphasises the divide between the SED and the SPD.

30 April. Iraq becomes the second non-Soviet bloc state to recognise East Germany.

28 September. The 6th Bundestag elections are inconclusive. The SPD with Willy Brandt as Chancellor candidate does not enjoy an overall majority, but agreement on an SPD/FDP coalition is announced on 3 October.

21 October. Willy Brandt is elected Chancellor by the Bundestag by a formal margin of only two votes. He is the first SPD Chancellor since Hermann Müller, 1928–30. He lists his four main tasks as securing the stability and growth of the economy, reforming education, developing relations with Poland and preparing for the signature of the nuclear non-proliferation treaty. The new cabinet no longer contains a minister for refugees and expellees.

21 October. Chancellor Brandt welcomes the suggestion of establishing diplomatic relations with Poland.

30 October. West Germany signs an agreement with Czechoslovakia, although it does not recognise the Czechoslovak government, enabling the payment of DM7.5 million to Czechoslovak victims of Nazi concentration camp experiments.

8 December. Talks open in Moscow on a possible agreement between West Germany and the Soviet Union to renounce the threat or use of force.

1970

14 January. Chancellor Brandt advises the Bundestag in the context of evolving inter-German relations:

> ... let us all realise that outside our nation there are not many people in this world who are enthused by the thought that the 60 million and the 17 million Germans – the economic potential of the one and of the other, let alone their armies – might merge.

5–6 February. The first round of talks to normalise Polish–West German relations opens in Warsaw.

16 February. Erich Honecker, Ulbricht's heir apparent, harshly criticises the SPD leadership.

27 July. Formal negotiations open in Moscow on the proposed treaty to renounce the use of force. The CDU/CSU had declined an invitation to be represented on the West German delegation, as the Brandt government had not accepted its demand that no treaty be signed in Moscow, until the Four-Power talks on Berlin had come to a satisfactory conclusion.

12 August. West Germany and the Soviet Union sign the Treaty of Moscow. They renounce the use of force and agree to respect the integrity of all European states within their existing frontiers, including that between East and West Germany and the Oder-Neisse frontier with Poland. Dr Kiesinger, the former Chancellor, maintains that the new government's policy is wrong because it is going to replace 'the previous West European concept by the Soviet concept for Europe'.

15 October. The CDU/CSU parliamentary group states that 'future European solutions must not be obstructed by the political cementing of demarcation lines and borders'.

7 December. Chancellor Brandt and Jozef Cyrankiewicz, the Polish prime minister, sign the Treaty of Warsaw, normalising relations between the two countries. The Treaty recognises the Oder-Neisse line as Poland's western frontier, and renounces the use, or threat, of force in their mutual relations.

Chancellor Brandt makes a major impact on opinion throughout eastern Europe by falling to his knees at the Warsaw ghetto memorial in a gesture of atonement.

1971

22 January. West Germany agrees to pay DM6.25 million to Hungarian victims of Nazi medical experiments and DM100 million spread over three years to the representative organisation of Hungarian victims of Nazi persecution.

3 May. Erich Honecker replaces Walter Ulbricht as First Secretary of the East German SED.

3 September. The western Allies and the Soviet Union sign the Four-Power Berlin Agreement. It foreshadows the signature of the 'Basic Treaty' by East and West Germany in the following year. (See section 5.2 for fuller particulars.)

20 October. Chancellor Brandt is awarded the Nobel Peace Prize for his Ostpolitik.

1972

27 April. The CDU/CSU moves the first 'constructive vote of no confidence' in the Bundestag in West German history. The initiative to instal Dr Rainer Barzel as Chancellor under Article 67 of the Basic Law fails by just two votes.

17–19 May. The Bundestag ratifies the 1970 Treaty of Moscow and Treaty of Warsaw.

8 June. West Germany and Egypt resume diplomatic relations, broken off by Egypt in 1965 when West Germany recognised Israel.

16 October. The Volkskammer adopts a citizenship law whereby East Germans who had left the country illegally before 1 January 1972 and lost their citizenship would not be prosecuted if they visited East Germany.

16 November. West Germany agrees in Geneva to pay DM100 million to Polish victims of Nazi concentration camp experiments.

19 November. The SPD wins the 7th Bundestag elections with Willy Brandt as Chancellor candidate. The SPD becomes the largest party in the Bundestag for the first time in West German history. The election had been held prematurely, again for the first time, because of the lack of a working majority for the coalition government.

21 November. East Germany becomes a member of UNESCO.

24 November. Finland unilaterally recognises East and West Germany simultaneously.

7–8 December. The NATO ministerial council decides in principle to establish relations with East Germany.

13 December. East Germany becomes a member of the UN Economic Commission for Europe.

14 December. The Bundestag re-elects Willy Brandt as Chancellor. His new government comprises thirteen SPD and five FDP members, as against eleven and three respectively in the previous government.

21 December. East and West Germany sign the 'Basic Treaty' on mutual relations, whereby West Germany effectively recognises East Germany. (See section 3.1 for fuller particulars.)

27 December. Belgium becomes the first NATO member state to establish diplomatic relations with East Germany.

1973

9 February. Britain and France announce that they have both established diplomatic relations with East Germany.

18–22 May. Leonid Brezhnev, General Secretary of the Soviet Communist Party, becomes the first Soviet General Secretary to visit West Germany. His visit is at the invitation of Chancellor Brandt and is preceded by a visit to East Germany on 12–13 May.

19 May. Brandt, Brezhnev, and their foreign ministers, Walter Scheel and Andrei Gromyko, sign a ten-year agreement on the development of economic, industrial, and technological co-operation, and Scheel and Gromyko sign an agreement on cultural co-operation.

7–11 June. Willy Brandt becomes the first Chancellor to pay a state visit to Israel. His first official act is to lay a wreath at the memorial to the victims of the Holocaust outside Jerusalem commemorating the six million Jewish victims of the Nazi annihilation and concentration camps.

20 June. The West German and Czechoslovak foreign ministers initial a treaty in Bonn recognising that the provisions of the 1938 Munich Agreement which led to the transfer of the Sudetenland from Czechoslovakia to Germany were 'null and void'.

18 September. Both East Germany and West Germany are admitted to the United Nations.

11 December. Chancellor Brandt and Lubomir Strougal, the Czechoslovak prime minister, sign the Treaty on Bilateral Relations between West Germany and Czechoslovakia, in Prague. They agree on the same day to establish diplomatic relations.

1974

24 April. Günter Guillaume, one of Chancellor Brandt's three personal assistants, is arrested in Bonn as an East German agent.

6 May. Willy Brandt resigns as West German Chancellor, admitting that he had known that his personal assistant, Günter Guillaume (q.v.) had been under suspicion for some months, and admitting political responsibility for negligence in the affair. Brandt nevertheless remains as SPD leader.

16 May. Helmut Schmidt is elected Chancellor by the Bundestag by 267 votes to 225. His first policy speech the following day stresses 'continuity and concentration'.

7 August. Syria resumes the diplomatic relations with West Germany broken off in May 1965 when West Germany recognised Israel.

28–31 October. Chancellor Schmidt visits the Soviet Union at the invitation of General Secretary Brezhnev. The final communiqué confirms the continued good relations between the two countries and formalises regular governmental consultations.

1975

18 January. West Germany resumes the diplomatic relations with Cuba broken off in 1963 under the Hallstein Doctrine when Cuba recognised East Germany.

27 February. Peter Lorenz, chairman of the CDU in West Berlin, is kidnapped three days before the West Berlin elections by the 'June 2 Movement'. He is freed on 5 March after five terrorist prisoners have been flown to Aden (South Yemen), accompanied by the former governing mayor, Pastor Heinrich Albertz.

1 August. Both East and West Germany sign the final act of the Helsinki Conference on European Security and Co-operation.

7 October. Erich Honecker and Leonid Brezhnev in Moscow sign a 25-year Treaty of Friendship, Co-operation and Mutual Assistance between East Germany and the Soviet Union.

9 October. The Polish and West German foreign ministers sign agreements in Warsaw on pension claims and credits and a protocol on the emigration of ethnic Germans.

25 October. Franz-Josef Strauss, chairman of the CSU, urges all Bundestag and Bundesrat members to vote against ratifying the reciprocal pensions agreement as it could lead to further reparations claims against West Germany.

3–4 November. The CDU/CSU minority Bundestag group votes to reject the agreements with Poland.

5 December. The Volkskammer ratifies October's Moscow Treaty.

1976

11 March. The Polish government concedes that more ethnic Germans would in due course be allowed to emigrate than the 120,000–125,000 over four years laid down in the October protocol.

12 March. The Bundesrat ratifies the Warsaw agreements and protocol unanimously.

9 May. Ulrike Meinhof commits suicide in prison. (See section 2.9, 'Red Army Faction' in *Glossary*, and *Biographies* for fuller particulars.)

18 August. An East German pastor commits suicide by setting himself alight in protest at the government's youth and education policy.

3 October. The SPD wins the 8th Bundestag elections with Helmut Schmidt as Chancellor candidate, but with a reduced vote. The FDP had given an election pledge that it would remain in coalition with the SPD.

1 November. The second-highest-ranking Luftwaffe general, Lt-General Walter Krupinski, and his deputy, Major-General Karl-Heinz Franke, are dismissed for remarks inconsistent with their duty to respect democracy. (See 'Generals affair' in the *Glossary* for fuller particulars.)

15 December. Helmut Schmidt is elected Chancellor by the Bundestag with 250 of the 493 valid votes cast. The new Cabinet has, as before, twelve SPD and four FDP members.

1977

16 August. Chancellor Schmidt and Giulio Andreotti, the Italian prime minister, cancel their meeting scheduled for Verona on 19 August in view of possible demonstrations over the Kappler affair. (See section 2.8 for fuller particulars.)

18 October. The three convicted 'hard core' RAF members are found dead or dying in their cells. (See section 2.9 for fuller particulars.)

1978

1 February. Georg Leber resigns as defence minister following the exposure of cases of illegal electronic monitoring undertaken by the Military Counter-Intelligence Service (*Militärischer Abschirmdienst*).

6 March. Erich Honecker meets Bishop Albrecht Schönherr, Evangelical Bishop for East Berlin and chairman of the East German Conference of Evangelical Church Leaders, in the first such church–state meeting for 20 years. It results in permission being given for religious broadcasts, and for some prison visiting by chaplains, together with a pledge of non-discrimination.

4–7 May. Leonid Brezhnev, President of the Supreme Soviet and General Secretary of the Soviet Communist Party, pays a state visit to West Germany. The Soviet Union and West Germany sign a 25-year economic co-operation agreement.

1979

16 May. West German plans to construct a large nuclear reprocessing plant at Gorleben are refused by the CDU Lower Saxony Land government. Exploratory drillings for underground nuclear waste storage are, however, allowed to proceed.

4 September. A West German ministry of defence White Paper argues that there is a 'menacing disparity' between the medium-range missile capabilities of NATO and the Warsaw Pact.

25 September. The East German Council of State announces a general amnesty between 10 October and 14 December for all offences except murder and war crimes, to celebrate the 30th anniversary of the state's foundation.

7 October. The *Bremer Grüne Liste* becomes the first Green group to clear the 5 per cent electoral hurdle to secure representation in a Landtag (Bremen).

17 December. It is announced that 21,928 East German prisoners have been released under the amnesty, as have 1,272 people convicted but awaiting sentence. 130 death sentences have been commuted to life imprisonment.

1980

12–14 January. The Greens (*Die Grünen*) are formally established as a West German political party at a conference in Karlsruhe. (See section 2.4 for fuller particulars.)

18 January. West German general, Gert Bastian, is dismissed for publicly opposing the deployment of new nuclear weapons in Western Europe.

20 June. 60,000 people, organised by delegates to the biennial congress of the West German Protestant Union, demonstrate in protest against the West German government's support for the deployment of new NATO missiles.

25 August. A pre-election demonstration by some 15,000 people in Hamburg against Franz-Josef Strauss, the CDU/CSU candidate, causes 102 police injuries.

21 September. A pastoral letter is read in all West German Roman Catholic churches criticising the government for its fast-growing borrowing requirement. Chancellor Schmidt maintains that the Church should stay out of politics, as it had since the mid-1960s, but Franz-Josef Strauss, the CDU/CSU Chancellor candidate, supports the bishops' letter.

26 September. A bomb explodes at the Munich October Festival, killing thirteen people and injuring over 200. It is attributed to the far right 'Hoffman military sport group'. (See section 2.9 for fuller particulars.)

5 October. The SPD/FDP coalition wins the 9th Bundestag elections with Helmut Schmidt as Chancellor candidate. The result is seen as a serious personal rebuff for Franz-Josef Strauss, the CDU/CSU candidate, who announces that he will confine himself henceforth to Bavaria and the CSU.

5 November. Helmut Schmidt is re-elected as Chancellor by the Bundestag by 266 votes to 222.

10–13 November. Erich Honecker makes his first official visit to a western country by visiting Austria.

1981

25 February. West Germany rejects Soviet President Brezhnev's proposed moratorium on the deployment of new medium-range missiles, arguing that it would only confirm the current Soviet advantage.

17 May. Chancellor Schmidt declares at an SPD meeting that he will personally 'stand or fall with the realisation of both parts of the NATO decision' on the deployment of nuclear weapons and a new round of American–Soviet arms limitation talks.

30 September. Chancellor Schmidt urges the SPD Bundestag group to dissociate itself from the peace rally planned for 10 October, but is opposed by Willy Brandt and Erhard Eppler. Schmidt describes their support for the rally as 'an internal declaration of war against the Government'.

10 October. Some 250,000 people from over 700 organisations demonstrate peacefully in Bonn against the armaments policies of NATO and the Warsaw Pact.

1982

25 January. Rainer Eppelmann, an East Berlin pastor, launches the Berlin Appeal. The petition calls on the Soviet Union and the western Allies to withdraw their forces of occupation from Germany and to guarantee non-intervention in the internal affairs of East and West Germany.

25 March. The Volkskammer passes a new law on East German military service whereby reservists are required to undergo 24 months' military training, divided into periods of up to three months in any one year, with effect from 1 May 1982. National service, however, remains at eighteen months.

21 April. The SPD Congress calls for increased taxation to finance a major investment programme to reduce West Germany's accelerating unemployment. The Congress proposal is unacceptable to the FDP.

17 September. The four FDP ministers resign from the Schmidt government.

1 October. The Bundestag passes by 256 votes to 235 a constructive vote of no confidence against Chancellor Schmidt in favour of Dr Helmut Kohl of the CDU.

4 October. Chancellor Kohl is appointed and announces his CDU/CSU/FDP coalition government. (See section 2.5 for particulars.)

10 October. The FDP fails to reach the 5 per cent threshold for representation in the Bavarian *Land* elections. The failure is attributed to its changed stance in Bonn.

5–6 November. Ingrid Matthäus-Maier is the first of five FDP Bundestag members to leave the party in protest at its change of stance. She joins the SPD, becoming its expert on taxation questions.

3 December. The Bundestag removes the former government's restrictions on the operation of the fast breeder reactor at Kalkar, having already agreed to spend DM600 million on nuclear projects there and at Schmehausen.

31 December. An unconfirmed report claims that an assassination attempt has been made on Erich Honecker as he is driven through Klosterfelde, near Berlin.

1983

2 February. The new West German government decides to proceed with construction of the remaining 40 miles of the 105-mile Rhine–Main–Danube canal between Bamberg on the Main and Regensburg on the Danube. The additional cost is estimated at some DM3 billion, and the project is controversial on both commercial and environmental grounds.

6 March. The CDU/CSU/FDP governing coalition wins the 10th Bundestag elections with Dr Helmut Kohl as Chancellor candidate. The Greens enter the Bundestag for the first time with 5.6 per cent of the vote.

24 March. Chancellor Kohl announces his proposed government. Franz Josef Strauss does not achieve his ambition of replacing Hans-Dietrich Genscher as foreign minister.

29 March. The Bundestag re-elects Helmut Kohl as Chancellor.

22 April. *Der Stern*, a popular West German magazine, claims that it has acquired 60 volumes of Hitler's diaries.

3–7 May. Erich Honecker pays his first official visit to the Soviet Union since 1976. Despite reports that there is a 'full identity of views on all questions discussed', the Soviet Union does not appear to have endorsed the East German policy of developing dialogue and links with the west.

6 May. The German Federal Archive describes the diaries as 'grotesquely primitive forgeries'. (See 'Hitler Diaries' in *Glossary* for fuller particulars.)

9–11 October. Chancellor Kohl makes an official visit to Saudi Arabia. Despite reports that West Germany is planning to supply a large number of Leopard 2 tanks to Saudi Arabia, which provoke Israeli warnings of a major deterioriation in relations, no specific arms agreements are reached.

18 November. An extraordinary SPD conference in Cologne votes to oppose the proposed deployment of American missiles by 283 votes to 14. Its stance is a reversal of its December 1979 endorsement of the 'twin track' approach, and is contrary to the advice of Helmut Schmidt. He announces shortly afterwards that he will not stand for the Bundestag or any senior party post again.

22 November. The Bundestag confirms by 286 votes to 226 its support for the deployment of American Cruise and Pershing II missiles in West Germany.

26 November. Pershing II missiles arrive at Mutlangen, east of Stuttgart.

29 November. The West German public prosecutor's office requests the Bundestag to lift the parliamentary immunity of Dr Otto Graf Lambsdorff, the economics minister, so that charges may be brought against him in connection with the so-called Flick affair. (See 'Flick affair' in *Glossary*.)

2 December. The Bundestag votes unanimously to lift Graf Lambsdorff's immunity. On 8 December, he becomes the first West German cabinet minister to be indicted while in office.

30 December. West Germany announces that the first Pershing II missiles are now operational.

31 December. Lt-General Günter Kiessling is dismissed from his post as a Deputy Supreme Commander of the Allied Forces in Europe by Manfred Wörner, the West German minister of defence. (See 'Kiessling affair' in *Glossary* for fuller particulars.)

1984

18 January. The Soviet Army newspaper, *Krasnaya Zvezda*, reports that 'enhanced range' missiles are now deployed in East Germany.

25–30 January. Chancellor Kohl visits Israel, provoking a number of demonstrations against the Israeli government's willingness to receive him.

30 January–1 February. Pierre Trudeau, prime minister of Canada, is the first leader of a NATO member state to visit East Germany.

1 February. Chancellor Kohl reinstates Lt-General Kiessling but also retains Manfred Wörner as defence minister.

6 June. Germany is not invited to the commemorations of the Normandy D-Day landings attended by western heads of state and government.

4 September. Erich Honecker cancels his planned visit to West Germany following Soviet pressure.

13 September. Giulio Andreotti, Italian Christian Democrat foreign minister (and many times prime minister) declares in a debate on German reunification in the Italian parliament that 'pan-Germanism [is] something which had to be overcome' and that 'there are two German states and the two German states should remain as such'.

22 September. The 'hereditary enmity' between Germany and France is again ceremonially declared over by the 'Verdun handshake'. (See section 3.2 for fuller particulars.)

4 October. West Germany temporarily closes its embassy in Prague following its occupation by some 40 East Germans seeking asylum.

1985

January. The West German government gives final approval to the construction of a nuclear reprocessing plant at Wackersdorff, Bavaria. A peaceful demonstration by more than 30,000 people is held in the village of Schwandorf nearby in protest.

24 March. Major Arthur Nicholson, a member of the American military liaison mission in Potsdam, East Germany, is shot dead by a Soviet guard near a restricted military area near Ludwigslust, East Germany.

22 April. Chancellor Kohl attends the site ceremony to commemorate the 40th anniversary of the liberation of the Bergen Belsen concentration camp.

23–24 April. Erich Honecker visits Italy. It is his first visit to a NATO member country.

25–26 April. East Germany is a signatory of the agreement renewing the Warsaw Pact for twenty years.

25 April. As a result of the Nicholson shooting, there is no official American representation at the ceremonies at Torgau, East Germany, to mark the 40th anniversary of the meeting of American and Soviet troops on the Elbe in the last days of the War.

5 May. Chancellor Kohl and American President Reagan visit the Bitburg military cemetery and Belsen to mark the impending 40th Anniversary of VE Day. The Bitburg visit fails to promote the hoped-for reconciliation. Critics, both in Germany and outside, conscious that the cemetery contained the graves of a number of SS officers, had urged that it be cancelled. The occasion is a major political embarrassment for President Reagan.

7 May. The SPD organises a commemoration in Nuremberg of the 'martyred towns' of the Second World War.

The American, British and French ambassadors and the West German representative boycott the East Berlin ceremonies commemorating the defeat of the Nazi regime. They allege that they put too much emphasis on the Soviet contribution and not enough on that of the western Allies.

8 May. They also boycott the wreath-laying ceremony at the Soviet memorial in West Berlin, allegedly because the presence of East German troops is contrary to the city's demilitarised status.

Richard von Weizsäcker, the West German president, acknowledges in a speech marking the 40th anniversary of VE Day that Germany bears responsibility for its Nazi past.

9–10 June. Former President Carstens and Dr Friedrich Zimmermann, the West German minister of the interior, attend the annual Sudeten German rally in Munich. (See 'Sudetenland' in *Glossary.*) The Czechs complain of the enhanced aggressiveness of the attacks on Czechoslovakia on this occasion.

10–11 June. Laurent Fabius, the French prime minister, is the first head of government of one of the western Allies to pay an official visit to East Germany.

14–16 June. Chancellor Kohl generates controversy by being the first Chancellor for twenty years to speak at the annual meeting of the Silesian Exiles' Association. He maintains that the Polish border issue is still legally open and can only be resolved by peaceful means through a final German peace treaty. The moderated slogan of the meeting is '40 years of expulsion – Silesia remains our future in a Europe of free peoples', and Chancellor Kohl's remarks are poorly received in Poland.

18 December. The West German government reaffirms its political endorsement of President Reagan's Strategic Defence ('Star Wars') Initiative (SDI) and agrees that negotiations be entered into with the Americans on the mutual transfer of research and technology by private firms.

1986

28–30 March. Protests involving up to 360,000 people are held throughout West Germany over Easter, opposing the government's energy policy, an agreement signed on 27 March on West German participation in the American Strategic Defence Initiative, and the deployment of American Cruise and Pershing missiles in West Germany.

4 April. The Soviet Union formally protests at West German SDI policy. West Germany maintains that it is only concerned with questions of feasibility.

3 June. Chancellor Kohl responds to the growing public concern over environmental issues by establishing a specific ministry for the environment. Walter Wallman is sworn in as West Germany's first environment minister on 6 June.

25 July. A letter from Franz-Josef Strauss as Bavarian *Ministerpräsident* to President Kurt Waldheim of Austria suggests that the Austrian request for reconsideration of the construction of the Wackersdorff nuclear reprocessing plant is 'almost an impertinence'. Wackersdorff is some 75 miles from the Austrian frontier.

13–16 October. President von Weizsäcker is the first West German head of state to visit Hungary.

1987

25 January. The CDU/CSU wins the 11th Bundestag elections but remains dependent on FDP support.

1 February. Hans Dietrich Genscher, West German foreign minister, urges the west not to make a 'mistake of historic proportions' by ignoring the Soviet disarmament proposals of 1986–87.

3 April. Alexei Antonov, a Deputy Chairman of the Soviet Council of Ministers, attends the 15th annual meeting of the West German–Soviet commission on economic, scientific and technological co-operation. His attendance confirms a greater warmth in Soviet–West German relations.

30 April. Pope John Paul II makes his second visit to West Germany. He celebrates beatification masses for two opponents of Nazism, but is criticised in some quarters for failing to come to terms with the limited response of the Roman Catholic Church to the Nazi regime.

3–5 June. Erich Honecker visits the Netherlands. It is the first visit there by an East German head of state.

6–11 July. Dr Richard von Weizsäcker, the West German president, makes a six-day official visit to the Soviet Union. He stresses that the implications of the division of Germany for individuals 'make us acutely conscious of the need for peace' and asks the Soviet Union to treat the estimated 60,000 ethnic Germans who wish to emigrate, more sympathetically.

7 July. Mikhail Gorbachev, General Secretary of the Soviet Communist Party, maintains in talks with President von Weizsäcker that no alternative to the existence of two German states can be countenanced.

17 July. East Germany abolishes the death penalty and announces a general amnesty effective from 8 October for all prisoners other than those sentenced for war crimes, spying or murder.

17 August. Rudolf Hess, Hitler's deputy until 1941, dies in Spandau Prison, Berlin. (See section 5.2 for fuller particulars.)

26 August. Chancellor Kohl provokes a furious reaction from Franz-Josef Strauss and the CSU by announcing without consultation that West Germany will destroy the 72 Pershing 1A missiles in its ownership if America and the Soviet Union come to an agreement to destroy their intermediate nuclear forces, the so-called 'double-zero' option. The Chancellor can rely on SPD support, and America and the Soviet Union reach agreement in Washington on 8 December.

31 August. Margarete Höke, a senior secretary in the West German president's office, is sentenced to eight years' imprisonment for passing secret defence and foreign policy documents to the Soviet Union for at least eleven years.

7–11 September. Erich Honecker pays an official 'working' visit to West Germany. It is the first official visit to be made there by an East German head of state. The joint communiqué issued during the visit proclaims that 'never again must war be allowed to emanate from German soil'. (See section 3.1 for fuller particulars.)

1988

3 March. Erich Honecker has 'very open and businesslike discussions' with Werner Leich, Evangelical-Lutheran Bishop of Thuringia and chair of the Conference of Evangelical Church Leaders in East Germany.

4–5 March. Some 300 demonstrators in Dresden demand the right to emigrate to West Germany.

5–6 March. Civil rights demonstrations are held simultaneously in East Berlin, Leipzig, Dresden and Wismar. 80 people are arrested.

15 March. Some 300 demonstrators in Leipzig protest against alleged infringements of civil rights.

The governing synod of the Evangelical-Lutheran Church of East Germany expresses solidarity with the growing number of people urging wider personal freedom.

28 March. Six men are charged in West Germany with spying for the Soviet Union. The chief federal prosecutor claims that the arrests are 'the biggest blow to the Soviet secret service since the establishment of the Federal Republic'.

11 May. Dr Hans-Jochen Vogel, chair of the SPD, meets Mikhail Gorbachev during a visit to Moscow at the invitation of the central committee of the Soviet Communist Party. He welcomes the creation of a working party comprising SPD Bundestag members and members of the Supreme Soviet.

15 June. Erich Honecker maintains in an interview published in Austria that the changes in the Soviet Union are attributable to specifically Soviet conditions and that the KPD (and later the SED) from 1945 onwards had never given unqualified endorsement to the Soviet model.

1 July. Manfred Wörner, formerly West German defence minister, becomes secretary-general of NATO.

28 September. Erich Honecker meets Mikhail Gorbachev in Moscow. The Soviet media pay the visit scant attention.

17 October. Erich Honecker meets the American president of the World Jewish Congress in East Berlin. East Germany agrees in principle to pay reparations to the Jewish community for the Nazi era.

24–27 October. Chancellor Kohl makes an official visit to the Soviet Union, accompanied by the largest West German delegation ever to visit a foreign state. The visit sees the signature of six intergovernmental agreements, thirty agreements between West German companies and Soviet state enterprises, and a credit agreement between a consortium of West German banks and the Soviet Union in the sum of DM3,500 million to aid the modernisation of Soviet industry.

9 November. President von Weizsäcker and Chancellor Kohl attend a 50th anniversary commemoration of *Kristallnacht* in a Frankfurt synagogue. The Chancellor is heckled when he expresses his distress at the passivity of most Germans when the Nazis unleashed their attacks on Jewish shops and synagogues in 1938.

10 November. Philipp Jenninger, Bundestag president, makes a speech during the Bundestag commemoration, which is interpreted by many as an apologia for Nazi persecution.

11 November. Jenninger resigns, claiming to have been misunderstood. He is defended by some prominent Jews. He is succeeded as Bundestag president by Rita Süssmuth.

20 November. East Germany bans the Soviet magazine *Sputnik*, alleging that it distorts history.

21 November. Five Soviet films are similarly excluded from a Soviet film festival in East Berlin.

1 December. Erich Honecker announces that the 12th SED Congress will be brought forward a year to May 1990. The announcement fuels speculation that he may than announce his retirement.

10 December. Peter-Kurt Würzbach, a state secretary in the ministry of defence, orders a ban on low-level NATO flights until the end of the year, following the crash of an American fighter into housing at Remscheid, near Düsseldorf, killing six and injuring nine.

14 December. Würzbach resigns following disagreement over his decision with the minister, Dr Rupert Scholz.

1989

31 May. Construction of the Wackersdorf nuclear reprocessing plant is formally abandoned by its private promoters.

7–8 July. The Bucharest Summit of Warsaw Pact members fails to agree over reform.

10 September. Hungary's declaration that thousands of East Germans 'on holiday' there may cross the border into Austria initiates a wave of East German emigration to the West.

1 October. Some 10,000 East Germans are permitted to leave the West German embassies in Warsaw and Prague and travel to the west.

2 October. President Gorbachev's impending visit is preceded by a march of some 12,000 protesters through Leipzig, many of whom nevertheless claim that they do not wish to emigrate.

3 October. East Germany temporarily suspends visa- and passport-free travel by its citizens to Czechoslovakia, the only state they have been able to enter without formality. The concession is reinstated from 1 November.

6–7 October. Gorbachev visits East Germany on its 40th anniversary as a state, and criticises the government's hostility to reform. He emphasises that 'matters affecting East Germany are decided not in Moscow but in Berlin'. Demonstrations continue in favour of the democratisation of public life and 500–700 marchers are arrested in East Berlin. Almost all are released within a week.

8 October. Some 30,000 marchers disperse in Dresden after the local SED leadership agrees to meet a delegation.

9 October. Some 50,000 marchers in Leipzig elicit agreement from the local SED that 'we all need a free exchange of ideas'.

10–11 October. The Politbüro meets in emergency session. It sees a split between the hardliners and the reformers associated with Dresden and Leipzig.

16 October. The weekly Monday march in Leipzig after 'peace prayers' doubles in size to 100,000–120,000 people. Similar marches are organised in Dresden, Magdeburg, Plauen, Halle and elsewhere.

18 October. Erich Honecker resigns his posts in favour of his preferred successor, Egon Krenz. Dr Günter Mittag and Joachim Herrmann, responsible for economic affairs and for the media and propaganda respectively, resign (are dismissed) from the Politbüro.

Speaking on television that evening, Egon Krenz estimates that more than 100,000 people have recently left East Germany and says, 'We have to recognise the sign of the times and react accordingly, otherwise life will punish us.'

23 October. The weekly march in Leipzig is attended by demonstrators, estimated at anything between 100,000 and 300,000 in number. They call for the removal of the Berlin Wall and for free elections.

24 October. Egon Krenz is confirmed as chairman of the Council of State by the *Volksversammlung* in East Berlin's Palace of the Republic. 26 members of the 499 members present vote against him and 26 abstain. Some 12,000 demonstrators outside chant 'Who asked us?'

27 October. The Council of State proclaims an amnesty for people trying to leave East Germany illegally and for participants in demonstrations to date.

29 October. The SED organises 'mass discussions' in East Berlin and other large centres.

30 October. The weekly Leipzig march attracts more than 300,000 people.

31 October. Egon Krenz meets Gorbachev in Moscow.

Harry Tisch resigns as chair of the East German trade union federation (FDGB). He is replaced by Annelis Kimmel.

2 November. Egon Krenz meets President Jaruzelski of Poland in Warsaw, together with Tadeusz Mazowiecki, the new Solidarity prime minister.

Heinrich Homann and Gerald Götting resign as chairs of the East German NDPD and CDU.

3 November. The LDPD calls for the resignation of the East German government.

4 November. An East Berlin rally attended by more than 500,000 people is addressed by leaders of all the political parties.

6 November. Leipzig experiences its largest demonstrations to date for the removal of the Wall and for general democratisation.

7 November. Hans Modrow, Dresden SED Secretary, and Wolfgang Berghofer, mayor of Dresden, march with some 70,000 protesters. The mayor calls for the government's resignation.

Willi Stoph, Chairman of the Council of Ministers (prime minister), resigns together with his whole cabinet.

8–10 November. The Politbüro resigns in its entirety at the opening of a special three-day session of the central committee of the SED. The newly elected Politbüro includes both Krenz and Modrow. Krenz acknowledges that the leadership is to blame for the crisis of confidence, and censures Günter Mittag in particular. Mittag and Joachim Herrmann are expelled from membership of the central committee for 'gross violations of internal party democracy and . . . for damaging the standing of the Party'.

An 'action programme' is approved, including amongst its provisions free elections, the assumption of power by the Volkskammer 'without tutelage', a democratic coalition government, parliamentary control of the defence and security organisations, civilian service rather than military service for conscientious objectors, a 'socialist planned economy guided by market conditions' and the restoration of internal democracy within the SED.

9 November. The border between East and West Germany, including the Berlin Wall, is opened.

10–11 November. Some two million East Germans visit West Berlin through breaches in the Wall. More than 99 per cent return home.

13 November. Hans Modrow, a reformer and formerly SED secretary in Dresden is elected by the Volkskammer to succeed Willi Stoph as East German prime minister.

14–16 November. Egon Krenz demands the expulsion from the Volkskammer of Erich Honecker and 26 other former leading members of the SED.

17–18 November. The Volkskammer approves Hans Modrow's new government, which comprises three portfolios each for the CDU and the LDPD, and two each for the DBD and the NDPD, with the balance of seventeen for the SED. It also endorses his policy statement based on the 10 November 'action programme'. Modrow is willing to co-operate with West Germany more closely than envisaged by the Basic Treaty, but maintains that 'speculation about reunification [is] as unrealistic as it is dangerous'.

23 November. Dr Günter Mittag is expelled from the SED.

26 November. The five East German National Front parties agree to hold round table talks with a range of opposition groups.

28 November. Chancellor Kohl submits to the Bundestag a ten-point plan for a German confederation which could ultimately result in German unification.

Prominent East German artists and intellectuals sign a petition 'For our country' which maintains that 'We still have a chance . . . to develop a socialist alternative to the Federal Republic.'

2 December. An arrest warrant is issued for Alexander Schalck-Golodkowski, formerly secretary of state at the ministry of foreign trade, accused of illegal arms dealing. He gives himself up five days later.

3 December. Up to 2 million people form a human chain across East Germany calling for democratic reform and prosecution of corrupt leaders and officials. The Politbüro elected in November resigns in its entirety together with the SED central committee. Dr Günter Mittag and Harry Tisch, leader of the official East German trade union federation (*FDGB*), are arrested for alleged abuse of office.

4 December. Protests by some 150,000–200,000 people in Leipzig reveal angrily opposing views over unification. Some protesters break into the area Office for National Security to investigate files. The government announces a joint investigation committee into corruption, with members drawn from government and all political parties and groups.

5 December. Erich Honecker is placed under house arrest for alleged abuse of office, but not detained in view of his health.

6 December. Egon Krenz resigns as chairman of the East German Council of State and National Defence Council.

7 December. Lt-General Wolfgang Schwanitz, head of the National Security Office, and the East German government warn of 'unforeseeable consequences' if protesters continue to attack security premises.

East German round table talks lead to agreement on general elections in 1990, subject to formal endorsement by the Volkskammer.

8 December. Gregor Gysi is elected leader of the SED.

Willi Stoph, General Erich Mielke, and two other Politbüro members are arrested on charges of corruption.

11 December. The weekly demonstration in Leipzig again reveals sharp disagreement over unification although it appears to enjoy majority support.

14 December. The East German government decides to replace the National Security Office (*Stasi*) with smaller units for intelligence and for protection of the constitution.

15 December. The East German government decides to abolish the factory-based workers' militia.

16–17 December. The SED changes its name to the SED–PDS. (See section 2.4 for fuller particulars of this and foregoing.)

19–20 December. Helmut Kohl and Hans Modrow agree in Dresden to conclude a 'joint treaty on co-operation and good neighbourliness' between West and East Germany by spring 1990.

22 December. East Germany repeals its mandatory currency exchange and visa requirements.

1990

4 January. Erich Honecker is released from house arrest.

1 February. Hans Modrow, returning from a brief visit to Moscow, puts forward a four-stage plan for a united, neutral Germany, declaring 'Germany should again become the unified fatherland of all citizens of the German nation.' The precondition of military neutrality is rejected by Chancellor Kohl.

5 February. Dr Christa Luft, East German economics minister and a deputy prime minister (PDS), warns a session of the round table that any adoption of the West German Mark by East Germany will reduce neither the wages gap nor emigration, but will instead lead to industrial closures and unemployment.

The leaders of eight opposition groups join the Modrow government as ministers without portfolio, putting the SED in a minority for the first time in East German history.

The Volkskammer and the round table ban electoral activity by the West German *Republikaner*. Neo-Nazis smash shop windows during the weekly demonstration in Leipzig.

6 February. Chancellor Kohl declares that he is ready to negotiate with East Germany on economic and monetary union immediately.

Karl Otto Pöhl, president of the West German Bundesbank, describes plans for such a union as a 'fantastical illusion'. He is to resign in 1991.

11 February. Following discussions with Chancellor Kohl, President Gorbachev states that the Soviet Union has no objection in principle to German unification. He adds, however, that unification should not disturb the present strategic balance between NATO and the Warsaw Pact and should contribute to a new European security system.

13–14 February. Hans Modrow and seventeen of his ministers, representing all parties in the government, visit Bonn. His key request arising from the round table talks for a 'solidarity contribution' of up to DM15 billion does not, however, receive an answer, ending any real prospect of a continuing East German identity. West Germany alleges that its counter-offer of a common currency founded on the West German Mark is the superior option. The East German government maintains after the visit that 'unity must not and cannot be a simple annexation'.

13 February. East and West Germany and the war-time Allies agree the 'two plus four' formula for unification talks, which are to commence after the East German elections on 18 March.

18 February. President von Weizsäcker of West Germany warns that East Germany will be 'swallowed' if German unity is made dependent on common use of the West German Mark.

6–7 March. The Volkskammer approves the law creating the *Treuhandanstalt*, which is to oversee the privatisation of East Germany's 8,000 state-owned industries.

14 March. Wolfgang Schnur resigns as the leader of *Demokratischer Aufbruch* (Democratic Awakening) after admitting that he had been co-operating with the *Stasi* for at least 20 years.

17 March. Warsaw Pact foreign ministers meet in Prague. The Soviet Union alone wants German neutrality. Czechoslovakia, Hungary and

Poland want to restrain Germany from becoming a great power acting on its own.

18 March. The CDU-led 'Alliance for Germany' wins the last elections for East Germany's Volkskammer.

1 April. Ibrahim Böhme resigns as chairman of the East German SPD following allegations that he had worked for the *Stasi.*

12 April. Lothar de Maizière forms an East German coalition government, including representatives of the SPD and the Liberals, now known as the *Bund freier Demokraten* (BfD – League of free Democrats) as well as of the Alliance for Germany.

17 April. The collision of two Canadian military aircraft near Karlsruhe renews the widespread public hostility to low-level NATO flights.

18 May. East and West Germany sign a treaty introducing West Germany's currency and applying its economic, financial and social legislation to East Germany with effect from 1 July.

1 July. The May treaty comes into effect.

23 August. The Volkskammer declares by 294 votes to 62 East Germany's accession to the jurisdiction of the Federal Republic as from 3 October, in accordance with Article 23 of the Basic Law.

31 August. Pursuant to the Volkskammer declaration, Günther Krause for East Germany and Wolfgang Schäuble for West Germany sign a second state treaty, which provides for unification on 3 October.

10 September. West Germany agrees to pay DM12 billion over four years for the upkeep and resettlement of Soviet troops then in Germany, and in addition to make available an interest-free loan of DM3 billion repayable after five years. Hans-Dietrich Genscher describes it as 'the price of unity'.

12 September. The Treaty on the Final Settlement with Respect to Germany (effectively the German Peace Treaty) is signed in Moscow by East and West Germany and the four war-time Allies, America, Britain, France and the Soviet Union. It gives the united Germany full sovereignty over its internal and external affairs.

20 September. The Treaty is ratified by the Volkskammer by 200 votes to 80, by the Bundestag by 442 votes to 47 and by the Bundesrat unanimously.

24 September. East Germany leaves the Warsaw Pact.

29 September. Thousands march from West to East Berlin in protest at the terms of unification.

3 October. East and West Germany are united as a federal state in accordance with the legal declaration of 23 August.

4 October. The Bundestag formally declares Berlin to be the German national capital.

1.3 Germany on unification

The division of Germany was bitterly attacked by western politicians and the media for four decades, but they spoke in the confidence that the division was permanent. It was a valuable stick with which to beat the Soviet Union in the endless propaganda battle. In reality, reunification was not something they particularly wanted, as Brandt, himself, was to admit in January 1970 (see section 1.2). Even Adenauer was reputedly none too sorry not to have to dilute his Roman Catholic Christian Democracy with the more Protestant traditions of the east, not to mention the radicalism of Berlin. His vision for Germany was of a country with its windows open to the west, an orientation to be cemented by reconciliation with France. Khrushchev was probably being simply more honest than most outside Germany when he maintained in March 1959 that 'nobody really wants the reunification of Germany at this moment – nobody at all'.

It had also been presumed that reunification, if it ever did come about, would arise either on the initiative of one or more of the Four Powers or from the collapse of East Germany, a collapse which the western Allies and West Germany long sought to engineer. The reality when it did come about was somewhat different. It was to be Miklós Németh, the Hungarian Communist prime minister, who was to take the crucial initiative from which all else followed by ordering the dismantling in May 1989 of the twin barbed wire fences along the Hungarian border with Austria, although admittedly he would not have done so if Gorbachev had not already encouraged reform both in the Soviet Union and throughout the Soviet bloc.

The realisation that the confidence that unification would never happen had been misplaced was a source of considerable anxiety, if not outright alarm, almost everywhere in Europe. It generated caution even in the United States, where secretary of state James Baker's position that German unity had to be a gradual process within a context of stronger international institutional links was remarkably similar in spirit, if not in detail, to the position of Gorbachev and Eduard Shevardnadze, the Soviet foreign minister. Poland feared immediately and with some cause for the security of its Oder-Neisse frontier. Amongst the western European leaders, Giulio Andreotti, now once again Italian prime minister, had maintained in the Italian parliament in 1984 that there were two

German states and that situation should remain (see section 1.2). President Mitterand of France urged in the December of 1989 that West Germany make its priority strengthening the EU, not unification with East Germany (see section 3.2). Ruud Lubbers, prime minister of the Netherlands, and Margaret Thatcher in Britain were decidedly cool.

The Germans themselves were caught similarly unawares. The West German government had embarked in the mid-1980s on the creation of a whole new government quarter in Bonn, implicitly accepting that unification was not going to happen in the foreseeable future. East Germany had achieved its foreign policy goal of worldwide recognition, even if America remained aloof, and Chancellor Kohl himself had acknowledged on the occasion of Honecker's visit in September 1987 that two states now existed on German soil. For all the proud boast that the fall of Communism was the first ever peaceful revolution on German soil, there is little evidence that it would have materialised without the stimulus of external events.

The perception that unification was a possibility became a perception that it was a probability and then that it was a certainty with such speed that remaining opponents, inside the two parts of Germany as much as outside, merely bowed to what they now perceived as the inevitable. The only power which could have prevented it, the Soviet Union, no longer had the will to do so, although Gorbachev had maintained as recently as July 1987 that no alternative to the existence of two German states could be countenanced (see section 1.2). Whereas the Soviet Union had insisted for decades that the price of unification on the basis of free elections was permanent neutrality and detachment from NATO, the price had now shrunk to loans and cash payments.

In theory, the Germans had three options. One was to retain two independent sovereign states indefinitely. Those who had bitterly attacked the 'unnatural' division of Germany into two separate halves had always tended to ignore the fact that the German-speaking peoples were already divided between four European states – the two Germanys, Austria and Switzerland – not to mention French Alsace-Lorraine and Italian Alto Adige. Moreover, German Imperial unity under the Kaiser from 1871–1918 had been on the basis of a very loose federation, with a king of Bavaria, prince of Mecklenburg, individual state railway systems in addition to the main Prussian and Imperial network, and for a time even some separate state postal systems. Truly centralised government had begun and ended with Hitler. On the other hand, the boundary was an arbitrary one which had divided communities, families and economic units. Its hardening into an Iron Curtain had greatly magnified those deficiencies and given the division, most obviously in Berlin, a fearsome quality which precluded any acceptance that it was natural. Moreover, even the hardline East German government had talked in terms of two states of a single German nation, and just as in the Soviet Union, intensive education had failed to create the distinctive new Communist man in whom ideologues had had so much faith. Even these handicaps might perhaps have been overcome if East Germany had not been so much poorer than West Germany. East Germany had acquired a personality of its own and enjoyed specific cultural and social strengths, which could have been built on. A continuing reformist government under Hans Modrow briefly seemed a possibility. The option was, however, undermined by the flood of emigrants to West Germany, attracted by its higher living standards and opportunities, and the demand of a majority of East Germans for approximation to West German standards within a very short period of time.

The same problems undermined the concept of a confederation, which was initially the preferred option. An East German identity could only survive on the basis of a massive injection of West German funds, which Modrow and his all-party government sought in February 1990 (see section 1.2). It was not forthcoming, and those Germans still with doubts about unification had to bow to the inevitable just as those abroad had done.

Chancellor Kohl appears to have appreciated the speed at which change was occurring more rapidly than his political opponents and many of his own supporters, or perhaps was temperamentally less inclined to caution, and put himself forward unreservedly as the Chancellor of unity. Optimism and confidence were the watchwords as he overrode the advice of the Bundesbank and pursued monetary union on the basis of exchanging one East German Mark (M) for one West German Mark (DM) at par rather than at the more economically defensible rate of two East Mark for one West Mark. With even greater confidence, West Germans were assured that unification would bring no increase in the tax burden.

The results can only really be assessed at several different levels. At one level, the Chancellor's critics were virtually all proved right. The warnings by West Germany's President von Weizsäcker and Christa Luft, the East German economics minister, that common use of the West German Mark would result in the 'swallowing' of East Germany and in unemployment and industrial closures (see section 1.2) rapidly proved all too true. The calculations of the cost of unification by Oskar Lafontaine, the SPD candidate for the 1990 Bundestag elections, similarly were to prove much more accurate than the Chancellor's. At a different level, it could be argued that giving all Germans confidence in their future and in that of their united country and currency, and conveying that confidence to the world at large, was the all-important task. From that perspective the reservations of the doubters may look rather irrelevant within a timescale of only ten to fifteen years. Certainly Germany in 1997/98 appeared to be emerging quite strongly from the recession associated with unification.

At yet another level, unification can be assessed as the ruthless suppression of a hated and perhaps feared rival. Currency union bankrupted East Germany as a functioning economy and plant closures soared, as did unemployment and short-term working. The conglomerates were broken up and much plant summarily demolished as obsolescent. Restructuring was drastic in all sectors and the East German economy was effectively rebuilt on West German foundations. The cost in both public and private investment has been enormous and infinitely greater than East Germany originally needed to keep itself afloat.

The benefits have been similarly enormous. Much East German plant is now as modern as any in the world and environmental standards have improved out of recognition. Nevertheless unification did not so much 'swallow' East Germany, as President von Weizsäcker predicted, but submerge it. Valued social rights such as the right to work were simply ignored and East Germany's own democratic awakening was stunted by the ridicule which its inexperienced politicians generated in Bonn. Within a very short time many of the East German *Länder* were being run by West German politicians advised by West German senior staffs, driven on the whole by the highest motives but nevertheless conveying a distinct air of benevolent colonialism.

The question as to how much, if any, of this matters cannot be answered objectively. Even some form of confederation would have entailed painful adjustments and West Germany was always bound to be the dominant partner. The inexperience of East Germans in so many fields demanded a constructive response. All those things are unquestionably true. At the same time the style of unification has had baleful consequences. However pleased East Germans may be to be free of the *Stasi* and free to travel, those benefits pall if they have no job. Frustrations are vented all too easily on foreigners of any description. If opinion polls are reliable, some 40 per cent of East Germans have no faith in democracy. Germany has also lost an alternative model. It is one thing to say that East Germany was repressive and authoritarian and an inferior model of economic and social development, something other to say that the heritage of a quarter of one's fellow citizens is devoid of value. Pluralism is about more than making a choice every four years between two major parties who agree on infinitely more than they disagree on. It is about an environment in which very different threads of experience interweave and enrich each other. It is also about trust and confidence. The history of Germany in the twentieth century has resulted in a country with an arguably excessive respect for conformity and orthodoxy. The Greens have introduced one corrective but Germany would benefit from more and the East German experience could have been employed constructively in this way. The concrete Wall and the barbed wire may have gone but the 'Wall in the head' of incomprehension between East Germans and West Germans (*Ossis und Wessis*) has not yet followed suit. Helmut Schmidt, the former West German Chancellor, has repeatedly underlined the extent to which all Germans, in the east as much as in the west, made the most of the unenviable cards they had been dealt by time, but his words have not always been heeded. Germany may yet live to regret its presumption that the West German way is the only way.

The issue is not academic. German political discourse is focused on European economic and monetary union, employment and the prospects for the economy, and it seems likely that such questions will dominate the 1998 elections if not monopolise them. In retrospect, though, it may well appear that the real problems were social rather than economic: the challenge of absorbing the millions of guest workers and the not unrelated question of Germany's place in the world.

Coming to terms with, rather than simply overriding, the different priorities of East and West Germany could have been a constructive step forward in this direction. It is surely not self-evident, for example, that access to a telephone is of greater value than access to a crèche? Germany is not a multi-ethnic state in the way that many of its neighbours are. It has not absorbed large numbers of immigrants, many of mixed blood, from its former colonies like Britain, France and the Netherlands, for the simple reason that it never had many, and lost those it had in 1919. The 'colonies' of Germany, in the sense of areas of economic expansion, settlement and cultural transfer, have been in central and eastern Europe and in Russia since the knights of the Teutonic Order sought to take their form of Christianity there rather than to the Holy Land in the thirteenth century. Ethnic Germans from those areas have always been considered 'German' and entitled to enter and settle in Germany, regardless of the fact that they may no longer speak the language or have any meaningful connection with it.

Guest workers, however, who in practice come mainly from Turkey and the former Yugoslavia, are in no sense considered 'German': the concept is ethnic not cultural. They, therefore, enjoy no political rights, even if they are by now second or even third generation residents. Arguments in favour of this situation can be found. Eberhard Diepgen, currently governing mayor of Berlin, fears the establishment of divisive national parties. Nevertheless, the situation seems unsustainable. The Turks are unlikely to return and many of the Yugoslavs may be literally unable to, even if they wished to. Germany's moral and political standing and even its ability to recognise such ambitions as securing a permanent seat on the UN Security Council could well be affected by the quality of its ultimate response.

1.4 Chronology of key events following unification

1990

12 October. Wolfgang Schäuble, interior minister, is shot and seriously wounded by Dieter Kaufmann, a disturbed drug addict, after a political rally at Oppenau, Baden-Württemberg. He recovers, but is henceforth confined to a wheelchair.

14 November. Germany and Poland sign a treaty pursuant to the 12 September Treaty on the Final Settlement confirming the Oder-Neisse line as their joint border and renouncing any German claims to territory lost as a result of the Second World War.

2 December. The CDU/CSU win the 12th Bundestag elections, with Helmut Kohl as Chancellor candidate, but remain dependent on FDP support.

1991

21 May. The Czechoslovak federal assembly approves legislation on the restitution of confiscated land. It excludes owners who had been 'transferred abroad' in 1945 and had not declared themselves Czechoslovak citizens (i.e. the Sudetens). (See 'Sudetenland' in *Glossary* for fuller particulars.)

17 June. Germany and Poland sign a Friendship Treaty which again recognises the Oder-Neisse border and which guarantees minorities' rights in both countries.

20 June. The Bundestag decides to move both itself and the seat of government from Bonn to Berlin.

2 July. Gerd Gies (CDU) resigns as *Ministerpräsident* of Saxony-Anhalt following accusations by his colleagues that he had made false allegations against three members of working for the East German security police.

5 July. The Bundesrat resolves by 38 votes to 30 to remain in Bonn. It nevertheless agrees to reconsider the decision in a few years' time.

9 July. Gerald Götting, chairman of the East German CDU, 1966–89, is sentenced to eighteen months' imprisonment for using Party funds to build a personal holiday home.

15 July. The last Soviet warship leaves German waters.

18 August. The remains of Frederick the Great of Prussia and his father are reburied with state honours at Schloss Sanssouci in Potsdam in the presence of Chancellor Kohl. It is interpreted as a move to restore the identity of Prussia, expunged as a *Land* by the Allies in 1947, and to dissociate Frederick from Nazi adulation.

6 September. Lothar de Maizière, formerly East German prime minister, resigns as deputy chairman of the CDU, and announces that he is to resign as chairman of the Brandenburg CDU also, following continued allegations that he had been a *Stasi* informer, 1981–88. He had already resigned from the government, and was to relinquish his Bundestag seat from 30 September. He is succeeded as deputy chairman by Angela Merkel from Mecklenburg-West Pomerania.

17–23 September. Nightly attacks on asylum applicants erupt across Saxony, led by representatives of the far right. They are at their most severe in Hoyerswerda, where the hostel is besieged and Molotov cocktails thrown.

29 September. The far-right DVU (German People's Union) wins 6.2 per cent of the vote and six seats in the Bremen elections, and thereby gains representation at *Land* level for the first time.

14 November. The Bundestag approves legislation on access by individuals to their own *Stasi* files. Such files had been maintained on one East German in three. They will, however, only be available to the press with the prior permission of the administering commission.

1992

20 January. Ingo Heinrich and Andreas Kühnpast, two former East German border guards, are convicted of manslaughter and attempted manslaughter respectively for killing Chris Gueffroy, the last person to die attempting to cross from East to West Germany.

The case was to go to appeal to determine whether West German law could be retrospectively applied to East Germany.

23 January. Josef Duchac (CDU) resigns as *Ministerpräsident* of Thuringia as a result of increasing concern over his relations with the former East German regime. He is succeeded by Bernhard Vogel (CDU), a former *Ministerpräsident* of the Rhineland-Palatinate.

4 February. Argentina reveals that it issued some 2,000 passports to German Nazi fugitives in the years after the War. They had included Josef Mengele, resident in Buenos Aires, 1959–85, an SS officer known as the 'Angel of Death' for his medical and genetic experiments in Auschwitz concentration camp. He had allegedly sent 400,000 Jews to their deaths in the gas chambers.

7 February. Wolfgang Berghofer, formerly mayor of Dresden, is sentenced to one year's imprisonment (suspended) and a fine of DM36,000 for falsifying results in the East German local elections of May 1989.

8–9 February. Two neo-Nazi attacks on hostels for asylum seekers result in the deaths of fifteen people, including eight children.

27 February. Chancellor Kohl and President Havel sign in Prague a treaty of good neighbourliness and co-operation between Germany and Czechoslovakia.

12 March. The Bundestag establishes a commission of inquiry into the former East German regime under the chairmanship of Rainer Eppelmann, a well-known dissident.

16 March. Alfred Gomolka (CDU) resigns as *Ministerpräsident* of Mecklenburg-West Pomerania, following criticism of his handling of the privatisation of the shipyards in the *Land*. He is succeeded by Berndt Seite, the CDU *Land* general secretary.

31 March. Gerhard Stoltenberg resigns as German defence minister following protests over the use of German armoured vehicles against the Kurds by the Turkish army. It had been revealed on 27 March that German tanks had been sold to Turkey illegally in late 1991.

Hans Modrow, formerly chairman of the East German Council of Ministers, is charged in Dresden with electoral fraud in the East German local elections of May 1989.

5 April. The far-right *Republikaner* win 10.9 per cent of the vote and fifteen seats in the Baden-Württemberg elections, and thereby gain representation at *Land* level for the first time.

The far-right DVU (German People's Union) wins 6.3 per cent of the vote and six seats in the Schleswig-Holstein *Land* elections.

22 April. The Czechoslovak federal assembly approves February's friendship treaty with Germany after ten hours of debate by 144 votes to 33 with 47 abstentions.

15 May. Six former East German leaders, including Erich Honecker, General Erich Mielke, head of the *Stasi*, Willi Stoph, prime minister, and Heinz Kessler, defence minister, are charged with manslaughter arising from the 'shoot-to-kill' order of May 1974, which had resulted in the deaths of more than 200 people trying to cross the inter-German border.

22 May. Germany and France agree to create a joint army corps of at least 35,000 soldiers to be operational by October 1995. The European Corps is to operate under the WEU for the defence of western Europe and for humanitarian and peacekeeping operations, and is envisaged as the core of a European army.

31 May. The unveiling of a statue in London by the Queen Mother to Sir Arthur 'Bomber' Harris, wartime head of Britain's Bomber Command, provokes considerable resentment in Germany.

5 June. The Bundestag approves an asylum bill reducing the period of inquiry into applicants from an average of nine months to six weeks. Germany had been receiving some 60 per cent of all refugees in the EU.

14 June. Brandenburg adopts in a referendum a new constitution which guarantees the right to work and housing.

26 June. The Bundesrat ratifies the Czechoslovak–German friendship treaty signed in February. Only the Bavarian representatives remain opposed.

30 June. Germany withdraws from the multinational European Fighter Aircraft project on grounds of cost and the changed security situation.

3 July. Ibrahim Böhme, chairman of the East German SPD in 1990, is expelled from the SPD for having joined the *Stasi* in the 1970s and informed on the East German SPD from 1989.

11 July. Peter-Michael Diestel, the last East German interior minister (CDU), and Gregor Gysi, chairman of the PDS, launch an all-party movement to represent the interests of former East Germans. 'Committees for justice' are planned at grass roots level to seek to reduce mass unemployment, deindustrialisation, the collapse of agriculture and the humiliation of individuals.

30 July. Erich Honecker is further charged with 49 cases of manslaughter and with misappropriation of state funds.

22–26 August. A reception centre for asylum applicants at Lichtenhagen near Rostock is attacked by several hundred neo-Nazis for five successive nights. The ground floor is set alight on 25 August. Many bystanders are sympathetic, and police reinforcements are not brought in for several days. 32 arrests are made in due course.

29 August. 15,000 demonstrators march in Rostock against racism.

29–30 August. Neo-Nazi attacks occur in at least fifteen towns, primarily but not exclusively in East Germany.

4–6 September. Attacks on a hostel for asylum applicants at Eisenhüttenstadt on two successive nights lead to the summoning of 200 police and border guards.

8 September. Chancellor Kohl advises the Bundestag that western Germany will have to transfer DM150 billion to eastern Germany annually 'for a long time to come'. He calls for a 'solidarity pact' to finance the increasing cost of unification.

8–11 September. A hostel in Quedlinburg, Saxony-Anhalt, is besieged for four nights. 71 attackers are arrested and local citizens help to guard the residents. Attacks nevertheless continue in Hemsbach, Baden-Württemberg, and in Wismar.

23 September. The government approves an emergency plan to help industry in eastern Germany and to safeguard 400,000 jobs by subsidising foreign construction contracts.

24 September. Markus Wolf, head of the *Stasi*, 1958–87, is charged with treason, espionage and corruption.

Romania agrees to accept back more than 43,000 of its citizens, 60 per cent of them gypsies, who have been living in Germany illegally. Germany pays DM30 million in reintegration aid.

25 September. The Rhine–Main–Danube canal is opened. Construction of the last 40 miles had been authorised in February 1983. (See section 1.2 for fuller particulars.)

3 October. A protest by several thousands against xenophobia, at the former Sachsenhausen concentration camp firebombed the previous month, is counter-balanced by right-wing xenophobic protests in Dresden and Arnstadt, Thuringia.

5 October. German plans for official commemoration of the 50th anniversary of its wartime development of rocket technology near Peenemünde do not come to fruition.

10 October. An extraordinary conference of interior and justice ministers at the federal and *Land* levels fails to agree on how to fight racist violence.

6 November. An agreement is announced whereby some 50,000 Jews living in eastern Europe and the former Soviet Union, who had been persecuted by the Nazi regime but who had not yet been able to claim compensation, will benefit from German payments of US$630 billion between 1992 and 2000.

8 November. 300,000 people support a rally of solidarity with foreigners attended by President von Weizsäcker, Chancellor Kohl and the *Land Ministerpräsidenten*, other than Max Streibl of Bavaria. Similar major rallies are organised in other large cities in November and December.

12 November. The trial opens in Berlin of the six former East German leaders charged in May with manslaughter. The court rules on 13 and 17 November respectively that Willi Stoph and General Mielke are too ill to stand trial. Honecker is considered to have not more than eighteen months to live.

22–23 November. Three Turks die in a racist attack on their homes at Mölln, Schleswig-Holstein. They bring the number of deaths from racist attacks during the year to seventeen.

1993

3 January. Jürgen Möllemann (FDP) resigns as Vice-Chancellor and economics minister over improper use of influence.

13 January. Erich Honecker is allowed to join his wife in Chile. (See section 2.8 and *Biographies* for fuller particulars.)

3 February. Volker Rühe, defence minister, announces that all major weapons expenditure is suspended so as to save DM860 million in 1993 and DM700 million in each of the following three years. The savings will assist higher spending on eastern Germany.

13 March. Federal government and opposition leaders, together with all the *Ministerpräsidenten*, agree on a public spending package which will be one element of the proposed 'solidarity pact' to help eastern Germany.

A 'solidarity surcharge' of 7.5 per cent is to be added to income tax from 1 January 1995, social spending is not to be reduced and public borrowing will rise by a further DM60 billion. Implementation of the agreement will permit the transfer of DM110 billion to eastern Germany in 1995.

17 March. The imposition of prison sentences in Berlin of 5 years 9 months and 2 years 9 months, for trying to blow up a Jewish memorial and to firebomb an asylum applicants' hostel respectively, mark a new severity by the courts towards right-wing extremism.

26–28 April. 85–90 per cent of eastern German steel, electrical and metal workers vote in favour of industrial action to support their claim for a 26 per cent pay rise. The rise would bring eastern pay levels up to western levels, as had been agreed by the employers' association and the union in March 1991.

3 May. Björn Engholm resigns as chair of the SPD, its Chancellor candidate, and *Ministerpräsident* of Schleswig-Holstein, following his admission that he had not told a parliamentary inquiry of his prior knowledge of a 'dirty tricks campaign' against him by his CDU *Land* opponent, Uwe Barschel.

6 May. Günther Krause (CDU), resigns as transport minister over financial irregularities. He had been the leading former East German in the cabinet.

7 May. Rudolf Seiters and Andzej Milczanowski, interior ministers, sign an agreement on the return of asylum applicants to Poland. Germany will give Poland DM120 million in 1993 and 1994 for the improvement of border controls and reception centres.

19 May. Heide Simonis in Schleswig-Holstein becomes the first woman *Ministerpräsident.*

23 May. The eastern German steelworkers strike approved on 26–28 April and effective from 3 May, is resolved on the basis of wage parity by 1996 rather than 1994.

25 May. *Die Republikaner* secure representation in the Bundestag for the first time with the defection of Rudolf Krause from the CDU. He had been *Land* interior minister in Saxony.

27 May. Hans Modrow, the former East German prime minister, is found guilty in Dresden of electoral fraud in the May 1989 communal elections. He receives a caution, as do three other defendants.

29 May. Five Turkish women and girls are killed in an arson attack on their home at Solingen in the Ruhr. Three others are seriously injured. Turks and Germans organise protest demonstrations in Solingen and elsewhere over the next three days.

31 May. Chancellor Kohl claims that the Solingen attacks reveal 'an unfathomable degree of brutalisation and contempt for humanity'.

4 July. Rudolf Seiters (CDU) resigns as interior minister, taking political responsibility for a bungled anti-terrorist operation.

16 September. Heinz Kessler, former East German defence minister, is sentenced in Berlin to seven and a half years' imprisonment in connection with the 'shoot-to-kill' policy.

26 October. General Mielke is found guilty in Berlin of two murders and one attempted murder in 1931. He had been found guilty of the same offences by the Nazis in 1934. It is argued that the Statute of Limitation does not apply because the relevant files were in Soviet hands, 1947–89.

28 November. Dr Werner Münch, *Ministerpräsident* of Saxony-Anhalt (CDU), and his government resign over overpayments to four of their number over the previous two years. The four, including Dr Münch, are all westerners.

6 December. Markus Wolf, former head of the *Stasi*, is sentenced to six years' imprisonment in Dusseldorf for treason and bribery. (See also section 2.8 (1995) and *Biographies* for fuller particulars.)

1994

24–25 March. The Lübeck synagogue is damaged by a firebomb.

12 May. More than 40 neo-Nazi youths attack five Africans in Magdeburg in broad daylight. Neither police nor public make a ready response.

20 May. The Bundestag approves a raft of measures against violence by the far Right and against organised crime.

The Bundestag approves a DM18 billion compensation fund for owners of property in eastern Germany confiscated by the Nazis or the East German regime.

23 May. Roman Herzog, the CDU candidate, is elected as Germany's next president by the Federal Assembly on the third ballot.

16 October. The CDU/CSU win the 13th Bundestag elections with Helmut Kohl as Chancellor candidate. However, they achieve their lowest share of the vote since 1949, and have an overall majority with their FDP coalition partners of only ten seats.

31 December. The *Treuhandanstalt* privatisation agency is wound up. Of the 4 million jobs in East German state enterprises in July 1990, 2.5 million had been lost.

1995

9 January. Seven former members of the SED Politbüro are charged with manslaughter in connection with deaths on the former inter-German border. They are: Egon Krenz, Horst Dohlus, Kurt Hager, Günther Kleiber, Erich Mückenberger, Günter Schabowski and Harry Tisch.

7 May. The Lübeck synagogue suffers a second arson attack.

29 June. The Bundestag approves a revised abortion bill. Although abortion remains illegal, it is not a punishable offence if carried out in the first three months of pregnancy and is preceded by counselling.

13 November. The trial opens in Berlin of Egon Krenz and the other Politbüro members.

1996

16 January. Ezer Weizmann, president of Israel, tells the Bundestag and Bundesrat that he cannot forgive in the name of the Jewish victims of Nazi extermination policies.

3 February. The Land *Ministerpräsidenten* unanimously oppose the reduction from 7.5 per cent to 5.5 per cent in the solidarity surcharge on income tax, proposed in the government's 'action programme for growth' of 30 January.

25 April. The government approves an austerity programme which seeks spending cuts of DM70 billion. The reduction in the solidarity surcharge will now be phased over two years. It comes into effect on 1 October.

9 August. Chancellor Kohl announces on television that he is hoping for a thorough revision of the German taxation system with effect from 1999.

10 October. Germany and the Federal Republic of Yugoslavia (Serbia and Montenegro) sign a repatriation agreement on the return of some 135,000 refugees, many of them Kosovo Albanians, over three years from 1 December 1996. The agreement specifies that the return will proceed with 'complete respect for the human rights and dignity' of those involved. Manfred Kanther, interior minister, maintains that the agreement underscores the fact that Germany is not a land for immigrants.

1997

9 January. 34 leading American artists, centred on the film industry, publish an open letter to Chancellor Kohl in the *International Herald Tribune* alleging German discrimination against scientologists and comparing their position with that of the Jews under Hitler.

6 March. Trade union leaders, alarmed by the February unemployment figures, call for a delay to European economic and monetary union (EMU), unless job creation is a feature of the revised Maastricht Treaty to be negotiated in Amsterdam.

3 April. Helmut Kohl announces that he is willing to stand as CDU/CSU Chancellor candidate in the 14th Bundestag elections due in September 1998.

15 May. Theo Waigel, finance minister, announces a plan to revalue Germany's gold and foreign exchange reserves so as to reduce government debt and to help Germany meet EMU criteria. The Bundesbank characterises the plan as creative accounting, and it is abandoned on 3 June.

6 June. The May unemployment figures show an adjusted total of 4.36 million, equivalent to 11.4 per cent of the work-force. It is the highest level of unemployment since the War.

The interior ministry announces that it is placing the Church of Scientology under observation on suspicion of its being an anti-democratic organisation.

10–11 August. Theo Waigel, finance minister, urges a renewed cabinet to 'clear dead wood'.

13–15 October. Chancellor Kohl indicates at a CDU Congress in Leipzig that Wolfgang Schäuble is his preferred successor.

25 November. The Bundestag agrees to move to Berlin in the summer of 1999. The government is expected to move at about the same time.

1998

5 February. The Federal Labour Office reports that the January unemployment rate has risen to 12.6 per cent, its highest monthly level since the war.

9 February. 155 prominent German economists publish a manifesto urging an 'orderly postponement' of economic and monetary union in view of the condition of the German economy.

2 March. The SPD confirms that Gerhard Schröder is to be its Chancellor candidate for the September 1998 elections.

26 March. The Bundestag begins consideration of a bill to grant foreigners an automatic right to German citizenship provided their families have lived in Germany for two generations. The bill has the support of the SPD and some members of the FDP, but is opposed by Chancellor Kohl. It falls following pressure from him on the FDP.

23 April. The Bundestag formally approves German participation in EMU by 575 votes to 35 with five abstentions.

26 April. The far-Right DVU wins 12.9 per cent of the vote and 16 seats in the Saxony-Anhalt *Land* elections. The results are seen as a major rebuff for Chancellor Kohl.

SECTION TWO

Government

2.1 Interim structures, 1945–48

It is easy to forget from the perspective of more than half a century later the scale of the devastation encountered by the victorious Allies as they advanced across Germany in the last months of the War. Adenauer was to note in his memoirs that more than 50 per cent of prewar dwellings in all major cities had been destroyed, a proportion rising to 80 per cent in some places. 40 per cent of all transport installations was in ruins. The practical necessity of imposing some sort of order was paramount. Marshal Zhukov, the Soviet commander, noted that the top priority of his troops in Berlin was to extinguish the fires that were raging everywhere, to make sure the corpses were recovered and buried, and to clear the city of mines. His American and British colleagues elsewhere in Germany would have said much the same. The dislocation in the countryside was often equally as great, although the physical devastation was obviously of a different order.

Such strictly practical considerations advanced in counterpoint to others of a more political and strategic nature in untidy fashion. Local military commanders did what seemed best to them in their particular circumstances, and of necessity employed Germans who had opposed or were at least not closely linked to the defeated regime. In practice that predominantly meant communists, socialists, and middle class opponents of Hitler on moral and/or religious grounds. At a higher level, the military authorities installed Germans whom they had identified in advance as potential leaders. Most had held office before Hitler, and been persecuted to a greater or lesser degree in the intervening period. The Americans had their 'White List' on which Dr Adenauer stood as number one. The Soviet Union had its Free Germany Committee organised in Moscow. The Allies rather inevitably tried to pick leaders whose world view seemed likely to echo their own. This did not always work as intended. Dr Adenauer, whom the Americans reappointed to the mayoralty of Cologne which he had held until 1933, was to be summarily dismissed by the British on 6 October 1945 for unsatisfactory performance of his duties. The future Chancellor was even prohibited from indulging in any kind of political activity for some months.

Such Germans were in an unenviable situation. Even if appointed to administrative, rather than purely advisory, posts they were prohibited from discussing the policy issues such as industrial dismantling and reparations which directly affected their countrymen, but could, like Dr Högner in Bavaria, be expected to witness the Nuremberg executions as witnesses for the German people. They slowly grew in legitimacy as consultative councils became advisory and then executive bodies, and as appointed members were confirmed or replaced in elections, first at the local (*Kreis*) level and progressively at higher levels. The new governmental structure at the local and regional level was, in fact, established with remarkable speed, largely because the Allies simply recreated many of the self-governing units into which Germany had traditionally been divided. Little regard was had to consistency in population or area, although some of the embryonic *Länder* were amalgamations of smaller units. Framework *Land* administrations were established in the Soviet Zone by July 1945 and, by the end of September, the three *Länder* in the American Zone all had their *Ministerpräsidenten* with executive authority, subject to overall American supervision. Indeed General Eisenhower was claiming on 29 September that the new *Land* governments already had more authority than their predecessors under the Nazi regime.

The great change at this regional level was the decision not to recreate Prussia. Indelibly associated in the Allied mind with authoritarianism and militarism, the core state in the nineteenth-century unification of Germany, which had stretched from Cologne to Kaliningrad (*Königsberg*), was not reborn in 1945 and was formally abolished by the Allies in 1947.

The creation of democratic legitimacy was a much more challenging and difficult task.

The first free elections in Germany since 1932 were held in January 1946 when electors in towns with fewer than 20,000 people in the American Zone voted for mayors and town councils. About 30 per cent of the electorate was, however, disenfranchised on account of its earlier membership of Nazi organisations and apathy was conspicuous. That was hardly surprising. Conditions were harsh and Eisenhower himself had noted that food consumption at sometimes a third below subsistence level was resulting in physical lethargy. Empathy with candidates endorsed by the Allies, who had agreed at Potsdam to the expulsion of some twelve million Germans from their homes, must have been minimal. The electorate voted because it was what the Allies wanted, and it could not argue with the will of the Allies.

The danger for the politicians was that they would be tarnished by association, as their predecessors had been in 1919, and that fear grew as conditions worsened through an adverse combination of circumstances. The combination of the exceptionally severe winter of 1946 followed by the drought of summer 1947, the reduction in industrial capacity through the dismantling of installations as reparations, and the presence of some twelve million displaced Germans, meant that conditions in the immediate postwar years barely improved and in many cases positively worsened. By the autumn of 1947 the Soviet Zone was suffering from mass hunger. It was only when Allied policy in the west was reversed and positive effort was put into rebuilding the German economy, and when Marshall Aid provided the necessary funding, that the new democratic institutions, first at the local and then at the national level, had any chance of being popularly accepted as an essential element of a prosperous and successful Germany.

The failure, or more probably the inability, of the Soviet Union to pursue a similar change of policy before 1953, clearly did much to undermine support in the east for the alternative structure of representative bodies organised under the auspices of the SED.

2.2 The establishment and development of the German Federal Republic

The constituent assembly convened on 1 September 1948 to draft a constitution for the envisaged West German state was not working in a vacuum. The western Allies had determined as early as 1945 that post-war German administration should be extensively decentralised in character, so as to make the rise of another Hitler as difficult as possible. *Land* governments had been established by all the Allies with remarkable speed. The Americans and the British had also created an Economic Council in January 1948 which, with its cabinet, court and upper chamber, had many of the characteristics of an embryonic governmental structure. The *Länder* themselves had been reinforced in the western zones by banking laws which had established central banks for each *Land* and decentralised the commercial banks. A new central reserve bank for the nine *Land* central banks, the *Bank deutscher Länder*, the precursor of the Bundesbank, had been established on 14 February 1948.

The *Land Ministerpräsidenten* had nevertheless received with considerable reserve the instruction of the Allied military governors on 1 July 1948 to convene the constituent assembly. They feared that the move would confirm the division of Germany and agreed with the leaders of the two main political parties before the assembly met that they should prepare a 'Basic Law' (*Grundgesetz*) rather than a constitution, so as to underline the new state's provisional nature. The Basic Law was finalised on 8 May 1949, but its provisional nature was again underlined by persuading the western Allies to agree to ratification by the Landtage, rather than by the electorate. Whether it would have been approved in a referendum at the time we cannot know, but contemporary opinion surveys suggest apathy rather than enthusiasm. It is more important that it has stood the test of time with considerable success.

The governmental system reflects traditional German practice in that the Chancellor governs outside rather than inside parliament. He does not have to seek the Bundestag's approval for his cabinet although he is himself appointed by the Bundestag. The Chancellor's office (*Kanzleramt*) is accordingly an important organ in the governmental structure, giving rise to the expression 'Chancellor democracy'. The presidency is ceremonial and procedural, but can carry considerable moral weight. The president is appointed by a Federal Assembly composed of all members of the Bundestag and an equivalent number of members appointed by the Landtage.

Germany is a federal state with powers divided between the national and *Land* governments both horizontally and vertically. The *Länder* are accordingly responsible for the execution of many national functions, but are themselves directly responsible for large sectors of public policy, including the control of education and the police. They have their own sources of finance, as of right. Representatives of the *Länder* form the upper house, the Bundesrat, whose consent is required for the enactment of legislation approved by the Bundestag, including the federal budget.

The Basic Law sought to prevent the rise of another Hitler not only by making Germany a federal, decentralised state but also by seeking to avoid the instability of German governments before 1933. A Chancellor (or a *Ministerpräsident*) cannot therefore be removed from office unless the Bundestag passes a 'constructive vote of no confidence'. That means that the incumbent cannot be removed, even if he or she can no longer command a majority, unless there is at the same time a majority for a specific replacement. Chancellor Kohl gained office through this route in 1982.

Electoral law pursues a similar objective by generally requiring parties to achieve 5 per cent of the vote to be represented in a Landtag or the Bundestag. This '5 per cent hurdle' may, however, be varied to allow for local circumstances, such as the existence of the Danish minority in Schleswig-Holstein. Each elector has two votes: the first for a specific candidate in a comparatively large geographical constituency, the second (*Zweitstimme*) for a national party list. It is common for the two votes to be given to different parties, with the FDP benefiting disproportionately from second votes, reflecting an apparent desire by the electorate to align politics towards the centre.

The political parties enjoy particular status as the embodiment of the public will in a state rooted in law, and enjoy considerable public funding to reflect their responsibilities for political education and the encouragement of public participation in the conduct of public affairs.

2.3 The establishment and development of the German Democratic Republic

Commentary

The key differences between the East and West German systems were not strictly speaking constitutional, but were focused on the electoral system and on different concepts of the role of the political parties. Although both systems maintained that power flowed from the people, Marxism as developed by Lenin taught that democracy could only be achieved with guidance, and that that guidance could best be provided by a Communist party, because such a party was rooted in the most politically advanced social class, namely the working class. The German middle class, in particular, was considered to have lost any moral claim to political power by its endorsement of the Nazi regime. The SED was therefore conceived from the beginning as being in the vanguard of political progress and, at an early stage, as having a different role from that of the other parties, even though that leading role was not recognised constitutionally until 1974. Elections were never conceived as a way of changing the balance of power between the different political parties but, at most, as a way of expressing approval, or disapproval, of a list of candidates. The allocation of seats in the Volkskammer was pre-arranged and held to be democratic, because it reflected what the SED, as the leading party within the National Front, interpreted as the desirable end state of affairs. Whether or not it corresponded to the will of the electorate at any particular time was essentially secondary, because the electorate might be ill-advised or ill-informed. The SED, on the other hand, like all orthodox Communist parties, was held to be scientific in its analysis and in its prescriptions.

This prime position for one party and one interpretation of history readily provoked another major difference. Whereas the whole West German system was rooted in the concept of law and legal relationships between institutions, East German institutions were always subordinate to the leading role of the SED. The administration of justice, as just one example, was always liable to be distorted by essentially political considerations.

The SED itself always claimed to be democratic in its internal structure, but its democracy took the form of 'democratic centralism'. In principle this meant that, when a decision had been taken by the majority vote at the lowest level of the Party, a delegate bound by that decision cast his or her vote accordingly at the next level up, until a final decision rooted in majorities at each constituent level was reached at the top. That final decision was then passed down again as binding on all levels of the Party down to the lowest. Even in theory that meant that there could be no adjustment to local opinion, preference or circumstance once policy had been fixed at the national level, and it was inherently undemocratic in the liberal sense, in that dissenting opinion was squeezed out at each successive stage of decision making.

The reality was even less democratic as a result of the related concentration of power at the top of the Party. The political bureau of the central committee (the *Politbüro*) directed the Party, as the Party directed the country, and the real power lay with the general secretary, who was responsible for all Party appointments and could therefore engineer majorities for preferred policy objectives. It was Ulbricht and then Honecker, not successive prime ministers, who really mattered, just as it was Stalin, Khrushchev, Brezhnev and Gorbachev who mattered in the Soviet Union from their holding of the same office. The danger in normal times without the stimulus of either Stalin-style purges or the alternation of parties in government was not so much one-man dictatorships as dictatorship by a self-perpetuating oligarchy. Its deepest practical fault was not brutality or sadism but an unquestioning rigidity unable to cope with changing circumstances.

Chronology

1947

6–7 December. The 1st People's Congress is held in the Soviet Zone, allegedly to prepare a German-formulated policy for Germany which could be submitted to the London conference of foreign ministers. The CDU leaders, Lemmer and Kaiser, decline to participate and lose their Soviet political permits. They subsequently move to West Germany.

1948

17–18 March. The 2nd People's Congress elects a German People's Council of 330 members, of whom 100 allegedly represent West Germany. It is led by a Praesidium comprising the chairmen of the participating parties and mass organisations.

1949

19 March. The People's Council approves a constitution for a German Democratic Republic and calls for elections to a 3rd People's Congress.

15–16 May. Single list elections are held to the 3rd Congress with the reluctant consent of parties other than the SED. 61.6 per cent of voters allegedly support the official list.

30 May. The 3rd Congress meets and nominates 330 members to sit in a new People's Council.

7 October. The People's Council turns itself into a provisional People's Chamber (*Volkskammer*) and adopts a liberal democratic constitution.

The German Democratic Republic (GDR) is proclaimed in East Berlin on the 32nd anniversary of the communist revolution in Russia. The high commissioners of the western Allies argue that it is the artificial creation of a 'popular assembly' which has no mandate for the purpose. On that basis, they refuse to recognise it and other non-Communist countries follow suit.

11 October. The parliaments of the five *Länder* elect representatives to sit in the *Länderkammer*, or upper chamber. Wilhelm Pieck is elected president of the GDR by a joint session of the two chambers.

12 October. The first East German government is announced, headed by Otto Grotewohl of the SED. His deputies are: Walter Ulbricht (SED), Otto Nuschke (CDU) and Professor Hermann Kastner (LDPD). The SED has a clear majority of ten to eight with the ministries of foreign affairs, work and health, and posts and telecommunications being allocated to the CDU, and finance and trade to the LDPD.

1950

8 February. The Volkskammer approves the establishment of a ministry of state security with unlimited powers. Later to be familiar as the *Stasi*, it is headed by Wilhelm Zaisser, chief of the *Volkspolizei* (People's police).

15 October. The East German elections on that day are preceded by warnings in *Neues Deutschland* two days before that those who do not vote for the National Front may be exposed as opponents of 'peace, German unity and the welfare of the people'. Open voting without ballot boxes is officially encouraged. The National Front had been established on 7 January. (See section 2.4 for fuller particulars.)

1952

23 July. The Volkskammer agrees to dissolve the five *Länder* and to replace them with fifteen *Bezirke* (districts), each with its own *Bezirkstag* and *Bezirksrat*. The reforms which also create 217 subordinate *Landkreise*, are to be implemented by 30 September.

1958

8 December. East Germany abolishes the 63-member upper house (*Länderkammer*) representing the *Bezirke*, including East Berlin.

1960

12 September. The Volkskammer unanimously amends the East German constitution by replacing the office of president with a Council of State.

1963

17 April. The Volkskammer approves legislation greatly increasing the power of the Council of State (*Staatsrat*), and decreasing that of the Council of Ministers (*Ministerrat*), which becomes an administrative rather than a policy-making body. Supervision of the judiciary is transferred from the ministry of justice to the Council of State.

31 July. The Volkskammer approves legislation setting the term of office of elected bodies, including itself, at four years, providing for the 'guarantee of the democratic execution' of elections by the Council of State, the replacement of at least one third of the total of sitting members at every election and the election at the same time of 'successor candidates'.

1968

26 March. The Volkskammer approves a new East German constitution, replacing that of 7 October 1949. It no longer provides for the rights of trade unions to strike, for the right to emigrate and for press freedom. It comes into force on 9 April.

1974

27 September. The Volkskammer unanimously amends the 1968 East German constitution. Article 1 emphasises that East Germany is 'a socialist state of workers and farmers. It is a political organisation of workers in town and country under the leadership of the working class and its Marxist-Leninist party'. Article 6(2) strengthens the bond with the Soviet Union, East Germany 'is linked irrevocably and for ever with the Soviet Union'.

1976

24 June. The Volkskammer fixes the legislative period for all East German representative bodies, including itself, at five years.

1989

1 December. By 420 votes to none, with five abstentions, the Volkskammer deletes the constitutional provision that the state is 'led by the working class and its Marxist-Leninist party'.

1990

5 April. The Volkskammer approves a constitutional amendment replacing the Council of State by a president.

22 July. The Volkskammer re-establishes the *Länder*, abolished in 1952.

2.4 The political parties

1945

30 April. Walter Ulbricht, Anton Ackermann and Gustav Sobottka are despatched to Germany by the party leadership headquarters in Moscow to operate Communist Party Central Committee Groups in Berlin, Saxony and Mecklenburg. No such groups were sent into the other zones and a Soviet document of 5 April suggests that their initial task was to organise the populace in the way the Soviet authorities wanted rather than to inaugurate immediate political activity among the Germans.

10 June. Marshal Zhukov permits the establishment and activity of all anti-Fascist parties in the Soviet Zone which have as their aim the securing of democratic foundations and civic freedoms.

11 June. The Communist Party (KPD) is the first party to issue its manifesto. It calls for a democratic parliamentary republic in which full rights for all men and women and full liberties for all anti-Fascist parties and organisations would be guaranteed. Representatives of the working people should assume the commanding heights of the state and the economy, and all those willing to help in the reconstruction effort should join together under the leadership of the united working class. Among its prominent signatories are Walter Ulbricht, Wilhelm Pieck, Anton Ackermann, Franz Dahlem and Gustav Sobottka.

15 June. The Central Committee of the Social Democrats (SPD) in Berlin issues a programme of action similar to that of the Communists, demanding 'the removal of all remnants of Fascist rule and the eradication of militarism from our hearts and minds'; a democratic anti-Fascist republic; the rebuilding of economic life on a Socialist basis; encouragement of the growth of free trade unions; new property laws with the aim of redistributing large estates for the benefit of the community; nationalisation of the banks, public utilities and primary industries. Signatories include Gustav Dahrendorf, Max Fechner, Otto Grotewohl, Karl Litke, Josef Orlopp, Hermann Schlimme and Richard Weimann.

19–22 June. The Communists and the Social-Democrats decide to collaborate closely with the aim of 'ensuring the liquidation of the vestiges of Nazism and building the country on sure foundations'. Joint action committees are set up in consequence at the local level, particularly in the Soviet Zone.

26 June. The Christian Democratic Union issues its appeal to the German people. The Berlin CDU had been created by certain former members of the German Democratic and Catholic Centre Parties, and by Christian and white collar trade unionists. Its leaders include Dr Walther Schreiber, Dr Andreas Hermes, Heinrich Krone, Jakob Kaiser and Ernst Lemmer. It declares its belief in the importance of private property, but recognises the need for the state ownership of mineral resources, including the mines, and of major industrial monopolies. It also accepts the importance of firm economic planning.

5 July. Publication in Berlin of the manifesto of the Liberal Democratic Party (LDPD), created by other former members of the Catholic Centre and Democratic Parties who place greater stress on private property and free enterprise while accepting the state control of certain enterprises. Its leaders include Dr Wilhelm Külz and Dr Eugen Schiffer.

6 July. First mass meeting of democratic parties since Hitler's rise to power takes place in the Tiergarten, Berlin, and is attended by representatives of the SPD, KPD, LDPD and CDU. A manifesto is adopted with unanimous approval stating that the representatives of the four parties 'mutually acknowledging the independence of each party [have decided to create] a strong united front of democratic parties in order to accomplish by united effort the great tasks facing us'. To this end a joint committee would be created which would meet at least twice a month and to which each party would send five representatives.

14 July. The four parties agree to set up the united front endorsed at the 6 July meeting. The Communists see some leaders, such as Otto Nuschke (CDU) and Wilhelm Külz (LDPD) as politicians with whom they can cooperate, but others in key positions as reactionaries contemplating little more than a new version of the Weimar Republic. It is agreed that all decisions and recommendations should be adopted unanimously and it is also recommended that similar committees be established at all levels. The KPD self-consciously pursues a popular front policy in accordance with principles evolved by the 7th World Congress of the Communist International in 1935.

17 August. A directive issued in the American Zone gives Military Government officers the power to approve the formation of democratic parties at the local (*Kreis*) level.

14 September. Field-Marshal Montgomery gives conditional permission for the formation of democratic political parties. The SPD, KPD, and CDU appear as the leading parties in the British Zone.

6–7 October. A conference of the SPD from all four zones is held in Hannover in the British Zone. Otto Grotewohl recognises Kurt Schumacher as the leader of the SPD in the three western zones and Schumacher recognises Grotewohl as its leader in the Soviet Zone.

16 October. General Eisenhower reports that the KPD and the SPD have emerged as the leading parties in the American Zone. In Bavaria a new party, the CSU, has been formed, parallel with the CDU elsewhere. It is described as the successor to the old Bavarian People's (Catholic) Party but, unlike the latter, is not linked to the Catholic hierarchy, rejects the participation of the clergy in political life, and admits Protestants to membership.

21 December. Dr Andreas Hermes is suspended from the leadership of the CDU. Dr Hermes had protested against measures of land expropriation carried out in the Soviet Zone, maintaining that proven non-Nazis whose lands were expropriated should be entitled to compensation. It was reported that his resignation was the direct result of intervention by the Soviet authorities.

At a meeting of the Central Committees of the KPD and SPD in the Soviet Zone in Berlin, it is decided to set up a committee of four members from each party to consider proposals for fusion of the two parties as a single organisation, *Einheitspartei der Arbeiter*. Both parties declare themselves in favour of a single electoral programme and call on local party organisations throughout Germany to collaborate with the aim of amalgamation. It is stated that the minimum programme of the proposed united party shall be 'the completion of the democratic renewal of Germany through the building up of anti-Fascism' and its maximum programme 'the development of Socialism . . . in the spirit of Marx and Engels'. The proposed party would thus be Marxist, but not Marxist-Leninist. The initiative for these negotiations comes in the main from the Communists, supported in their attitude by the Soviet authorities.

1946

8 January. Dr Kurt Schumacher, head of the SPD in the American Zone, declares in Frankfurt that the SPD in the western zones will not unite with the KPD, which they consider as the representative of a foreign imperialist power.

An SPD conference in the British Zone held in Hannover rejects almost unanimously a fusion with the KPD on the ground that similar experiments elsewhere had ended in failure. It also rejects the obligatory character of any decisions taken by the SPD's Central Committee in Berlin.

2–3 March. A KPD conference in Berlin maintains that the anti-Fascist, democratic regeneration of the whole of Germany 'lays the foundations of the unity of Germany and the safeguarding of peace'.

March–April. Unification of the KPD and the SPD in the Soviet Zone takes place from the bottom upwards with the two parties first taking separate votes on the unification issue, then holding joint meetings and setting up factory, local, district and provincial organisations and electing leading committees consisting of an equal number of former KPD and SPD members.

19 April. The Central Committee of the SPD in Berlin organises what it alleges is the Party's 40th national Congress in the Theater am Schiffbauerdamm. Schumacher exercises all the pressure he can to prevent western delegations from attending. He does not, however, succeed in preventing some who favour an immediate merger with the KPD from being present.

A parallel 15th Congress of the KPD also votes for an immediate merger.

21–22 April. The KPD and SPD merge at the Unification Congress held in Berlin's Admiralspalast, later Metropol, Theatre to form the SED. The 3,000 delegates from all four zones represent 620,000 Communists and 680,000 Social Democrats. Wilhelm Pieck, till then leader of the KPD, and Otto Grotewohl, till then leader of the SPD in the Soviet Zone, are elected SED chairmen. Walter Ulbricht is elected deputy chairman.

20 October. The SED gains only 29.8 per cent of the municipal election vote in the Soviet sector of Berlin, compared with 43.6 for the SPD. All elections in which the SED participates henceforth are single-list contests.

1947

3 February. Publication of the Ahlen Programme of the CDU in the British Zone, advocating an 'economic system based on communal ownership [as the] capitalist economic system has not lived up to the vital political and social interests of the German people'. The programme is to be abandoned under Adenauer in favour of Professor Erhard's social market economy. (See *Glossary* for fuller particulars.)

20–24 September. The 2nd SED Congress sees Party membership reach nearly 1.8 million. Ulbricht advises the Congress that the SED is becoming a 'party of a new type', a formula which meant similarity to the developed Soviet model.

1948

17 June. Establishment in the Soviet Zone of the National Democratic Party of Germany (NDPD) and the Democratic Peasants' Party of Germany (DBD).

The NDPD was aimed at former nominal Nazis and medium- and higher-ranking military personnel as well as the middle classes more widely. The political impact of both groups was to remain very small.

15–16 September. The executive committee (*Vorstand*) of the SED rejects any concept of a specifically German road to socialism, and endorses the Soviet model based on Leninist democratic centralism. The SED gives primacy to factory over territorial organisation.

11–12 December. The Liberal parties in the western zones amalgamate as the Free Democratic Party (*Freie Demokratische Partei – FDP*), and issue the Heppenheim Proclamation on the guidelines for future Party policy.

1949

5 January. The western KPD separates from the SED for organisational reasons.

25–28 January. The executive committee abandons the principle of parity between the constituent elements of the SED, and establishes a political bureau (*Politbüro*) with seven full and two candidate members.

1950

7 January. The East German 'People's Congress' movement turns itelf into a National Front encompassing all the permitted political parties, but with a predominant position for the SED. The Front appoints a *Nationalrat* (national council) on 3 February.

29 January. Professor Hugo Hickmann, CDU chairman in Saxony, resigns following the storming of the party offices and press accusations of hostility to the National Front.

9 July. Agreement is reached on the 'single list' of candidates to be sponsored by the East German National Front. It specifies in advance the proportion of seats to be allocated to each party.

20–24 July. The 3rd SED Congress adopts a second revised party statute whereby the executive committee (*Vorstand*) is replaced by a Central Committee, the Politbüro replaces the former Central Secretariat, and effective power passes to the General Secretary of the Central Committee. Although technically elected by the Central Committee, the Politbüro is to prove over the years a self-perpetuating oligarchy.

1 September. *Neues Deutschland* announces that six leading members of the SED have been expelled from the Party. They are: Paul Merker, state secretary in the ministry of agriculture and until the previous SED Congress a member of the Politbüro and Central Committee, Leo Bauer, Bruno Goldhammer, Willy Kreikemeyer, Lex Ende and Maria Weiterer. All those purged had been emigrants in the west during the War and, as such, were now suspect to the Soviet Union. Ongoing purges of the SED membership as a whole reflect similar suspicions and the fear both of Titoism and of the influence of the eastern bureau of the West German SPD. The SED nevertheless avoids the more hysterical reactions of many other Communist-dominated states.

12 September. The East German CDU expels three of its leading members for 'criminal activities and anti-State and anti-Party actions'.

1 November. East Germany introduces one year 'Lenin courses' to prepare 1,200,000 potential members of the SED.

The *Sozialistische Reichspartei* (SRP) is founded by Otto Remer (see *Biographies*) and Count Westarp in West Germany. It is anti-democratic and seeks to revive the Nazi movement.

1951

13 December. Bundestag members of the Bavarian and Centre Parties unite to form the 'Federal Union', so as to ensure continued group recognition in the Bundestag.

1952

9 July. Ulbricht announces that the Central Committee of the SED has decided that 'the planned construction of socialism should begin' in East Germany. He adds, in accordance with Stalinist orthodoxy, that 'the intensification of the class struggle is inevitable'.

23 October. The SRP is declared unconstitutional. It had held sixteen seats in the Lower Saxony Landtag and eight in the Bremen House of Burgesses, together with one in the Bundestag, but had decided to dissolve itself before the court ruling.

1953

13 May. Franz Dahlem, head of the SED's organisational and staff department, is expelled from the party for 'political laxity' and 'an unpartylike attitude towards his own mistakes'.

15 July. Ulbricht dismisses the East German justice minister, Max Fechner, for declaring that it is legal to strike. He is also expelled from the SED on 27 July.

August. Hans Jendretzky, First Secretary of the Berlin SED, is dismissed and ceases to be a candidate member of the SED Central Committee.

1954

23 January. Rudolf Herrnstadt, chief editor of *Neues Deutschland*, 1949–53, and Wilhelm Zaisser, East German minister of state security, 1950–53, are expelled from the SED for factionalism at the 17th Plenum of the Central Committee. They had been relieved of their posts on 24 July 1953.

30 March. Opening of the 4th SED congress. Ulbricht and Grotewohl attack bureaucracy and Honecker reports protests in the Free German Youth against the Oder-Neisse border with Poland.

There is, however, no party programme, probably because of uncertainty as to the future thrust of Soviet policy.

A third SED statute, similar to the Soviet Communist Party statute of October 1952, replaces that approved in 1950. For the first time, it stresses the SED's claim to leadership in all spheres of East German life.

1956

23 February. Sixteen of the 48 FDP members of the Bundestag, including the four cabinet ministers, leave the parliamentary party in protest against an FDP 'revolt' against the Chancellor in North Rhine-Westphalia. The sixteen create a Free People's Party (*Freie Volkspartei* – *FVP*).

24 June. The Free People's Party holds its first Congress in Bochum but merges with the *Deutsche Partei* (German Party) with effect from 21 January 1957.

27–29 July. The Central Committee of the SED rehabilitates Anton Ackermann, Franz Dahlem and others who have been subject to disciplinary action.

17 August. The KPD is declared unconstitutional by the West German Constitutional Court.

29 November. Wolfgang Harich, a member of the SED and an academic at East Berlin's Humboldt University, is arrested for seeking to develop a more popular form of socialism. He is sentenced to ten years' imprisonment the following March for allegedly establishing an anti-state group.

1957

30 January–1 February. Ulbricht advises the Central Committee of the SED that 'We are going on the offensive.'

17 April. Otto Blumenstein, the former SPD mayor of Moxa, East Germany, receives five years' imprisonment for unauthorised contact with the West German SPD.

14–16 November. Ulbricht's authoritarian style of leadership is rehabilitated by his attendance at the Moscow Conference of Communist Parties, which is hostile to revisionism and places increased emphasis on the necessity for strict Party discipline throughout the Communist world.

1958

3–6 February. The SED Central Committee expels Karl Schirdewan from the Central Committee and the Politbüro, Ernst Wollweber from the Committee and Professor Fred Oelssner from the Politbüro. They had been accused in a report prepared by Erich Honecker, then a member of the secretariat, of forming an opportunist group attempting to change the political line of the SED. In practice they had urged a measure of liberalisation in response to Khruschev's denunciation of Stalin and the Hungarian uprising of 1956. Ulbricht's authority is henceforth to remain unquestioned until his removal at Soviet behest in 1971.

1959

3 November. The federal executive of the *Deutsche Partei* (German Party) rejects a suggested merger with the CDU and tries to keep its identity as allegedly West Germany's only conservative party.

13–15 November. The SPD adopts its Bad Godesberg Programme. It commits the Party to accepting market principles and the profit motive, and renounces its traditional hostility to the church.

21 December. *Neues Deutschland*, the SED newspaper, largely rehabilitates Stalin in its celebration of his birthday.

1960

1 July. Nine of the fifteen members of the DP in the Bundestag join the CDU, including two cabinet ministers (Seebohm and von Merkatz). The DP Bundestag group accordingly loses formal recognition.

2 July. The party directorate resolves that the DP shall continue as an independent party.

17 December. The German Peace Union is founded in Stuttgart to contest the forthcoming Bundestag elections. It advocates an end to West German nuclear armament, the military neutrality of the two Germanys, a nuclear-free zone in central Europe and immediate negotiations with East Germany.

1961

15 January. Heinrich Hellwege, chairman of the DP, announces his resignation to join the CDU.

15 April. The congresses of the All-German Bloc (Refugee Party – BHE) and the *Deutsche Partei* (German Party – DP) agree to a merger. The new party is to be known as the All-German Party (DP-BHE).

30 October. The merger is abandoned in view of the failure of the new party to obtain the 5 per cent of the vote in the Bundestag elections necessary for representation.

1963

15–21 January. The 6th SED Congress proclaims that East Germany is starting a new phase in its development, the 'complete and comprehensive building of socialism'. It unanimously adopts the SED's first fundamental programme, which is similar to that adopted by the Soviet Communist Party at its 22nd Congress earlier the same year. It also adopts a revised 4th statute, replacing that approved in 1954, which likewise follows the Soviet model. The SED statute envisages a confederation between two 'equal and sovereign' German states and the 'free city' of West Berlin.

1964

28 November. Foundation of the extreme right-wing *Nationaldemokratische Partei Deutschlands* (National Democratic Party of Germany – NPD) in West Germany. It elects Fritz Thielen, a cement manufacturer and a member of the Bremen House of Burgesses for the former DP, as chairman and Adolf von Thadden, of aristocratic origins and a former Bundestag member for the extreme right-wing German Reich Party, as vice-chairman.

1966

June. The NPD adopts its political programme in Karlsruhe. It opposes the political, military and economic integration of Europe, aid to developing countries and the exposure of young people to unhealthy influences.
11 November. Fritz Thielen maintains in a letter to all foreign journalists in Bonn that the NPD is neither 'extremist', 'revanchist', nor 'Nazi'.

1967

10 March. Fritz Thielen, NPD chairman, expels Adolf von Thadden, deputy chairman, and others, in a conflict between Thielen's nationalist group rooted in the former DP and von Thadden's far-right group rooted in the DRP. The legality of the expulsion and the counter-expulsion of Thielen the same day is to remain in dispute.
18–22 April. The 7th SED Congress sees repeated attacks by Ulbricht on the West German SPD and on 'revisionism'.
8 May. Fritz Thielen resigns from the NPD and founds the *Nationale Volkspartei* (National People's Party) in his home city of Bremen.

1968

26 September. A new German Communist Party (*Deutsche Kommunistische Partei – DKP*) is founded in Frankfurt. It is allowed to organise in West Germany on the basis of a pledge to respect the Basic Law.

1971

16 January. The *Deutsche Union* is launched in Hannover by three defectors from the FDP who had initially switched to the CDU/CSU. Its aim is to derail Brandt's Ostpolitik. Its leader is Siegfried Zoglmann.

The *Deutsche Volksunion*, a right-wing group, is launched simultaneously by Dr Gerhard Frey, the editor and publisher of *Deutsche National-Zeitung*, an extreme right-wing weekly. Dr Frey alleges that the *Volksunion* will not fight elections but will provide a home for centre and right-wing voters following the poor performance of the NPD.
21 April. The congratulatory telegram from the Soviet Communist Party to the SED on the 25th anniversary of its foundation pointedly ignores Ulbricht.
3 May. Ulbricht resigns just before the 8th SED Congress, but is awarded the honorific of SED chairman and remains head of state and a member of the Politbüro.

1974

30 October. Formation of the BFD as a political party with Ernst Scharnowski as chairman. He is former chairman of *Deutscher Gewerkschaftsbund* (*DGB*) (Trade Unions' Confederation) in Berlin and a former member of the SPD. The party is supported financially by the Axel

Springer publishing house, and seeks to promote the concept of a single German nation. It regards East Germany as merely a Soviet dominion and fears the sacrifice of Berlin in any Four-Power agreement. The CSU is the only existing party to welcome the BFD, and Klaus Schütz, the governing mayor of West Berlin, announces that he will be alert to any organisational link with the NPD.

1976

18–22 May. 9th SED Congress in Berlin.

22 May. Congress adopts a new party programme, a 5th party statute, and the five-year plan for economic development, 1976–80. The new statute replaces the fourth, introduced in 1963.

The party programme declares that:

> The socialist state and socialist democracy guarantee to all citizens political freedoms and social rights – the right to work, the right to recreation, to free education and medical care, to material security in old age and in case of illness or the loss of ability to work, equal rights of citizens irrespective of racial or national affiliations, ideology, religious belief and social position, and equal rights for men and women in all sectors of public, economic and cultural life.
>
> [*Source*: Keesing's Contemporary Archives, p. 27875]

1980

12–14 January. Delegates from some 250 organisations come together to form the Green Party (*Die Grünen*) as a West German political party at a conference in Karlsruhe. The most important constituent groups are Green Action Future (*Grüne Aktion Zukunft – GAZ*), Green List Ecology (*Grüne Liste Umweltschutz – GLU*) and the Action Group of Independent Germans (*Aktionsgemeinschaft Unabhängiger Deutscher – AUD*). The conference permits, at the request of Communist groups, parallel membership of other political parties.

22–23 March. A second Green Party conference approves a party programme. It includes calls for the dissolution of both NATO and the Warsaw Pact, the breaking up of large economic and industrial concerns, a 35-hour working week and unlimited freedom to strike. August Haussleiter, Petra Kelly and Norbert Mann are elected as the national executive.

1983

26 November. Foundation of a new extreme right-wing party, *Die Republikaner*, in Munich.

1987

6 March. Dr Gerhard Frey establishes the *Deutsche Volksunion/Liste D* in a Munich beer cellar. Unlike his group founded in January 1971 (see above), the new DVU will fight elections, initially in Bremen in September.

1988

30 August–2 September. The SPD Congress in Münster resolves to promote the role of women in the party by a range of measures including the establishment of a third, necessarily female, deputy chair, fixed minimum percentages of women in party posts and in the Bundestag (40 per cent by 1994 and 1998 respectively), and an immediate increase from ten to fourteen in the number of women on the 40-strong party executive.

1989

9 February. The neo-Nazi National Gathering (*Nationale Sammlung*) is banned. It had been founded by Michael Kühnen in mid-1988 and had an estimated 170 members. Kühnen responds by founding the Popular Will Initiative.

3–5 March. The Greens' party congress in Duisburg is dominated by the realist wing (*Realos*), which favours co-operation with the SPD, while the option is open.

12 July. The group within the Greens, some 25,000 strong, concerned with older people and known as the Grey Panthers splits off as the Greys (*die Grauen*). The new party is led by Trude Unruh.

11–13 September. The CDU party conference in Bremen ratifies Chancellor Kohl's replacement of Heiner Geissler by Volker Rühe as secretary-general. The change is seen as a move to appease the right and to reduce the appeal of the extreme right *Republikaner.*

8 October. A new East German SPD is established.

24 November. An East German Green Party is founded. It aims to prevent East Germany from becoming a 'selfish and affluent throw-away society'.

25 November. An East German FDP is founded, which rejects the co-operation between the LDPD and the SED.

3 December. An SED working committee chaired by Herbert Kroker, and including Gregor Gysi, Markus Wolf and Wolfgang Berghofer, expels Honecker and Stoph from the SED.

8–9 December. The SED holds an emergency Congress. Gregor Gysi is elected as leader with the approval of 95.32 per cent of the delegates. The title of general secretary is dropped in favour of chairman. Hans Modrow, Wolfgang Berghofer and Wolfgang Pohl are elected deputy chairmen.

15–16 December. The East German CDU at an extraordinary conference adopts a Christian programme featuring a market economy underpinned by western investment.

16 December. *Demokratischer Aufbruch* (Democratic Awakening) at a meeting in Leipzig turns itself into a formal political party with Wolfgang Schnur as chair. Its goals include a 'social and ecologically sustainable market economy' and German unification.

16–17 December. The Congress changes the name of the SED to SED–PDS (*Sozialistische Einheitspartei Deutschlands–Partei des Demokratischen Sozialismus*). It is to become simply the PDS on 4 February 1990.

18–20 December. The SPD party congress adopts the Berlin Programme for the 1990 Bundestag elections. The programme proposes a confederation between East and West Germany as the precursor of a federal relationship, the withdrawal from Europe of both American and Soviet forces, and the establishment of nuclear-weapons-free zones. It envisages increased workers' rights, progressive reduction of the working week to 30 hours to fight unemployment, the full integration of environmental considerations in all other policies, and better rights for women.

1990

13–14 January. *Die Republikaner* hold a party congress in Rosenheim, Bavaria. The adopted programme calls for the immediate unification of East and West Germany with Berlin as capital. German unity takes precedence over Europe for which the aim is 'not a united Europe, but a Europe of the fatherlands'.

20 January. Twelve East German conservative parties and groups combine to found the *Deutsche Soziale Union* (German Social Union – DSU) in Leipzig.

4 February. The East German FDP is formally established as a sister party to the West German FDP.

5 February. The East German CDU under Lothar de Maizière, Democratic Awakening under Wolfgang Schnur and the DSU under Hans-Wilhelm Ebeling, agree in West Berlin to fight the East German election campaign jointly as the *Allianz für Deutschland* (Alliance for Germany).

7 February. New Forum, Democracy Now, and Initiative for Peace and Human Rights, agree in East Berlin to fight the campaign jointly as *Wahlbündnis 90* (Electoral Alliance 90). They favour gradual unification and a demilitarised Germany.

9–10 February. The East German LDPD is renamed the LDP at an extraordinary party congress in Dresden.

12 February. The LDP, some members of the DFP (German Forum Party) and the East German FDP, form the *Bund freier Demokraten* (League of Free Democrats) in West Berlin to avoid a split in the centre vote in the coming East German elections.

22–25 February. The East German SPD at its national electoral congress favours a social market economy with protection for the disadvantaged and proposes a German Unity Council under the chairmanship of Willy Brandt to prepare a new all-German constitution.

late March. The DKP holds its 10th party congress in Dortmund. Herbert Mies, party chairman from 1973 until his resignation in October 1989, is replaced by a council of Helga Rosenberg, Rolf Priemer, Heinz Stehr and Anna Frohnweiler. The 'congress of renewal' adopts a new party statute valid for just one year and favouring both Marxist-Leninism and German unification. The party had been supported previously by the East German SED.

9–10 June. The Greens' party congress in Dortmund is dominated by the fundamentalist wing (*Fundis*). The Greens continue to oppose the state treaty on German economic and monetary union and premature all-German elections. They favour an all-German confederal party but depart from the East German Greens in favouring an alliance with other East German citizens' groups.

30 June. Franz Schönhuber is expelled from *Die Republikaner*, at the instigation of its extreme neo-Nazi wing.

4 July. He is readmitted to the party.

7 July. He is re-elected as party leader by 373 votes to 179.

11 August. The East and West German Liberal Parties merge as the '*FDP–die Liberalen*' at a congress in Hannover.

27–28 September. The East German SPD merges with the West German SPD.

1991

30 August. The CDU sees severe tension between many of its leaders in eastern Germany and members led by the general secretary, Volker Rühe, who argue that new leaders are necessary who will represent a clean break with the past and stand unreservedly for reform.

1993

16–17 January. The Greens and *Bündnis 90* (Alliance 90) agree to merge at parallel congresses in Hannover. They are to be known formally as Alliance90/The Greens, but normally as simply The Greens.

29–31 January. The first session of the 3rd party Congress of the PDS adopts a ten-point party programme:

1. The democratisation of society including the workplace and the media. Extended legally enforceable rights of co-decision for trade unions, community groups, citizens' initiatives and democratic movements representing women, the disabled, environmentalists, etc. Extension of basic rights to work, housing, education and social security. Equal rights for men and women and the disabled, and a duty on the state and on society to eliminate all forms of discrimination based on sexual orientation. The right of women to abortion.

The extension of citizens' rights, including the right to vote, to foreigners living in Germany.

2. Opposition to all expressions of far-right extremism and neo-Fascism.
3. An elected East German committee to represent the interests of former East German nationals. No restitution of confiscated property to the great landowners or to war or Nazi criminals.
4. Real local self-administration.
5. A revised approach to the organisation of work and an economic policy directed at full employment.
6. Basic social security including adequate housing.
7. Social and ecological reform of the economy.
8. Equal opportunities for women and equal pay for equal work. Use of legal quotas to that end. Reduction of the voting age to sixteen. A minimum quota of 6 per cent for the handicapped in places of employment.
9. Access to education, culture and science.
10. Resistance to threats to the planet through a rigorous environmental policy and an end to the production and development of new weapons, as well as of arms exports and military aid.

24 April. The DSU decides to extend its coverage to the whole of Germany. The CSU general-secretary walks out of the congress in protest.

1994

13 March. The third session of the 3rd party Congress of the PDS in Berlin adopts an election manifesto for the 13th Bundestag elections. It is based on the party programme and rooted in the premise that the domination of capital must be overcome as it denies self-determination, individual development and social cohesion.

22 June. The SPD adopts its manifesto for the 13th Bundestag elections at an election congress in Halle. Its chief goals are work, social justice and a healthy environment for everyone. It envisages a solidarity pact for employment, innovation and environmentally sustainable growth which will extend the present social market economy to an ecological and social market economy. A major instrument of that extension will be the ecological tax reform, first proposed in 1990, which will simultaneously reduce the burden on employment, improve the environment and increase the international competitiveness of German industry. Ecologically significant investment will form part of an all-German future investment programme.

The SPD aims to phase out nuclear energy, because of the hazards and the problem of waste, but also to reduce carbon dioxide emissions from the burning of fossil fuels by at least a quarter by 2005 under a national climate protection programme. Solar energy will be massively promoted, together with other renewable energy sources, but the modernisation and cleaning up of coal-powered plant will also be pursued so as to increase the competitiveness of domestic coal and to avoid undue reliance on imported fuels.

All forms of transport should be integrated so as to maximise energy saving and minimise environmental impact. The 30km speed limits in residential areas should be extended and a speed limit introduced on motorways. The freedom from fuel tax of aircraft kerosene should be reduced Europe-wide.

The construction of an additional 100,000 social dwellings annually will be promoted in the first two years. High priority is also given to real equality between men and women and a fairer distribution of the tax burden.

2.5 Office holders

Heads of state

Presidents of West Germany 1949–90, and of united Germany thereafter

1949–59	Theodor Heuss (FDP)
1959–69	Heinrich Lübke (CDU)
1969–74	Gustav Heinemann (SPD)
1974–79	Walter Scheel (FDP)
1979–84	Karl Carstens (CDU)
1984–94	Richard von Weizsäcker (CDU)
1994–	Roman Herzog (CDU)

Presidents of East Germany 1949–60, and 1990

1949–60	Wilhelm Pieck (SED)
1990	Sabine Bergmann-Pohl

Chairmen of the East German Council of State (Staatsrat)

1960–73	Walter Ulbricht (SED)
1973–76	Willi Stoph (SED)
1976–89	Erich Honecker (SED)
1989	Egon Krenz (SED)
1989–90	Manfred Gerlach (LDPD)

Heads of government

Chancellors of West Germany 1949–90, and of united Germany thereafter

1949–63	Konrad Adenauer (CDU)
1963–66	Ludwig Erhard (CDU)
1966–69	Kurt Georg Kiesinger (CDU)
1969–74	Willy Brandt (SPD)
1974–82	Helmut Schmidt (SPD)
1982–	Helmut Kohl (CDU)

Chairmen of the Council of Ministers (prime ministers) of East Germany 1949–90

1949–64	Otto Grotewohl
1964–73	Willi Stoph
1973–76	Horst Sindermann
1976–7 November 1989	Willi Stoph
13 November 1989–18 March 1990	Hans Modrow
18 March 1990–3 October 1990	Lothar de Maizière

General (First 1954–76) Secretaries of the East German Socialist Unity Party (SED) 1950–89

July 1950–May 1971	Walter Ulbricht
May 1971–October 1989	Erich Honecker
18 October 1989–30 November 1989	Egon Krenz

(The SED is totally reorganised and reformed as the Party of Democratic Socialism)

Party chairmen

Christlich Demokratische Union Deutschlands (CDU–East)

1945	Dr Andreas Hermes
1945–47	Jakob Kaiser
1948–57	Otto Nuschke
1966–89	Gerald Götting
1989–90	Lothar de Maizière

Christlich Demokratische Union Deutschlands (CDU–West)

1946–66	Dr Konrad Adenauer
1966–67	Professor Ludwig Erhard
1967–71	Dr Kurt Georg Kiesinger
1971–73	Dr Rainer Barzel
1973–	Dr Helmut Kohl

Christlich-Soziale Union (CSU)

1949–54	Dr Hans Ehard
1955–61	Dr Hanns Seidel
1961–88	Franz-Josef Strauss
1988–	Dr Theo Waigel

Deutsche Kommunistische Partei (DKP)

1973–89   Herbert Mies
1990–   Anna Frohnweiler, Rolf Priemer, Helga Rosenberg and Heinz Stehr (joint)

Deutsche Partei (DP)

1945–61   Heinrich Hellwege
1947–56   Dr Hans-Christof Seebohm (co-chairman)

Freie Demokratische Partei (FDP)

1948–49   Professor Theodor Heuss
1949–57   Dr Thomas Dehler
1957–60   Dr Reinhold Maier
1960–68   Dr Erich Mende
1968–74   Walter Scheel
1974–85   Hans Dietrich Genscher
1985–88   Dr Martin Bangemann
1988–93   Dr Otto Graf Lambsdorff
1993–95   Dr Klaus Kinkel
1995–   Wolfgang Gerhardt

Die Grünen (The Greens)

In rotation

Kommunistische Partei Deutschlands (KPD)

1945–46   Wilhelm Pieck

Kommunistische Partei Deutschlands (KPD–West)

1945–56   Max Reimann

Partei des Demokratischen Sozialismus (PDS)

1989–93   Gregor Gysi
1993–   Professor Lothar Bisky

Sozialistische Einheitspartei Deutschlands (SED)

1946–54   Wilhelm Pieck and Otto Grotewohl (joint)
(post suspended)
1971–73   Walter Ulbricht

Sozialdemokratische Partei Deutschlands (SPD)

1945–52	Dr Kurt Schumacher
1952–63	Erich Ollenhauer
1964–87	Willy Brandt
1987–91	Dr Hans-Jochen Vogel
1991–93	Björn Engholm
1993–95	Rudolf Scharping
1995–	Oskar Lafontaine

Sozialdemokratische Partei Deutschlands (SPD–East)

1945–46	Otto Grotewohl
February–April 1990	Ibrahim Böhme
April–June 1990	Markus Meckel
June–September 1990	Wolfgang Thierse

Foreign ministers

West Germany 1951–90, and united Germany thereafter

1951–55	Dr Konrad Adenauer (CDU) (acting)
1955–61	Dr Heinrich von Brentano (CDU)
1961–66	Dr Gerhard Schröder
1966–69	Willy Brandt (SPD)
1969–74	Walter Scheel (FDP)
1974–92	Hans-Dietrich Genscher (FDP)
1992–	Dr Klaus Kinkel (FDP)

East Germany 1949–90

1949–53	Georg Dertinger (CDU)
1953	Anton Ackermann (SED) (acting)
1953–65	Dr Lothar Bolz (NDPD)
1965–75	Otto Winzer (SED)
1975–90	Oskar Fischer (SED)

Governments

The Adenauer government 20 September 1949–October 1953

Chancellor: Dr Konrad Adenauer (CDU)
Vice-Chancellor and ERP Affairs: Dr Franz Blücher (FDP)
Foreign Affairs: Dr Konrad Adenauer (CDU) (from 15 March 1951)
Interior: Dr Gustav Heinemann (CDU) (until 10 October 1950)
　　　　　Dr Robert Lehr (CDU) (from 13 October 1950)
Justice: Dr Thomas Dehler (FDP)
Finance: Dr Fritz Schäffer (CSU)

Economic Affairs: Professor Ludwig Erhard (CDU)
Agriculture and Food: Dr Wilhelm Niklas (CSU)
Labour: Dr Anton Storch (CDU)
Transport: Dr Hans-Christof Seebohm (DP)
Housing: Eberhard Wildermuth (FDP) (until March 1952)
         Fritz Neumayer (FDP) (from 17 July 1952)
All-German Affairs: Jakob Kaiser (CDU)
Refugees: Dr Hans Lukaschek (CDU)
Posts and Telegraphs: Dr Hans Schubert (CSU)
Co-ordination with the Bundesrat: Heinrich Hellwege (DP)

The Adenauer government 20 October 1953–October 1956

Chancellor:
     Dr Konrad Adenauer (CDU) (and foreign minister until 6 June 1955)
Vice-Chancellor and Minister for European Economic Co-operation:
     Dr Franz Blücher (FDP)
Foreign minister: Dr Heinrich von Brentano (CDU) (from 7 June 1955)
Interior: Dr Gerhard Schröder (CDU)
Finance: Dr Fritz Schäffer (CSU)
Economic Affairs: Professor Ludwig Erhard (CDU)
Defence: Theodor Blank (CDU) (from 7 June 1955)
Agriculture: Dr Heinrich Lübke (CDU)
Labour: Dr Anton Storch (CDU)
Transport: Dr Hans-Christof Seebohm (DP)
Posts: Dr Siegfried Balke (non-party) (from 9 December 1953)
Housing: Dr Viktor-Emmanuel Preusker (FDP)
All-German Affairs: Jakob Kaiser (CDU)
Justice: Fritz Neumayer (FDP)
Refugee Questions: Professor Theodor Oberländer (BHE)
Bundesrat Affairs: Heinrich Hellwege (DP) (until 6 June 1955)
         Dr Hans-Joachim von Merkatz (DP) (from 7 June 1955)
Family and Youth Questions: Dr Franz-Josef Würmeling (CDU)
Ministers without portfolio:
    Franz-Josef Strauss (CSU)
    Dr Robert Tillmans (CDU) (until 12 November 1955)
    Waldemar Kraft (BHE)
    Dr Hermann Schäfer (FDP)
Nuclear issues: Franz-Josef Strauss (CSU) (from 12 October 1955)

The Adenauer government 16 October 1956–October 1957

Chancellor: Dr Konrad Adenauer (CDU)
Vice-Chancellor and Minister for Economic Co-ordination:
     Dr Franz Blücher (FPP)

Foreign Affairs: Dr Heinrich von Brentano (CDU)
Interior: Dr Gerhard Schröder (CDU)
Finance: Dr Fritz Schäffer (CSU)
Economics: Professor Ludwig Erhard (CDU)
Defence: Franz-Josef Strauss (CSU)
Agriculture: Dr Heinrich Lübke (CDU)
Labour: Dr Anton Storch (CDU)
Transport: Dr Hans-Christof Seebohm (DP)
Housing: Dr Viktor-Emmanuel Preusker (FPP)
All-German Affairs: Jakob Kaiser (CDU)
Justice and Bundesrat Affairs: Dr Hans-Joachim von Merkatz (DP)
Refugee Affairs: Professor Theodor Oberländer (CDU)
Atomic Energy Questions: Dr Siegfried Balke (CSU)
Family Affairs: Dr Franz-Josef Würmeling (CDU)
Posts: Ernst Lemmer (CDU) (from 14 November 1956)

The Adenauer government 24 October 1957–November 1961

Chancellor: Dr Konrad Adenauer (CDU)
Foreign Affairs: Dr Heinrich von Brentano (CDU)
Interior: Dr Gerhard Schröder (CDU)
Justice: Dr Fritz Schäffer (CSU)
Finance: Franz Etzel (CDU)
Economics and (from 30 October) **Vice-Chancellor:**
   Professor Ludwig Erhard (CDU)
Defence: Franz-Josef Strauss (CSU)
Food and Agriculture: Dr Heinrich Lübke (CDU) (until September 1959)
                Werner Schwarz (CDU) (from 30 September 1959)
Labour and Social Affairs: Theodor Blank (CDU)
Transport: Dr Hans-Christof Seebohm (DP, subsequently CDU)
Housing: Paul Lücke (CDU)
All-German Questions: Ernst Lemmer (CDU)
Bundesrat Affairs: Dr Hans-Joachim von Merkatz (DP, subsequently CDU)
Refugees: Professor Theodor Oberländer (CDU) (until 4 May 1960)
           Dr Hans-Joachim von Merkatz (CDU) (from 26 October 1960)
Atomic Energy and Power: Professor Siegfried Balke (CSU)
Family and Youth Questions: Dr Franz-Josef Würmeling (CDU)
Federal Properties: Dr Hermann Lindrath (CDU)
Posts: Richard Stücklen (CSU)

The Adenauer government 14 November 1961–October 1963

Chancellor: Dr Konrad Adenauer (CDU)
Vice-Chancellor and Economics: Professor Ludwig Erhard (CDU)
Foreign Affairs: Dr Gerhard Schröder (CDU)
Interior: Hermann Höcherl (CSU)

Justice: Dr Wolfgang Stammberger (FDP) (until 10 December 1962)
Dr Ewald Bucher (FDP) (from 11 December 1962)
Finance: Dr Heinz Starke (FDP) (until 10 December 1962)
Dr Rolf Dahlgrün (FDP) (from 11 December 1962)
Defence: Franz-Josef Strauss (CSU) (until 30 November 1962)
Kai-Uwe von Hassel (CDU) (from 11 December 1962)
Food and Agriculture: Werner Schwarz (CDU)
Labour: Theodor Blank (CDU)
Transport: Dr Hans-Christof Seebohm (CDU)
Housing: Paul Lücke (CDU)
All-German Questions: Ernst Lemmer (CDU) (until 10 December 1962)
Dr Rainer Barzel (CDU) (from 11 December 1962)
Bundesrat and *Länder* Affairs:
Dr Hans-Joachim von Merkatz (CDU) (until 10 December 1962)
Alois Niederalt (CSU) (from 11 December 1962)
Refugees: Wolfgang Mischnick (FDP)
Atomic Energy: Professor Siegfried Balke (CSU) (until 10 December 1962)
Family and Youth Questions:
Dr Franz-Josef Würmeling (CDU) (until 10 December 1962)
Dr Bruno Heck (CDU) (from 11 December 1962)
Federal Treasury: Hans Lenz (FDP) (until 10 December 1962)
Dr Werner Dollinger (CSU) (from 11 December 1962)
Posts: Richard Stücklen (CSU)
Economic Co-operation: Walter Scheel (FDP)
Public Health: Dr Elisabeth Schwarzhaupt (CDU)
Special Responsibilities: Dr Heinrich Krone (CDU)
Scientific Research: Hans Lenz (FDP) (from 11 December 1962)

The Erhard government 17 October 1963–October 1965

Chancellor: Professor Ludwig Erhard (CDU)
Vice-Chancellor and Minister for All-German Affairs:
Dr Erich Mende (FDP)
Foreign Affairs: Dr Gerhard Schröder (CDU)
Interior: Hermann Höcherl (CSU)
Justice: Dr Ewald Bucher (FDP) (until 25 March 1965)
Dr Karl Weber (CDU) (from 27 March 1965)
Finance: Dr Rolf Dahlgrün (FDP)
Economy: Kurt Schmücker (CDU)
Defence: Kai-Uwe von Hassel (CDU)
Food and Agriculture: Werner Schwarz (CDU)
Labour: Theodor Blank (CDU)
Transport: Dr Hans-Christof Seebohm (CDU)
Posts and Telecommunications: Richard Stücklen (CSU)

Housing and Urban Development: Paul Lücke (CDU)
Bundesrat and *Länder* Affairs: Alois Niederalt (CSU)
Refugees: Dr Hans Krüger (CDU) (until 31 January 1964)
          Ernst Lemmer (CDU) (from 17 February 1964)
Family Affairs: Dr Bruno Heck (CDU)
Scientific Research: Hans Lenz (FDP)
Treasury: Dr Werner Dollinger (CSU)
Development Aid: Walter Scheel (FDP)
Health: Dr Elisabeth Schwarzhaupt (CDU)
Minister without Portfolio for special tasks: Dr Heinrich Krone (CDU)

The Erhard government 26 October 1965–27 October 1966

Chancellor: Professor Ludwig Erhard (CDU)
Vice-Chancellor and Minister for All-German Affairs:
   Dr Erich Mende (FDP)
Foreign Affairs: Dr Gerhard Schröder (CDU)
Interior: Paul Lücke (CDU)
Justice: Dr Richard Jaeger (CSU)
Finance: Dr Rolf Dahlgrün (FDP)
Economy: Kurt Schmücker (CDU)
Defence: Kai-Uwe von Hassel (CDU)
Agriculture: Hermann Höcherl (CSU)
Labour: Hans Katzer (CDU)
Transport: Dr Hans-Christof Seebohm (CDU)
Posts and Telecommunications: Richard Stücklen (CSU)
Housing: Dr Ewald Bucher (FDP)
Bundesrat and *Länder* Affairs: Alois Niederalt (CSU)
Refugees and Expellees: Dr Johann Baptist Gradl (CDU)
Family and Youth: Dr Bruno Heck (CDU)
Science: Dr Gerhard Stoltenberg (CDU)
Treasury: Dr Werner Dollinger (CSU)
Development Aid: Walter Scheel (FDP)
Health: Dr Elisabeth Schwarzhaupt (CDU)
Chairman of the Federal Defence Council: Dr Heinrich Krone (CDU)
Federal Chancellor's Office: Dr Ludger Westrick (CDU)

The Kiesinger government 1 December 1966–October 1969

Chancellor: Dr Kurt Georg Kiesinger (CDU)
Vice-Chancellor and Foreign Affairs: Willy Brandt (SPD)
Interior: Paul Lücke (CDU) (until 26 March 1968)
          Dr Ernst Benda (CDU) (from 2 April 1968)
Justice: Dr Gustav Heinemann (SPD) (until 25 March 1969)
          Professor Horst Ehmke (SPD) (from 26 March 1969)

Finance: Franz-Josef Strauss (CSU)
Economic Affairs: Professor Karl Schiller (SPD)
Food, Agriculture and Forestry: Hermann Höcherl (CSU)
Labour: Hans Katzer (CDU)
Defence: Dr Gerhard Schröder (CDU)
Transport: Georg Leber (SPD)
Posts and Telecommunications: Dr Werner Dollinger (CSU)
Housing: Dr Lauritz Lauritzen (SPD)
Refugees and Expellees:
  Kai-Uwe von Hassel (CDU) (until 5 February 1969)
  Heinrich Windelen (CDU) (from 7 February 1969)
All-German Affairs: Herbert Wehner (SPD)
Bundesrat and *Länder* Affairs: Professor Carlo Schmid (SPD)
Family and Youth: Dr Bruno Heck (CDU) (until 1 October 1968)
                  Aenne Brauksiepe (CDU) (from 2 October 1968)
Scientific Research: Dr Gerhard Stoltenberg (CDU)
Federal Property: Kurt Schmücker (CDU)
Development Aid: Hans-Jürgen Wischnewski (SPD) (until 1 October 1968)
                  Dr Erhard Eppler (SPD) (from 2 October 1968)
Health: Käte Strobel (SPD)

The Brandt government 21 October 1969–December 1972

Chancellor: Willy Brandt (SPD)
Foreign Minister and Vice-Chancellor: Walter Scheel (FDP)
Interior: Hans-Dietrich Genscher (FDP)
Justice: Gerhard Jahn (SPD)
Finance: Alex Möller (SPD)
Economic Affairs (and Finance from 13 May 1971):
  Professor Karl Schiller (SPD) (until 2 July 1972)
  Helmut Schmidt (SPD) (from 7 July 1972)
Food, Agriculture and Forestry: Josef Ertl (FDP)
Labour and Social Welfare: Walter Arendt (SPD)
Defence: Helmut Schmidt (SPD) (until 6 July 1972)
          Georg Leber (SPD) (from 7 July 1972)
Transport, Posts and Telecommunications: Georg Leber (SPD) (until
  6 July 1972)
Housing and Town Planning:
  Dr Lauritz Lauritzen (SPD) (and foregoing from 7 July 1972)
Inter-German Relations: Egon Franke (SPD)
Health, Family and Youth Affairs: Käte Strobel (SPD)
Education and Science:
  Professor Hans Leussink (non-party) (until 27 January 1972)
  Dr Klaus von Dohnanyi (SPD) (from 15 March 1972)
Economic Co-operation: Dr Erhard Eppler (SPD)

Minister without Portfolio at the Chancellery:
  Professor Horst Ehmke (SPD)

The Brandt government 15 December 1972–May 1974

Chancellor: Willy Brandt (SPD)
Foreign Minister and Vice-Chancellor: Walter Scheel (FDP)
Interior: Hans-Dietrich Genscher (FDP)
Justice: Gerhard Jahn (SPD)
Finance: Helmut Schmidt (SPD)
Economic Affairs: Dr Hans Friderichs (FDP)
Food, Agriculture and Forestry: Josef Ertl (FDP)
Labour and Social Welfare: Walter Arendt (SPD)
Defence: Georg Leber (SPD)
Transport: Dr Lauritz Lauritzen (SPD)
Housing and Town Planning: Dr Hans-Jochen Vogel (SPD)
Inter-German Relations: Egon Franke (SPD)
Health, Family and Youth Affairs: Dr Katherina Focke (SPD)
Research and Technology: Professor Horst Ehmke (SPD)
Education and Science: Dr Klaus von Dohnanyi (SPD)
Economic Co-operation: Dr Erhard Eppler (SPD)
Minister without Portfolio at the Chancellery: Egon Bahr (SPD)
Minister without Portfolio with special duties:
  Professor Werner Maihofer (FDP)

The Schmidt government 16 May 1974–February 1978

Chancellor: Helmut Schmidt (SPD)
Vice-Chancellor and Foreign Affairs: Hans-Dietrich Genscher (FDP)
Interior: Professor Werner Maihofer (FDP)
Justice: Dr Hans-Jochen Vogel (SPD)
Finance: Dr Hans Apel (SPD)
Economics: Dr Hans Friderichs (FDP)
Food, Agriculture and Forestry: Josef Ertl (FDP)
Labour and Social Affairs:
  Walter Arendt (SPD) (until 15 December 1976)
  Dr Herbert Ehrenberg (SPD) (from 16 December 1976)
Defence: Georg Leber (SPD)
Transport, Posts and Telecommunications: Kurt Gscheidle (SPD)
Housing and Town Planning: Karl Ravens (SPD)
Inter-German Relations: Egon Franke (SPD)
Health, Family and Youth Questions:
  Dr Katharina Focke (SPD) (until 15 December 1976)
  Antje Huber (SPD) (from 16 December 1976)
Education and Science: Helmut Rohde (SPD)

Research and Technology: Hans Matthöfer (SPD)
Economic Co-operation:
  Dr Erhard Eppler (SPD) (until 4 July 1974)
  Egon Bahr (SPD) (from 8 July 1974 until 15 December 1976)
  Marie Schlei (SPD) (from 16 December 1976)

The Schmidt government 3 February 1978–April 1982

Chancellor: Helmut Schmidt (SPD)
Vice-Chancellor and Foreign Affairs: Hans-Dietrich Genscher (FDP)
Interior: Professor Werner Maihofer (FDP) (resigned 6 June 1978)
        Gerhard Baum (FDP) (from 8 June 1978)
Justice: Dr Hans-Jochen Vogel (SPD) (until 26 January 1981)
        Dr Jürgen Schmude (SPD) (from 27 January 1981)
Finance: Hans Matthöfer (SPD)
Economics: Dr Otto Graf Lambsdorff (FDP)
Food, Agriculture and Forestry: Josef Ertl (FDP)
Labour and Social Affairs: Dr Herbert Ehrenberg (SPD)
Defence: Dr Hans Apel (SPD)
Transport, Posts and Telecommunications: Kurt Gscheidle (SPD)
(Transport deleted from portfolio 5 November 1980)
Transport: Dr Volker Hauff (from 5 November 1980)
Housing and Town Planning: Dr Dieter Haack (SPD)
Inter-German Affairs: Egon Franke (SPD)
Health, Family and Youth Questions: Antje Huber (SPD)
Education and Science:
  Dr Jürgen Schmude (SPD) (until 26 January 1981)
  Björn Engholm (SPD) (from 27 January 1981)
Research and Technology:
  Dr Volker Hauff (SPD) (until 4 November 1980)
  Dr Andreas von Bülow (SPD) (from 5 November 1980)
Economic Co-operation: Rainer Offergeld (SPD)

The Schmidt government 27 April 1982–October 1982

Chancellor: Helmut Schmidt (SPD)
Vice-Chancellor and Foreign Affairs: Hans-Dietrich Genscher (FDP)
Interior: Gerhard Baum (FDP)
Justice: Dr Jürgen Schmude (SPD)
Finance: Manfred Lahnstein (SPD)
Economics: Dr Otto Graf Lambsdorff (FDP)
Food, Agriculture and Forestry: Josef Ertl (FDP)
Labour and Social Affairs: Heinz Westphal (SPD)
Defence: Dr Hans Apel (SPD)
Posts and Telecommunications: Hans Matthöfer (SPD)

Transport: Dr Volker Hauff (SPD)
Regional Planning, Building and Urban Development:
    Dr Dieter Haack (SPD)
Inter-German Affairs: Egon Franke (SPD)
Health, Family and Youth Questions: Anke Fuchs (SPD)
Education and Science: Björn Engholm (SPD)
Research and Technology: Dr Andreas von Bülow (SPD)
Economic Co-operation: Rainer Offergeld (SPD)

The Kohl government 4 October 1982–March 1987

Chancellor: Dr Helmut Kohl (CDU)
Vice-Chancellor and Foreign Affairs: Hans-Dietrich Genscher (FDP)
Interior: Dr Friedrich Zimmermann (CSU)
Justice: Hans Engelhard (FDP)
Finance: Dr Gerhard Stoltenberg (CDU)
Economic Affairs: Dr Otto Graf Lambsdorff (FDP) (until 26 June 1984)
                Dr Martin Bangemann (from June 1984)
Commerce: Dr Werner Dollinger (CSU) (until 29 March 1983)
Food, Agriculture and Forestry:
    Josef Ertl (FDP) (until 29 March 1983)
    Ignaz Kiechle (CSU) (from 30 March 1983)
Labour and Social Affairs: Dr Norbert Blüm (CDU)
Defence: Dr Manfred Wörner (CDU)
Posts and Telecommunications: Dr Christian Schwarz-Schilling (CDU)
Regional Planning, Building and Urban Development:
    Dr Oskar Schneider (CSU)
Inter-German Affairs: Dr Rainer Barzel (CDU) (until 29 March 1983)
                Heinrich Windelen (CDU) (from 30 March 1983)
Youth, Family and Health Affairs:
    Dr Heiner Geissler (CDU) (until 25 September 1985)
    Professor Rita Süssmuth (CDU) (from 26 September 1985)
Education: Dr Dorothee Wilms (CDU)
Research and Technology: Dr Heinz Riesenhuber (CDU)
Economic Co-operation: Dr Jürgen Warnke (CSU)
Environment, Nature Conservation and Reactor Safety:
    Walter Wallmann (CDU) (from 6 June 1986)
Transport: Dr Werner Dollinger (CSU) (from 30 March 1983)
Head of Federal Chancellery:
    Dr Wolfgang Schäuble (CDU) (from 15 November 1984)

The Kohl government 11 March 1987–12 April 1989

Chancellor: Dr Helmut Kohl (CDU)
Vice-Chancellor and Foreign Affairs: Hans-Dietrich Genscher (FDP)

Interior: Dr Friedrich Zimmermann (CSU)
Justice: Hans Engelhard (FDP)
Finance: Dr Gerhard Stoltenberg (CDU)
Economic Affairs:
  Dr Martin Bangemann (FDP) (until 28 November 1988)
  Helmut Haussmann (FDP) (from 29 November 1988)
Food, Agriculture and Forestry: Ignaz Kiechle (CSU)
Labour and Social Affairs: Dr Norbert Blüm (CDU)
Defence: Dr Manfred Wörner (CDU) (until 17 May 1988)
        Dr Rupert Scholz (CDU) (from 18 May 1988)
Posts and Telecommunications: Dr Christian Schwarz-Schilling (CDU)
Regional Planning, Building and Urban Development:
  Dr Oskar Schneider (CSU)
Inter-German Relations: Dr Dorothee Wilms (CDU)
Youth, Family and Health Affairs:
  Professor Rita Süssmuth (CDU) (until 25 November 1988)
  Ursula-Maria Lehr (CDU) (from 29 November 1988)
Education and Science: Dr Jürgen Möllemann (FDP)
Research and Technology: Dr Heinz Riesenhuber (CDU)
Economic Co-operation: Hans Klein (CSU)
Transport: Dr Jürgen Warnke (CSU)
Environment, Nature Conservation and Reactor Safety:
  Walter Wallmann (CDU) (until 6 May 1987)
  Dr Klaus Töpfer (CDU) (from 7 May 1987)
Head of Federal Chancellery: Dr Wolfgang Schäuble (CDU)

The Kohl government 12 April 1989–18 May 1992

Chancellor: Dr Helmut Kohl (CDU)
Vice-Chancellor and Foreign Affairs: Hans-Dietrich Genscher (FDP)
Interior: Dr Wolfgang Schäuble (CDU) (until 25 November 1991)
        Rudolf Seiters (CDU) (from 26 November 1991)
Justice: Hans Engelhard (FDP) (until January 1991)
        Dr Klaus Kinkel (Ind. then FDP) (from 17 January 1991)
Finance: Dr Theo Waigel (CSU)
Economic Affairs: Helmut Haussmann (FDP) (until 3 December 1990)
              Dr Jürgen Möllemann (FDP) (from 17 January 1991)
Food, Agriculture and Forestry: Ignaz Kiechle (CSU)
Labour and Social Affairs: Dr Norbert Blüm (CDU)
Defence: Dr Gerhard Stoltenberg (CDU) (until 31 March 1992)
        Volker Rühe (CDU) (from 1 April 1992)
Posts and Telecommunications: Dr Christian Schwarz-Schilling (CDU)
Building: Gerda Hasselfeldt (CSU) (until January 1991)
        Irmgard Adam-Schwätzer (CSU) (from 17 January 1991)

Inter-German Relations:
Dr Dorothee Wilms (CDU) (until December 1990)
Youth, Family and Health Affairs:
Ursula-Maria Lehr (CDU) (until January 1991)
Health: Gerda Hasselfeldt (from 17 January 1991)
Women and Youth: Dr Angela Merkel (CDU) (from 17 January 1991)
Family and the Elderly: Hannelore Rönsch (CDU) (from 17 January 1991)
Education and Science: Dr Jürgen Möllemann (FDP) (until January 1991)
Rainer Ortleb (FDP) (from 17 January 1991)
Research and Technology: Dr Heinz Riesenhuber (CDU)
Economic Co-operation:
Jürgen Warnke (CSU) (until January 1991)
Carl-Dieter Spranger (CSU) (from 17 January 1991)
Transport: Dr Friedrich Zimmermann (CSU) (until January 1991)
Günther Krause (CDU) (from 17 January 1991)
Environment, Nature Conservation and Reactor Safety:
Dr Klaus Töpfer (CDU)
Minister at the Chancellery:
Rudolf Seiters (CDU) (until 25 November 1991)
Friedrich Bohl (CDU) (from 26 November 1991)
Government spokesman: Hans Klein (CSU)

The Kohl government 19 May 1992 –

Chancellor: Dr Helmut Kohl (CDU)
Vice-Chancellor and Economics:
Dr Jürgen Möllemann (FDP) (until 3 January 1993)
Foreign Affairs: Dr Klaus Kinkel (FDP)
Interior: Rudolf Seiters (CDU) (until 4 July 1993)
Manfred Kanther (CDU) (from 12 July 1993)
Justice:
Sabine Leutheusser-Scharrenberger (FDP) (until 14 December 1995)
Eduard Schmidt-Jortzig (FDP) (from 15 December 1995)
Finance: Dr Theo Waigel (CSU)
Economic Affairs: Dr Günter Rexrodt (FDP) (from 19 January 1993)
Food, Agriculture and Forestry:
Ignaz Kiechle (CSU) (until 18 January 1993)
Jochen Borchert (CDU) (from 19 January 1993)
Labour and Social Affairs: Dr Norbert Blüm (CDU)
Defence: Volker Rühe (CDU)
Posts and Telecommunications:
Dr Christian Schwarz-Schilling (CDU) (until 14 December 1992)
Wolfgang Bötsch (CSU) (from 19 January 1993)
Construction: Irmgard Adam-Schwätzer (CSU) (until 16 November 1994)

Regional Planning and Urban Development:
  Dr Klaus Töpfer (CDU) (from 17 November 1994 until 31 December 1997)
  Eduard Oswald (CSU) (from 1 January 1998)
Health: Gerda Hasselfeldt (CDU) (until 27 April 1992)
        Horst Seehofer (CSU) (from 6 May 1992)
Family, Youth, Women and the Elderly:
  Claudia Nolte (CDU) (from 17 November 1994)
Family and the Elderly:
  Hannelore Rönsch (CDU) (until 16 November 1994)
Women and Youth: Dr Angela Merkel (CDU) (until 16 November 1994)
Education and Science:
  Rainer Ortleb (FDP) (until 3 February 1994)
  Karl-Hans Laermann (FDP) (from 4 February 1994)
Research and Technology:
  Dr Heinz Riesenhuber (CDU) (until 18 January 1993)
  Matthias Wissmann (CDU) (19 January 1993–6 May 1993)
  Paul Krüger (CDU) (6 May 1993–16 November 1994)
Education and Science, Research and Technology:
  Dr Jürgen Rüttgers (CDU) (from 17 November 1994)
Economic Co-operation: Carl-Dieter Spranger (CSU)
Transport: Günther Krause (CDU) (until 6 May 1993)
        Matthias Wissmann (CDU) (from 6 May 1993)
Environment, Nature Conservation and Reactor Safety:
  Dr Klaus Töpfer (CDU) (until 16 November 1994)
  Dr Angela Merkel (CDU) (from 17 November 1994)
Minister at the Chancellery: Friedrich Bohl (CDU)

The Politbüro

The Congress elections were actually of the Central Committee, which then went on privately to elect the Politbüro, as shown. Appointments and dismissals between Congresses equally lay with the Central Committee. Announcements of results were not necessarily systematic.

Elected at the 3rd SED Congress on 20 July 1950:

Franz Dahlem
Friedrich Ebert
Otto Grotewohl
Hermann Matern
Professor Fred Oelssner
Wilhelm Pieck
Heinrich Rau

Walter Ulbricht
Wilhelm Zaisser

Elected at the 4th SED Congress on 30 March 1954:

Full members
Friedrich Ebert
Otto Grotewohl
Hermann Matern
Professor Fred Oelssner
Wilhelm Pieck
Heinrich Rau
Karl Schirdewan
Willi Stoph
Walter Ulbricht

Candidate members
Erich Honecker
Bruno Leuschner
Erich Mückenberger
Alfred Neumann
Herbert Warnke

Elected at the 6th SED Congress on 15 January 1963

Full members
Friedrich Ebert
Paul Fröhlich
Otto Grotewohl
Professor Kurt Hager
Erich Honecker
Bruno Leuschner
Hermann Matern
Erich Mückenberger
Alfred Neumann
Professor Albert Norden
Willi Stoph
Walter Ulbricht
Paul Verner
Herbert Warnke

Candidate members
Erich Apel
Hermann Axen
Karl-Heinz Bartsch

Georg Ewald
Gerhard Grüneberg
Dr Werner Jarowinsky
Dr Günter Mittag
Margarete Müller
Horst Sindermann

Elected at the 7th SED Congress on 17 April 1967

Full members
Friedrich Ebert
Paul Fröhlich
Gerhard Grüneberg
Professor Kurt Hager
Erich Honecker
Hermann Matern
Dr Günter Mittag
Erich Mückenberger
Alfred Neumann
Professor Albert Norden
Willi Stoph
Walter Ulbricht
Paul Verner
Herbert Warnke

Candidate members
Hermann Axen
Georg Ewald
Dr Werner Jarowinsky
Margarete Müller
Horst Sindermann

Elected at the 8th SED Congress on 15 June 1971:

Full members
Hermann Axen
Friedrich Ebert
Gerhard Grüneberg
Professor Kurt Hager
Erich Honecker
Werner Krolikowski
Werner Lamberz
Dr Günter Mittag
Erich Mückenberger
Alfred Neumann

Professor Albert Norden
Horst Sindermann
Willi Stoph
Walter Ulbricht
Paul Verner
Herbert Warnke

Candidate members
Georg Ewald
Walter Halbritter
Dr Werner Jarowinsky
Günther Kleiber
Erich Mielke
Margarete Müller
Harry Tisch

Elected at the 9th SED Congress on 22 May 1976:

Full members
Hermann Axen
Friedrich Ebert
Werner Felfe
Gerhard Grüneberg
Professor Kurt Hager
General Heinz Hoffmann
Erich Honecker
Werner Krolikowski
Werner Lamberz
Erich Mielke
Dr Günter Mittag
Erich Mückenberger
Konrad Naumann
Alfred Neumann
Professor Albert Norden
Horst Sindermann
Willi Stoph
Harry Tisch
Paul Verner

Candidate members
Horst Dohlus
Joachim Herrmann
Dr Werner Jarowinsky
Günther Kleiber

Egon Krenz
Ingeborg Lange
Margarete Müller
Gerhard Schürer
Werner Walde

Elected at the 10th SED Congress on 11 April 1981:

Full members
Hermann Axen
Horst Dohlus
Werner Felfe
Professor Kurt Hager
Joachim Herrmann
General Heinz Hoffmann
Erich Honecker
Werner Krolikowski
General Erich Mielke
Dr Günter Mittag
Erich Mückenberger
Konrad Naumann
Alfred Neumann
Horst Sindermann
Willi Stoph
Harry Tisch
Paul Verner

Candidate members
Dr Werner Jarowinsky
Günther Kleiber
Egon Krenz
Ingeborg Lange
Margarete Müller
Günter Schabowski
Gerhard Schürer
Werner Walde

Elected at the 11th SED Congress on 21 April 1986:

Full members
Hermann Axen
Hans-Joachim Boehme
Horst Dohlus
Werner Eberlein
Werner Felfe

Professor Kurt Hager
Joachim Herrmann
Erich Honecker
Dr Werner Jarowinsky
General Heinz Kessler
Günther Kleiber
Egon Krenz
Werner Krolikowski
Siegfried Lorenz
General Erich Mielke
Dr Günter Mittag
Erich Mückenberger
Alfred Neumann
Günter Schabowski
Horst Sindermann
Willi Stoph
Harry Tisch

Candidate members
Ingeborg Lange
Gerhard Müller
Margarete Müller
Gerhard Schürer
Werner Walde

*Elected at a special session of the SED central committee,
8–11 November 1989:*

Full members
Werner Eberlein
Wolfgang Herger
Dr Werner Jarowinsky
General Heinz Kessler
Egon Krenz
Siegfried Lorenz
Hans Modrow
Wolfgang Rauchfuss
Günter Schabowski
Gerhard Schürer

Candidate members
Margarete Müller
Gunter Sieber
Hans-Joachim Willerding

2.6 Election results

The Bundestag

1st Bundestag elections
(14 August 1949; Turn-out 78.5%)

	%	Seats
CDU	25.2	115
CSU	5.8	24
SPD	29.2	131
FDP	11.9	52
DP	4.0	17
KPD	5.7	15
ZP	3.1	10
Others	9.2	35

2nd Bundestag elections
(6 September 1953; Turn-out 86%)

	%	Seats
CDU	36.4	191
CSU	8.8	52
SPD	28.8	151
FDP	9.5	48
DP	3.3	15
BHE	5.9	27
ZP	0.8	3

3rd Bundestag elections
(15 September 1957; Turn-out 87.8%)

	%	Seats
CDU	39.7	215
CSU	10.5	55
SPD	31.8	169
FDP	7.7	41
DP	3.4	17

4th Bundestag elections
(17 September 1961; Turn-out 87.7%)

	%	Seats
CDU	35.8	192
CSU	9.6	50
SPD	36.2	190
FDP	12.8	67

5th Bundestag elections
(19 September 1965; Turn-out 86.8%)

	%	Seats
CDU	38.0	196
CSU	9.6	49
SPD	39.3	202
FDP	9.5	49

Chancellor candidates:
CDU/CSU   Ludwig Erhard
SPD   Willy Brandt

6th Bundestag elections
(28 September 1969; Turn-out 86.7%)

	%	Seats
CDU	36.6	193
CSU	9.5	49
SPD	42.7	224
FDP	5.8	30

Chancellor candidates:

SPD	Willy Brandt
CDU/CSU	Kurt Georg Kiesinger

7th Bundestag elections
(19 November 1972; Turn-out 91.1%)

	%	Seats
CDU	35.2	177
CSU	9.7	48
SPD	45.8	230
FDP	8.4	41

Chancellor candidates:

SPD	Willy Brandt
CDU/CSU	Rainer Barzel

8th Bundestag elections
(3 October 1976; Turn-out 90.7%)

	%	Seats
CDU	38.0	190
CSU	10.6	53
SPD	42.6	214
FDP	7.9	39

Chancellor candidates:

SPD	Helmut Schmidt
CDU/CSU	Helmut Kohl

9th Bundestag elections
(5 October 1980; Turn-out 88.6%)

	%	Seats
CDU	34.2	174
CSU	10.3	52
SPD	42.9	218
FDP	10.6	53

Chancellor candidates:
SPD   Helmut Schmidt
CDU/CSU   Franz-Josef Strauss

10th Bundestag elections
(6 March 1983; Turn-out 89.1%)

	%	Seats
CDU	38.2	191
CSU	10.6	53
SPD	38.2	193
FDP	7.0	34
Greens	5.6	27

Chancellor candidates:
CDU/CSU   Helmut Kohl
SPD   Hans-Jochen Vogel

11th Bundestag elections
(25 January 1987; Turn-out 84.3%)

	%	Seats
CDU	34.5	174
CSU	9.8	49
SPD	37.0	186
FDP	9.1	46
Greens	8.3	42

Chancellor candidates:
CDU/CSU   Helmut Kohl
SPD   Johannes Rau

12th Bundestag elections
(2 December 1990; Turn-out 77.8%)

	%	Seats
CDU	36.7	268
CSU	7.1	51
SPD	33.5	239
FDP	11.0	79
Alliance 90/		
Greens	5.0	8
PDS	2.4	17

Note: A special 5% threshold was applied to constituencies in the former East Germany.
Chancellor candidates:
CDU/CSU   Helmut Kohl
SPD   Oskar Lafontaine

13th Bundestag elections
(16 October 1994; Turn-out 79.0%)

	%	Seats
CDU	34.2	244
CSU	7.3	50
SPD	36.4	252
FDP	6.9	47
Alliance 90/		
Greens	7.3	49
PDS	4.4	30

Chancellor candidates:
CDU/CSU   Helmut Kohl
SPD   Rudolf Scharping

The Volkskammer

(18 March 1990 (the last); Turn-out 93.4%)

	%	Seats
Alliance for Germany		
(CDU, DSU and Democratic Awakening)	47.9	192
SPD	21.9	88
PDS	16.5	66
BfD	5.2	21
Alliance 90	3.0	12
Democratic Farmers	2.2	9
Greens	2.0	8
Others	1.1	5

2.7 Membership of political parties and other organisations

Membership of the political parties

(Statistics as at 31 December of relevant year)

West Germany

	CDU	CSU	SPD	FDP	Greens
1946	—	69 370	711 448		
1950	—	—	683 896		
1952	210 000	—	627 817		
1954	215 000	—	585 479		
1955	245 000	—	589 051		
1957	—	43 500	626 189		
1960	—	52 501	649 578		
1962	248 000	—	646 584		
1963	250 000	—	648 415		
1964	279 770	—	678 484		
1965	—	70 302	710 448		
1966	280 781	—	727 890		
1967	285 804	—	733 004		
1968	286 541	73 618	732 446	57 034	
1969	303 532	76 655	778 945	58 750	
1970	329 239	93 220	820 202	56 531	
1971	355 745	109 785	847 456	53 302	
1972	422 968	106 951	954 394	57 757	
1973	457 393	111 913	973 601	63 205	
1974	530 500	122 794	990 682	70 938	
1975	590 482	132 591	998 471	74 032	
1976	652 010	144 433	1 022 191	79 162	
1977	664 214	159 475	1 006 316	79 539	
1978	675 286	165 710	997 444	80 928	

West Germany (*cont.*)

	CDU	CSU	SPD	FDP	Greens
1979	682 781	169 274	981 805	82 546	
1980	693 320	174 420	986 872	84 208	
1981	705 116	175 295	956 490	86 884	
1982	718 889	178 523	926 070	73 952	
1983	734 555	185 428	925 630	71 643	29 022
1984	730 395	184 228	916 485	68 872	32 078
1985	718 590	182 852	916 386	65 762	37 024
1986	714 089	182 369	912 854	63 946	38 170
1987	705 821	184 293	910 063	64 905	39 479
1988	676 747	182 738	911 916	64 417	37 879
1989	662 598	185 853	921 430	65 485	37 956

Notes:
1. CDU figures 1952–64 are Party estimates.
2. SPD figures up to 1960 exclude Bremen and up to 1955 exclude the Saar.

Minor parties
DKP   47 513 (1989)
KPD   70 000 (approx) (1956)

East Germany

	SED	CDU	DBD	LDPD	NDPD
1946	1 298 412	149 912	—	124 484	—
1950	1 750 000	194 934	50 000	171 300	41 000
1954	1 413 313	136 000	98 000	115 000	172 000
1961	1 610 769	—	—	—	—
1966	1 769 912	110 000	80 000	80 000	110 000
1971	1 909 859	—	—	—	—
1976	2 043 697	100 000	90 000	70 000	80 000
1981	2 172 110	120 000	—	—	—
1982	2 202 277	125 103	103 000	82 000	91 000
1985	2 293 289	131 000	110 500	96 000	101 500
1987	2 328 331	140 000	115 000	104 000	110 000
1989	1 780 000	137 196	125 000	110 000	110 000

Germany

	CDU	CSU	SPD	FDP	Greens	PDS
1991	751 163	184 513	919 871	137 853	38 054	172 579
1992	713 846	181 758	885 958	103 488	35 845	146 742
1993	685 343	177 289	861 480	94 197	39 335	131 406
1994	671 497	176 250	849 374	87 992	43 418	123 751
1995	657 643	179 647	817 650	80 431	46 054	114 940
1996	645 786	—	793 797	75 038	—	—
1997[1]	635 000	—	781 100	—	—	—

1. As of 31 October for CDU and 30 September for SPD

Religious affiliation

Religious affiliation in West and East Germany (%)

	1950 %	1961 %
West Germany		
Protestant	51.1	51.1
Roman Catholic	45.2	44.1
Jewish	—	0.04
East Germany		
Protestant	80.5	59.4[1]
Roman Catholic	11.0	8.1[1]

1. 1964 figure

Religious affiliation in Germany

	Total numbers
Germany	
Protestants	28 197 000 (1994)
Roman Catholics	27 465 000 (1994)
Jews	53 797 (1995)

Religious affiliation by *Land* (%)

Länder (available data)	1950 %	1961 %	1987 %
Baden–Württemberg			
Protestant	49.4	48.9	39.3[1]
Roman Catholic	47.2	46.8	43.8[1]
Bavaria			
Protestant	26.5	26.5	23.9
Roman Catholic	71.87	71.3	67.2
Berlin (East)			
Protestant	70.7[2]	—	—
Roman Catholic	10.5[2]	—	—
Berlin (West)			
Protestant	73.2	73.1	—
Roman Catholic	11.2	11.4	—
Bremen			
Protestant	84.9	84.1	61.0
Roman Catholic	8.9	9.9	10.0
Hamburg			
Protestant	78.25	76.3	50.2
Roman Catholic	6.5	7.4	8.6
Hesse			
Protestant	64.1	63.4	52.7
Roman Catholic	32.2	32.1	30.4
Lower Saxony			
Protestant	—	76.9	66.12
Roman Catholic	—	18.8	19.6
Mecklenburg–West Pomerania		(adherents in 1995)	
Protestant	—		390 200
Roman Catholic	—		73 000
North Rhine–Westphalia			
Protestant	41.1	42.8	35.2
Roman Catholic	54.8	52.1	49.4
Rhineland–Palatinate			
Protestant	40.7	41.9	37.7
Roman Catholic	57.7	56.2	54.5
Saarland			
Protestant	—	24.9	20.3[3]
Roman Catholic	—	73.3	72.3[3]
Schleswig–Holstein			
Protestant	88.0	88.2	73.3
Roman Catholic	6.0	5.6	6.2

1. 1996 figure
2. 1946 figure
3. 1994 figure

2.8 Key legislative and constitutional judgments

1950

19 September. The West German government decides under the *Berufsverbot* to dismiss from public service all members of the Communist Party (KPD) and of twelve other extreme groups of left and right, including the SRP. The decision extends to all public servants including postmen and railwaymen, and the *Länder* governments are asked to act similarly.

1951

28 September. The West German Constitutional Court comes into existence in Karlsruhe in accordance with the provisions of the Basic Law.
16 November. The West German government asks the Constitutional Court to declare both the KPD and the SRP unconstitutional under Article 21 of the Basic Law.

1952

16 May. The Court rejects an application from the SPD for an interim injunction to restrain Chancellor Adenauer from signing either the contractual agreements with the western Allies or the EDC treaty.
10 June. The Court opens its hearings on an application from the SPD and the Federal Union, with the support of the *Land* governments of Bavaria, Hesse, and Lower Saxony, asking it to declare that any legislation enabling or requiring West Germans to undertake military service is 'formally and materially' incompatible with the Basic Law.
15 July. The Court issues an interim injunction on the SRP restraining it from engaging in propaganda activity.
23 October. The Court declares the SRP unconstitutional and a successor body to the Nazi Party.

1955

4 May. The West German Constitutional Court rejects an SPD petition that the Franco-German Saar agreement is unconstitutional.

1956

17 August. The West German Constitutional Court declares the KPD unconstitutional. It is banned the following month.

1957

23 January. The West German Constitutional Court dismisses petitions by the Bavarian Party and the All-German People's Party that the '5 per cent' clause of the 1956 electoral law is unconstitutional. The petitioners had maintained that it was an infringement of the right to vote and of the free establishment of political parties under Article 21 of the Basic Law. **9 April.** The Court finds that the Saar Communist Party is equivalent to the banned West German party and orders the Saar *Land* government to ban it accordingly.

1959

28 February. The Court finds a pamphlet published by Friedrich Nieland, a Hamburg timber merchant, alleging that the Jews had been exterminated by 'international Jewry', a danger to the democratic order, and orders that it be banned and all copies confiscated. The case had been dismissed in November 1958 by the Hamburg *Land* Court under the presidency of Dr Enno Budde, who was later revealed as having a pronounced anti-semitic and pro-Nazi record both before and after the War.

1961

25 May. West Germany bans the neo-Nazi Ludendorff Movement. Originally founded by Field-Marshall Ludendorff of First World War fame, it had been continued by his widow and had some 6,000 members.

1966

5 August. The West German Constitutional Court divides equally over whether the police action against the offices of *Der Spiegel* and the warrants for the arrest of its publisher, editors and some staff had been unconstitutional. It is therefore unable to determine a violation of the constitution. (See '*Spiegel* affair' in *Glossary* for fuller particulars.)

1973

23 May. The CSU government of Bavaria applies to the Constitutional Court for an interim injunction to prevent the Basic Treaty from coming into force.
5 June. The Court rejects the application.
13 June. Bavaria submits a second petition to the Court for an interim injunction.
18 June. The second petition is unanimously rejected by the Court.
19 June. The Court commences its deliberations into the main case brought by Bavaria arguing against the constitutionality of the Basic Treaty.
31 July. The West German Constitutional Court rules that the Basic Treaty does not conflict with the Basic Law.

1974

9 July. Beate Klarsfeld is sentenced in Cologne to two months' imprisonment for her participation in the attempted kidnapping of Kurt Lischka in Cologne on 22 March 1971. Lischka had been sentenced by the French *in absentia* to life imprisonment for war crimes, but could not be tried again in West Germany for the same offence. The judgment generates widespread protest.

1975

21 February. Against expectations, the CDU/CSU-dominated Bundesrat ratifies a Franco-German agreement of 2 February 1971 permitting West German courts to retry German war criminals convicted of murder by French courts, *in absentia*. The CDU/CSU had opposed ratification in the Bundestag on account of the alleged age of defendants and witnesses.

1977

12 July. Dr Klaus Croissant, defence lawyer to a number of alleged RAF (Red Army Faction) members and suspected by some of involvement in their activities, applies for French political asylum alleging that he cannot practise in West Germany and that he is afraid for his freedom.

15 August. Herbert Kappler, a former SS colonel and Gestapo chief in Rome sentenced to life imprisonment in Italy in 1948 for war crimes, is smuggled out of a Rome military hospital by his wife. The West German government confirms that Kappler is already in the country.

18 August. The Italian government requests the West German government to extradite Kappler, as West Germany is a signatory of the European Extradition Convention, 1957.

21 September. West Germany rejects the extradition request on the grounds that the Basic Law prohibits the extradition of West German citizens. (Kappler died at his home in Soltau, Lower Saxony, on 9 February 1978.)

2 October. The 'isolation from contact law' (*Kontaktsperrengesetz*) comes into force, having taken just five days to pass through the legislative process. It enables certain prisoners to be forbidden any contact with each other or with the outside world, including any contact with their defence lawyers, for a renewable period of 30 days.

16 November. The French courts grant the West German request for Dr Croissant's extradition despite many legal, political and public protests.

1979

3 July. The Bundestag approves a bill to abolish the Statute of Limitation for war crimes and the Bundesrat agrees three days later. The Statute had declared that no new prosecution for murder might be brought later than twenty years after the alleged crime, and its abolition removed any time limit for the trial of serious war criminals.

1982

27 January. The neo-Nazi 'Socialist People's Movement of Germany/ Party of Labour' is banned. It has some 90 members.

1983

7 December. The neo-Nazi *Aktionsfront Nationaler Sozialisten/Nationale Aktivisten* (*ANS/NA*) is banned.

15 December. The Constitutional Court requires the West German 1982 census law and forms to be amended, notably the clause permitting data to be given to the police for the updating of their address files. The census, originally planned for 27 April 1983, had generated a number of 'boycott initiatives'.

22 December. The Constitutional Court rejects petitions seeking an injunction to prevent the deployment of American Cruise and Pershing II missiles in West Germany, and rules that their deployment is constitutional.

1985

25 April. The *Auschwitz-lie* law comes into effect. It makes it an offence subject to a maximum penalty of two years' imprisonment 'to insult and defame victims of the Nazi regime and other [German] dictatorships'. The bill as originally proposed by the SPD/FDP made no reference to the victims of other dictatorships, and the SPD opposed the bill as revised at CSU insistence, because it could be taken to include all those Germans expelled from eastern Europe after 1945. (See section 8.3 for fuller particulars.)

25 June. The new SPD government of the Saar becomes the first *Land* government to abandon the *Berufsverbot* provisions of 19 September 1950. Other SPD *Länder* welcome the initiative, but the West German government keeps the provisions in force for federal civil service employment.

1988

18 May. The West German cabinet approves a new security law (*Vermummungsverbot*) which makes the wearing of masks in demonstrations a criminal offence.

1989

9 February. The neo-Nazi National Gathering (*Nationale Sammlung*) is banned.

12 October. The West German Constitutional Court rules against permitting foreigners with long-term residential qualifications to vote in local elections. The case had been brought by the CDU and the ruling obliges Schleswig-Holstein to abandon its proposed enabling legislation.

1991

23 April. The Constitutional Court rules that landowners and industrialists whose property was confiscated by the Soviet military government, 1945–49, cannot claim its return.

24 April. The Court rules that the government has the legal right to dismiss up to 600,000 former East German civil servants, who had been given temporary contracts on unification but had not then been declared redundant.

1992

21 July. The SPD decides to refer to the Constitutional Court the government decision of 15 July to send forces to the Adriatic.

15 October. A Bundestag vote to amend the Basic Law by restricting the right of asylum to those persecuted on political grounds fails to achieve the requisite two-thirds majority of members.

27 November. The neo-Nazi Nationalist Front, which had been founded in 1985 and has 130 members, is banned. Other similar groups are banned in the following weeks.

1993

12 January. The Constitutional Court rules that the continued imprisonment of Erich Honecker, who is suffering from liver cancer and is believed to have only three to six months to live, violates human dignity and basic human rights.

8 April. The Constitutional Court rules by five votes to three that German forces may participate in advance warning and control systems (AWACS) flights over Bosnia. It thus permits the first deployment of German combat troops outside the NATO area since the Second World War. The status of 'collective self defence', however, remains undefined.

26 May. The Bundestag approves by 521 votes to 132 with one abstention an amendment of Article 16 of the Basic Law, whereby the right of asylum is normally withdrawn from those arriving from 'safe' countries.

28 May. The Constitutional Court rules by six votes to two that the 1992 legislation unifying the approach to abortion in eastern and western Germany is unconstitutional. It also declares the 1972 East German law permitting abortion on demand until the twelfth week of pregnancy to be unconstitutional.

23 June. The Constitutional Court rejects an SPD submission that German troops in Somalia must be withdrawn as thay are now on a combat rather than a humanitarian mission.

12 October. The Court unanimously finds the Maastricht Treaty on European union compatible with the Basic Law, provided the convergence criteria for EMU are met.

1994

15 March. The Court rules that denying that the extermination of the Jews occurred does not of itself constitute incitement to racial hatred.

19 April. The Constitutional Court opens hearings into petitions by the SPD against force deployments in the Adriatic, Somalia, and over Bosnia. The last, concerning the implementation of the no-fly zone, is also referred by the FDP.

24 April. The Court rules that denying that the extermination of the Jews occurred is to deny a fact, and is thus a denial of the right to freedom of speech.

12 July. The Court rules that the despatch of German forces on active service abroad as part of a system of collective defence or security is in accordance with the Basic Law provided the Bundestag approves each specific case.

1995

23 May. The Court rules that former East German spies who operated exclusively from East German territory cannot now be prosecuted in the federal courts. Charges against more than 6,300 agents have to be dropped, and the six-year sentence of December 1993 on Markus Wolf is overturned. (See Markus Wolf in *Biographies*.)

10 August. The Court rules that Bavaria is contravening the Basic Law by hanging crucifixes in state schools. The ruling gives rise to demonstrations.

1996

14 May. The Court confirms that the 1993 changes to the legislation on asylum are compatible with the Basic Law.

1998

2 April. The Court dismisses two petitions designed to prevent the start of European economic and monetary union on 1 January 1999. The petitioners, led by Professor Karl Albrecht Schachtschneider and by Manfred Brunner, a noted Eurosceptic, had alleged that the government had 'fudged' the convergence criteria laid down by the Maastricht Treaty.

2.9 Terrorism

1952

27 March. A parcel bomb addressed to Chancellor Adenauer explodes under police investigation in Munich. An explosives expert later dies of his injuries.

1967

2 June. The killing of Benno Ohnesorg in West Berlin leads to the foundation of the 'June 2 [terrorist] Movement'. (See section 5.2 for fuller particulars.)

1968

2 April. The RAF opens its large-scale terrorist campaign with arson in a Frankfurt department store. (See 'Red Army Faction' in *Glossary* for fuller particulars.)

14 May. Andreas Baader is sentenced in Frankfurt to three years' imprisonment with hard labour for the arson attack.

1970

14 May. Andreas Baader is liberated by the RAF, while visiting a Berlin educational institute under guard.

1972

11 May. Bombs explode at the headquarters of the US Army Fifth Corps in Frankfurt. One officer is killed and thirteen people are injured. The RAF claims responsibility.

16 May. Bombs explode in the city police headquarters in Augsburg and in a car park adjacent to the Bavarian police office in Munich.

19 May. Two major explosions badly damage the headquarters of the Axel Springer publishing group in Hamburg and seriously injure six people. Six further unexploded bombs are found later. Axel Springer had been a leading campaigner against the RAF.

24 May. Two large bombs explode almost simultaneously at the American Army's European Command headquarters in Heidelberg. Three soldiers are killed and five other people are injured.

1 June. Andreas Baader, Holger Meins and Jan-Carl Raspe are arrested as the 'hard core' of the RAF, following a gun battle in Frankfurt.

7 June. Gudrun Ensslin, a further 'hard core' RAF member, is arrested in Hamburg. She had earlier been found guilty of participation with Andreas Baader in the Frankfurt arson case of April 1968.

16 June. Ulrike Meinhof, one of the RAF leaders, is arrested in Langenhagen, near Hanover.

25 June. Iain MacLeod, a Scottish businessman, is accidentally killed by police searching for RAF members.

5 September. Eleven Israeli athletes are killed by Arab terrorists at the Munich Olympic Games.

29 October. Two Arabs hijack a West German airliner between Damascus and Frankfurt and, by threatening to blow it up, obtain the freedom of three Arabs detained after the Munich killings.

1974

9 November. Holger Meins, allegedly a core RAF member, dies on hunger strike in Wittlich prison (Rhineland-Palatinate). He had been in prison awaiting trial since June 1972 on charges of complicity in five cases of murder and 54 of attempted murder. His death provokes demonstrations in a number of large West German cities, and widespread concern at the conditions of imprisonment, which are described by some as 'isolation torture'.

10 November. Günter von Drenkmann, President of the West Berlin Supreme Court, is assassinated at his home in Berlin Charlottenburg. The RAF claims responsibility.

20 November. The RAF is believed to be responsible for a bomb explosion outside the home of Dr Gerd Ziegler, a Hamburg judge.

26 November. The police launch 'operation winter journey' and arrest about 40 suspected RAF members and sympathisers.

30 November. The RAF claims responsibility for the attempted murder of Walter Leisler Kiep, CDU treasurer, near his home in Kronberg, Taunus.

1975

27 February. Peter Lorenz, chairman of the West Berlin CDU, is kidnapped by the 'June 2 Movement'.

5 March. Peter Lorenz is freed, broadly on the Movement's terms. (See section 1.2 for fuller particulars of this and foregoing.)

24 April. Six terrorists seize the West German embassy in Stockholm in an unsuccessful attempt to secure the release of 26 West German prisoners, including Ensslin, Baader, Meinhof and Raspe. Three people are killed – the economic and military attachés and one terrorist – and some 30 injured. The captured terrorists are returned to West Germany.

21 May. The trial opens in a specially built courtroom in Stammheim high security prison, Karlsruhe, of the four RAF leaders: Andreas Baader,

Gudrun Ensslin, Ulrike Meinhof, and Jan-Carl Raspe. Among other charges, all four are accused of murder and bank robbery.

23 September. A medical commission appointed by the presiding judge reports that the four defendants in the 'hard core' RAF trial are not in its opinion physically or mentally capable of following the trial for more than three hours daily and that their health may deteriorate rapidly if they do not receive immediate treatment compatible with the trial and their conditions of imprisonment.

1976
9 May. Ulrike Meinhof commits suicide in prison.

1977
20 January. Dr Theodor Prinzing is removed from the presidency of the court trying the three remaining 'hard core' members of the RAF by his eight colleagues who accept that the defendants could feel reasonable doubt as to his impartiality.

7 April. Dr Siegfried Buback, West Germany's Chief Federal Prosecutor, is assassinated in Karlsruhe. His chauffeur and a policeman are also killed. The 'Ulrike Meinhof Commando' claims responsibility.

28 April. The new president of the court, Dr Eberhard Foth, sentences Andreas Baader, Gudrun Ensslin and Jan-Carl Raspe to life imprisonment for four cases of murder with an additional fifteen years for 34 cases of attempted murder and the formation of a criminal organisation.

30 July. Dr Jürgen Ponto, Chief Executive of the Dresdner Bank, is killed in the course of an attempted kidnapping from his home in Oberursel near Frankfurt. '*Roter Morgen*' claims responsibility.

25 August. The RAF mounts an unsuccessful attempt to destroy the Chief Federal Prosecutor's office.

5 September. Dr Hanns-Martin Schleyer, president of the West German Federal Union of German Industry and of the Federation of German Employers' Associations, is kidnapped near Cologne. His chauffeur and three police guards are killed.

13 October. A Lufthansa jet aircraft is hijacked between Palma de Mallorca and Frankfurt in an attempt to secure the release of terrorists.

18 October. The jet is successfully stormed at Mogadishu, Somalia, by a special West German police unit.

The three convicted 'hard core' RAF members are found dead or dying in their cells.

19 October. The body of Dr Schleyer is discovered in the boot of a German-registered car in Mulhouse, France. The RAF claims that his death is in no way commensurate with those at Mogadishu and those of the 'hard core' RAF members.

12 November. Ingrid Schubert, a leading RAF member serving thirteen years for armed robbery and membership of a criminal organisation, commits suicide in Stadelheim prison, Munich.

1978

11 April. The trial opens in Berlin Moabit prison of leading members of the June 2 Movement, accused of the murder of Günter von Drenkmann in November 1974.

6 September. Willy Peter Stoll, one of the three most wanted terrorists, is killed by police in Düsseldorf while resisting arrest. A former assistant to Dr Croissant, the defence lawyer, he was believed to be implicated in the murders of Dr Buback, Dr Ponto and Dr Schleyer.

1979

19 January. Bombs severely damage television transmitters in Koblenz and Münster during the transmission of a programme on the Holocaust. The far right claims responsibility.

16 February. Dr Klaus Croissant is sentenced to 30 months' imprisonment in Stuttgart for abusing his status as a defence lawyer. He is also banned from practising for four years. He is released on 5 December under an amnesty.

1980

22 February. A bomb badly damages a Stuttgart hall where there is an exhibition on the Auschwitz concentration camp.

26 September. A bomb explodes outside the main entrance at the Munich October Festival killing thirteen people and injuring over 200. It is attributed to the far-right 'Hoffmann military sport group' (*Wehrsportsgruppe Hoffmann*) banned in January of that year.

1981

11 May. Heinz Herbert Karry, FDP Minister for Economic Affairs in the SPD/FDP Hesse *Land* government, is assassinated at his home in Frankfurt. He had vigorously supported the controversial extension of the Rhine/Main airport near Frankfurt opposed both by environmentalists and the left wing of the SPD. Political motivation is considered likely.

31 August. A bomb severely damages the headquarters at Ramstein of the NATO Allied Air Forces, Central Europe, and the United States Air Force, Europe, injuring 20 people.

1985

19 June. A bomb explosion at Frankfurt/Main Airport kills three people and injures two. Several Arab and left-wing groups claim responsibility.

1986

9 July. Professor Karl Heinz Beckurts, director of research and technology at Siemens, is killed by a bomb as he is driven to work near Munich. His chauffeur is also killed and an RAF group claims responsibility.

10 October. Gerold von Braunmühl, director of the political section of the Foreign Ministry, is shot dead outside his Bonn home. The 'Ingrid Schubert Commando of the Revolutionary Front of West Europe' claims responsibility.

1988

20 September. Hans Tietmeyer, then a state secretary at the finance ministry and later Bundesbank president, escapes an assassination attempt, together with his driver, in Bad Godesberg. The 'Khaled Aker Commando' of the RAF claims responsibility.

Tietmeyer was involved in the organisation of the annual joint meeting of the World Bank and the International Monetary Fund in West Berlin, which extremists had sworn to prevent from happening.

1989

12 May. A hunger strike by up to 33 RAF prisoners against 'isolation torture' is called off after limited concessions by those *Länder* controlled by the SPD. The strike, begun in February, had been accompanied by sympathetic fire bomb attacks in Frankfurt, Münster, West Berlin and elsewhere.

30 November. Alfred Herrhausen, chief executive of the Deutsche Bank, chairman of the supervisory board of Daimler-Benz (a major manufacturer of armaments as well as cars) and a prominent economic adviser to Chancellor Kohl, is killed by a car bomb in Bad Homburg. The RAF claims responsibility.

1990

3 March. An assassination attempt on Ignaz Kiechle, the food minister, is called off by the RAF as a result of failed co-ordination.

1991

13 January. RAF members fire shots at the American embassy in Bonn in protest at the American role in the Gulf War.

1 April. Detlev Rohwedder, director of the *Treuhandanstalt* privatisation agency, is assassinated at his home in Düsseldorf by the RAF. He is succeeded in post by Birgit Breuel. It is the last of the 32 murders attributed to the RAF, and appears to mark the end of organised German terrorism against individuals.

1992

13 April. The RAF declares that it will cease its attacks on leading business and political figures if some of its members serving particularly long terms of imprisonment are released. Dr Kinkel had stated in the January that the government was 'prepared for reconciliation'.

15 May. Günter Sonnenberg is released on probation after serving fifteen years of a life sentence. He had been seriously injured on arrest.

14 September. Klaus Croissant, the former RAF defence lawyer, is charged with supplying the *Stasi* with political information between 1981 and 1987.

1993

26–27 March. An RAF bomb destroys a new prison in Hesse.

1998

20 April. The RAF announces (on Hitler's birthday) that it is abandoning its guerilla struggle against the state.

SECTION THREE

Germany's foreign policy

3.1 Inter-German relations 1949–90

1950
30 November. Otto Grotewohl, the East German prime minister, writes to Chancellor Adenauer proposing conversations between their two governments on the establishment of an all-German Constituent Council. The proposal arises from a meeting of Cominform and East German foreign ministers held in Prague on 21–22 October.
11 December. East German radio invites Chancellor Adenauer to use its network to address the Germans of East Germany.

1951
15 January. Chancellor Adenauer replies indirectly to Otto Grotewohl in a statement which argues that any all-German assembly must be freely elected on the basis of freely constituted political groupings. The Chancellor also requires the prior disbandment of the *Volkspolizei* (People's Police).
21 January. Dr Schumacher, leader of the SPD, supports the Chancellor and maintains that the real Soviet aim is to get reparations from West Germany.

1952
8 May. Otto Grotewohl, East German prime minister, declares that the signing of the Treaties of Bonn and Paris by West Germany and the western Allies will 'produce in Germany the same conditions as exist in Korea' and might lead to 'a fratricidal war of German against German'.
12 May. Ulbricht threatens Chancellor Adenauer and his government with 'reprisals at the hands of the German people' if they sign the Treaties, and maintains that those Bundestag members in support will be 'blacklisted' and one day 'suitably punished'.
27 May. East Germany responds to the signing of the Treaties of Bonn and Paris (see section 1.2 for fuller particulars) by erecting a literal 'Iron Curtain' of barbed wire, minefields and watchtowers and by creating a security zone three miles deep the length of its frontier with West Germany. The security zone also extends along the Baltic coast. West Germans and West Berliners will henceforward need East German entry permits.
East Germany also cuts off telephone communications with West Berlin.

1954

7 April. The Bundestag unanimously refuses to recognise the Soviet Union's right to establish an East German state.

1955

9 December. Dr Heinrich von Brentano, the West German foreign minister, proclaims the 'Hallstein Doctrine' whereby West Germany declares that it will terminate diplomatic relations with any state, other than the Soviet Union, which recognises East Germany.

1956

27 June. East Germany announces that travel restrictions between East and West Germany are to be greatly relaxed.

1957

13 February. Chancellor Adenauer maintains in a broadcast that the German people must remember 'clearly and distinctly' that there is 'only one German State' and that the 'so-called Democratic Republic [is] not a State but an occupation zone under Soviet rule, whose people must have their freedom restored to them'.

19 October. West Germany severs relations with Yugoslavia in accordance with the Hallstein Doctrine. (See section 3.3 for fuller particulars.)

1958

1–3 October. A unanimous Bundestag resolution formally protests against the continued persecution of the people of East Germany and the refusal to allow free movement across the joint border.

1963

12 January. Cuba recognises East Germany. West Germany severs relations with Cuba in accordance with the Hallstein Doctrine. (See section 3.3 for fuller particulars.)

15–21 January. Ulbricht puts forward at the 6th SED Congress in East Berlin a seven-point plan for the normalisation of relations between East and West Germany.

1964

23 September. West Germany approves a permanent 'technical agreement' between East Germany and the West Berlin Senate permitting limited visits by West Berliners to relations in East Berlin. (See section 5.2 for fuller particulars.) West Germany insists that the agreement involves recognition of neither East Germany nor East Berlin as its capital.

1966

11 February. The SED writes to the West German SPD proposing a debate between party representatives on the future of Germany.

18 March. The SPD responds positively but on terms which the SED is unlikely to accept. The initiative lapses with the formation of the 'grand coalition'.

1968

10 March. East Germany bans members of the NPD and other neo-Nazis from staying in, or travelling through, East Germany. The NPD had had significant successes in West German *Land* elections in the previous fifteen months.

13 April. The March ban is extended to all West German ministers and senior officials.

26 April. East German border guards prevent Klaus Schütz, governing mayor of West Berlin and then president of the Bundesrat, from driving on the autobahn across East Germany.

11 June. East Germany requires all West Germans travelling across East Germany to hold a passport and transit visa, and all those visiting East Germany to hold a passport with entry and exit visas. West Berliners are to hold identity cards with a transit or entry visa, as appropriate.

1969

28 October. Chancellor Brandt reiterates the West German position on the unity of the German people with the same right to self-determination as any other people, but reverses established policy by recognising the existence of two German states. Nevertheless, 'They are not foreign countries to each other; their relations with each other can only be of a special nature.' Recognition of East Germany by West Germany under international law remains out of the question. He offers East Germany negotiations at government level without discrimination on either side, which should lead to contractually agreed co-operation.

12 November. Willi Stoph, the East German prime minister, says that East Germany is ready to negotiate for a normalisation of relations and adds that such a normalisation is an absolute necessity.

17 December. The Volkskammer resolves that the two German states should take the necessary measures to establish 'relations on the basis of peaceful co-existence'.

18 December. Ulbricht writes to President Heinemann suggesting that Stoph and Brandt meet in January 1970 to negotiate the establishment of normal relations between East and West Germany, and proposing a draft treaty to that end. President Heinemann refers the letter to the West German government.

1970

14 January. Chancellor Brandt defines to the Bundestag West Germany's approach to the normalisation of relations with East Germany. He maintains that:

> [a nation] rests on a people's enduring sense of solidarity. Nobody can deny that in this sense there is and will be one German nation as far as we can think ahead . . . the path that leads to German self-determination . . . will be a long and thorny one. Its length and difficulties must not restrain us from seeking, in the present phase of history, if that is possible, regular neighbourly relations between the two states in Germany . . . However, the two state and social structures that have now been existing on German soil for more than two decades, reflect completely different and incompatible ideas of what the unity of Germany, what a common future, should look like and how it could be reached . . . On this point we are agreed with Ulbricht – there can be no intermingling, no dubious compromise, between our system and what has become a set order on the other side . . .
>
> [*Source*: Keesing's Contemporary Archives, pp. 23834–5 (adapted)]

19 March. Willi Stoph and Willy Brandt meet in Erfurt, East Germany, in the first top-level government meeting between the two states since their foundation. The local populace welcomes Brandt enthusiastically.

21 May. Stoph and Brandt meet in Kassel, West Germany.

12 August. The Treaty of Moscow between West Germany and the Soviet Union respects the existing frontiers of East Germany. (See section 1.2 for fuller particulars.)

14 August. The East German Council of Ministers endorses the Moscow Treaty, hiding its chagrin that it does not require West Germany to recognise East Germany under international law and leaves open the possibility of ultimate unification.

7 December. The Treaty of Warsaw between West Germany and Poland respects the Oder-Neisse line as the East German frontier with Poland. (See section 1.2 for fuller particulars.)

1971

3 September. Signature of the Four-Power Berlin Agreement. (See section 5.2 for fuller particulars.)

30 September. East Germany and West Germany sign a protocol on postal services and telecommunications and agree to establish a colour television relay system.

17 December. East and West Germany sign a transit agreement. (See section 5.2 for fuller particulars.)

1972

26 May. East and West Germany sign a treaty on traffic.

21 December. The Basic Treaty is signed between East Germany and West Germany. They agree under Article 1 to develop normal good-neighbourly relations on the basis of equality, and under Article 2 to act in accordance with the UN Charter. They renounce the threat or use of force under Article 3 and undertake not to represent the other abroad under Article 4. Further Articles envisage co-operation in a wide range of fields.

East Germany thereby receives recognition from West Germany of its separate identity and equality but not of its identity as a foreign state under international law.

1973

2 February. Helmut Kohl, as prime minister of the Rhineland-Palatinate, declares in a Bundesrat debate on the admission of the two Germanys to the United Nations that the CDU would continue not to ratify the 1972 Basic Treaty on the grounds that it would significantly reduce Germany's ability to maintain the basis for ultimate reunification. In particular, acceptance of East Germany as a separate German state had endangered West Germany's historic right, as the only freely elected state on German soil, to speak for all Germans.

The CDU/CSU majority rejects the bill to ratify the Basic Treaty on its first reading by 21 votes to 20.

25 May. West Germany completes the ratification of the Basic Treaty.

13 June. The East German Volkskammer unanimously ratifies the Basic Treaty.

20–21 June. The Basic Treaty comes into force.

1974

2 May. East and West Germany establish permanent representation in each other's capitals.

1975

26 March. A consular agreement is signed in East Berlin between the Austrian ambassador and the East German foreign minister. It is the first such agreement with a western country. It has the effect of recognising an East German nationality and had been opposed by the West German government which claimed that the existence of one German nationality had not been suspended since 1945 and that it was not compromised by the 1972 Basic Treaty.

West Germany had exercised the right of consular protection since 1949 for all Germans domiciled within the frontiers of the German state as at 31 December 1937. Austria's particular concern was the

10,000–15,000 Austrians living in East Germany, many of whom had been born after the *Anschluss* and who could not therefore prove their Austrian status.

15 December. Christel Guillaume is transferred to East Germany in an exchange of prisoners.

1977

19 June. Chile releases a Communist Party leader, Jorge Montes, in exchange for eleven East German political prisoners. West Germany collaborates 'for humanitarian reasons'.

1978

10 November. A substantial agreement is signed between East and West Germany on improving the transit routes between West Berlin and West Germany. It includes a new 128km length of autobahn between West Berlin and Hamburg to be paid for by West Germany, and the renovation and reopening of the Teltow canal. The agreement also provides for the release by East Germany of all savings of pensioners who have emigrated to West Germany.

1979

19 January. Lt Werner Stiller of the East German security service defects to the west with extensive information on alleged East German spies and contacts. Arrests follow.

8 February. It is officially estimated in a reply to a Bundestag question that some 3,500–4,000 East European spies are operating in West Germany and that some four-fifths of them are working for East Germany.

18 June. Lothar Lutze and Renate Lutze are sentenced in Düsseldorf to twelve years' and six years' imprisonment respectively for particularly significant spying for East Germany.

1980

17 April. The meeting in West Germany between Chancellor Schmidt and Dr Günther Mittag, a member of the Politbüro and Erich Honecker's chief economic adviser, is the highest level political contact between the two Germanys since 1970.

22 August. The meeting between Erich Honecker and Chancellor Schmidt in East Germany, scheduled for 28–29 August, is cancelled by the Chancellor. The unrest in Poland and alterations to the programme are among the likely reasons.

1981

28 October. An exchange of prisoners, including Günter Guillaume and Renate Lutze, is concluded between East and West Germany.

11–13 December. Chancellor Schmidt pays an official visit to East Germany. It is the first top-level East–West German meeting on German soil since 1970. Honecker urges Schmidt to recognise an East German nationality, to resolve a border dispute over a section of the River Elbe and to agree to raise the two countries' missions to each other to embassy status. Schmidt maintains that the visit has increased the calculability of inter-German relations, but there is little progress on the issues in dispute.

1982

25 March. The Volkskammer passes a new law on the East German state border, which is declared inviolable. It establishes in law for the first time that border guards are under orders to shoot any person trying to escape to West Berlin or West Germany, if a warning shout or shot is ignored.

20 November. The autobahn between Hamburg and West Berlin, the construction of which had been agreed in 1978, is officially opened.

1983

28 April. Erich Honecker postpones his forthcoming visit to West Germany, citing 'the situation which West Germany had brought about with regard to relations between the two German states, as also expressed in various press commentaries' there.

28 May. Erich Honecker and Hans-Jochen Vogel, SPD Bundestag leader, meet at the hunting lodge by Lake Wehrbellin in East Germany where Honecker had met Schmidt in 1981.

August. President Carstens of West Germany rejects Erich Honecker's invitation to attend the official celebrations of the 500th anniversary of Martin Luther's birth, to be held in East Berlin in November 1983.

5 September. Erich Honecker and Helmut Schmidt, the former West German Chancellor, meet in East Berlin.

14 September. Erich Honecker and Dr Richard von Weizsäcker, mayor of West Berlin, meet in East Berlin.

31 October. A West German Green Party delegation meets Erich Honecker.

1984

13 February. Erich Honecker and Chancellor Kohl meet in Moscow before President Andropov's funeral.

10 March. Sixteen Bundestag members meet members of the Volkskammer at the invitation of its president, Horst Sindermann. It is the first meeting to be held between members of the two chambers and is opposed by the West German CDU.

14 March. Erich Honecker and Hans-Jochen Vogel meet again in East Berlin.

11–17 March. The Leipzig trade fair is attended by Dr Otto Graf Lambsdorff, the West German economics minister, the *Ministerpräsidenten* of three West German *Länder* and Eberhard Diepgen, CDU mayor of West Berlin.

15 March. Chancellor Kohl in his state of the nation speech argues 'that a normalisation of intra-German relations still remains far away'.

10 July. The two national airlines, Lufthansa and Interflug, establish scheduled (as distinct from chartered) flights between West and East Germany and agree to recognise each other's domestic and international tickets.

1 August. A commentary in *Neues Deutschland*, the East German newspaper, to mark the ninth anniversary of the Helsinki declaration, argues that dialogue between the two blocs 'must be maintained' and that East Germany will continue its approach 'unswervingly'.

4 September. Erich Honecker cancels his visit to West Germany scheduled for 26–29 September. The cancellation is preceded by a number of articles in the eastern European and Soviet press criticising West German 'revanchism'.

20–21 September. Talks are held in Bonn between representatives of the SPD and the SED on a chemical-weapons-free zone in Central Europe.

5 October. Erich Honecker maintains in *Pravda*, the Soviet newspaper, that ties between East and West Germany can only be formed by 'two sovereign equal states which do not depend on each other and which manage their domestic and foreign affairs themselves'.

5–6 December. The SPD–SED September talks are continued in East Berlin.

13–14 December. A conference between representatives of the SPD and the SED on peaceful co-existence and security is held in Bonn.

1985

19 June. The 1984 talks between the SPD and the SED result in a proposed draft treaty to establish a chemical-weapons-free zone in Central Europe comprising East and West Germany, Belgium, Netherlands, and Luxembourg, Czechoslovakia and Poland.

late September. Talks are held between the SPD and the SED on the establishment of a nuclear-weapons-free zone in Central Europe.

1 November. The East–West German border is declared free of mines, although the border fence has been reinforced.

1986

14–16 February. The SPD–SED September talks are continued.

19–21 February. Horst Sindermann, the president of the Volkskammer, visits West Germany at the invitation of the SPD Bundestag group. He talks with Chancellor Kohl, Hans-Jochen Vogel, the SPD Bundestag leader, and Philipp Jenninger, the Bundestag president.

23 April. Saarlouis, West Germany, and Eisenhüttenstadt, East Germany, conclude the first inter-German town twinning agreement, to come into effect later in the year.

6 May. East and West Germany sign a cultural agreement after thirteen years of negotiation.

21 October. An SPD–SED working party produces a joint paper, endorsed also by the Czechoslovak Communist Party, proposing the establishment over three years of a 300km-wide nuclear-weapons-free corridor along the West German border with East Germany and Czechoslovakia.

1987

25–30 March. Two West German Army officers observe Soviet–East German manoeuvres in East Germany for the first time. They are part of an international delegation pursuant to the 1986 Stockholm conference on confidence- and security-building measures and disarmament in Europe.

1 April. Lothar Lutze is released by West Germany in an East–West spy exchange.

18 August. Manfred Rotsch, a Soviet spy, is released by West Germany in a spy exchange. He is considered to be the last major spy held by West Germany.

27 August. The SPD and the SED produce a joint eighteen-page declaration of goals, 'Conflicting ideologies and common security'. It aims to set in motion processes of disarmament and open debate on the rival political systems.

7–11 September. Erich Honecker pays an official visit to West Germany. It is the first official visit to be made there by an East German head of state. His delegation includes Dr Günter Mittag, the Politbüro member responsible for economic affairs, Oskar Fischer, foreign minister, and Dr Gerhard Beil, minister of foreign trade. Talks are held in Bonn with Chancellor Kohl, Dr Martin Bangemann, economics minister, Dr Dorothee Wilms, minister for inter-German relations, and Dr Wolfgang Schäuble, head of Chancellery, which are described by both sides as 'concrete, open and constructive'. A joint communiqué issued on the second day proclaims that 'never again must war be allowed to emanate from German soil.' Philipp Jenninger, president of the Bundestag, nevertheless expresses to Erich Honecker CDU reservations over greater contact with the Volkskammer, arising in part from the implications for West Berlin Bundestag members.

Erich Honecker also visits Cologne, Düsseldorf, Wuppertal, where he visits the birthplace of Friedrich Engels, Essen, his own place of birth in Neunkirchen and his sister's home in Wiebelskirchen, both in the

Saarland, Trier, where he visits the birthplace of Karl Marx, and Dachau concentration camp.

The visit also sees the signature of significant agreements on environmental and scientific co-operation, and on the exchange of information on nuclear safety.

1988

19 January. East and West Germany agree to link their electricity grids using a new power line from Helmstedt to Berlin.

(The critical contacts between East and West Germany immediately prior to unification are detailed in section 1.2 from mid-1988 onwards.)

3.2 West Germany and the west

1950

14 January. Chancellor Adenauer expresses disquiet at reports that France is seeking to acquire the Saar coal mines on a long lease of perhaps 50 years. He fears the adverse impact of any unilateral change on German public support for European integration.

19 January. Dr Johannes Hoffmann, leader of the Saar government, maintains that the Saar wishes to maintain its economic union with France and that it is 'indifferent to the evidence of reviving German nationalism'. His government's aim for the Saar is economic prosperity and political autonomy. The Saar Landtag on the same day adopts emergency legislation 'to protect the democratic order of the Saar' from the 'wave of propaganda' coming from Germany.

3 March. Robert Schuman, French foreign minister, and Dr Johannes Hoffmann, Saar prime minister, conclude a series of agreements which supersede all previous agreements and are to remain in force pending a German peace treaty. They are described by Chancellor Adenauer as calculated to endanger Franco-German relations and a violation of the Potsdam principles. (N.B. France was not represented at Potsdam.) Dr Schumacher claims that they create a 'new Alsace-Lorraine'.

2 May. The Saar legislative assembly accepts an invitation from the Council of Europe to become an associate member.

8 May. Chancellor Adenauer welcomes the Schuman Plan for the pooling of French and German coal and steel production, formally launched on the following day, as 'magnanimous'. Dr Schumacher for the SPD also welcomes it in principle as a 'healthy European development'.

9 May. Robert Schuman, French foreign minister, launches the Schuman Plan for a European Coal and Steel Community (ECSC). Belgium, France, Italy, Luxembourg, the Netherlands, and West Germany open negotiations with the goal of ensuring continual peace by a merging of their essential interests.

West Germany accepts an invitation from the Council of Europe parallel to that accepted by the Saar on 2 May.

1951

6 March. West Germany gains the conditional right to conduct its own foreign relations. (See section 1.2 for fuller particulars.)

18 April. West Germany and the five other states sign the Treaty of Paris to establish the ECSC. Its aim is to contribute towards economic expansion, growth of employment and a rising standard of living in member states, through common action in the coal and steel sector.

2 May. The Council of Europe accepts West Germany as a full member.

21 May. The Saar government dissolves the Democratic Party of the Saar as anti-constitutional and confiscates its property. Chancellor Adenauer expresses the hope that Saarlanders will 'fight such an undemocratic measure by all legitimate means of protest' and Dr Schumacher, leader of the SPD, describes the ban as 'proof of the existence of an oppressive police regime in the Saar'. His deputy is to describe the Saar regime as 'in reality a French protectorate' and the Saar as threatening to become a new Danzig (Gdansk).

3–8 December. Chancellor Adenauer makes the first official visit to Britain of a German head of government since Chancellor Brüning in 1931. It inspires some minor demonstrations. He describes his reception by the British press as 'cool but not unfriendly'.

1952

10 August. The ECSC comes formally into existence.

1954

23 October. Chancellor Adenauer and Pierre Mendès-France, the French prime minister, sign a statute proposing the Europeanisation of the Saar.

1955

29 March. Chancellor Adenauer and H. C. Hansen, the Danish prime minister, conclude an agreement in Bonn regulating the status of the Danish minority in Schleswig-Holstein and of the German minority in Denmark. It exempts the Danish minority from the results of the '5 per cent' clause in *Land* elections, and restores the pre-1954 level of grant to Danish language schools.

1–3 June. The Messina Conference of members of the European Coal and Steel Community agrees to work towards the creation of a European common market and the foundation of a European atomic energy agency.

15 June. A Franco-German Chamber of Commerce is established in Paris pursuant to the La Celle-St Cloud discussions between Chancellor Adenauer and Pierre Mendès-France, the French prime minister, in October 1954.

23 October. The Saar rejects by a majority of more than two to one in a plebiscite the statute proposing Europeanisation signed twelve months previously. The three new pro-German parties corresponding to the CDU, SPD and FDP and grouped as the *Heimatbund* had campaigned for reunion with Germany, as had the Saar Communist Party.

1956

27 October. Germany and France sign the treaty regulating the Saar question.

14 December. The Bundestag unanimously ratifies the Franco-German treaty on the Saar, a convention between West Germany, France and Luxemburg on the canalisation of the Mosel, a Franco-German convention on the utilisation of the Rhine between Basle and Strasbourg, and a treaty varying the membership of the ECSC assembly. All four complete the West German legislative process on 22 December.

1957

25 March. West Germany and the five other members of the ECSC sign the Treaty of Rome establishing the European Economic Community (EEC), popularly known as the Common Market, and the European Atomic Energy Community (EAEC or EURATOM) with effect from 1 January 1958. The aim is gradually to integrate the nations' economies and to move towards closer political unity.

7–9 May. Harold Macmillan becomes the first British prime minister to visit West Germany since its establishment as a state.

1958

29 May. A compromise agreement is reached after some six months of dispute on the West German contribution to the cost of maintaining British forces in West Germany from 1 April 1958 to 31 March 1961.

14 September. Chancellor Adenauer and General de Gaulle, again in power in France, meet for the first time at the General's home in Colombey-les-Deux-Eglises. Their joint declaration maintains that:

> We are convinced that close co-operation between [West Germany and France] is the basis of all constructive work in Europe . . . We believe that this co-operation must be organised and that it must include the other nations of Western Europe with which our countries have close ties . . . We hope that it can be extended to the greatest possible number of European states.

8–9 October. Harold Macmillan visits Bonn informally to maintain regular personal contacts with Chancellor Adenauer.

20–22 October. President Heuss makes the first state visit to Britain by a German head of state since the Kaiser in 1907. His reception is occasionally cool.

1959

8 April. Chancellor Adenauer reveals in a broadcast that he has protested to Harold Macmillan about the negative trend of British opinion towards Germany.

3 August. West Germany signs new agreements on the status of foreign NATO forces stationed there with America, Belgium, Britain, Canada, France, and the Netherlands. They replace the temporary conventions operative since 1955.

7 August. A West German–Norwegian agreement, signed in Oslo, provides for the payment of DM60 million to Norwegian victims of Nazi persecution.

24 August. A West German–Danish agreement, signed in Copenhagen, provides for the payment of DM16 million to Danish victims of Nazi persecution. The SPD abstains in the subsequent ratification vote in the Bundestag, claiming that the payments to both Denmark and Norway are insufficient.

1960

17 January. Some 30,000 people march in London in protest at recent anti-semitic incidents in West Germany. (See sections 1.2 and 2.8 for fuller particulars.) The protest document calls on West Germany to remove from office all former active Nazis still occupying important positions in the civil service, the law, education and the armed services.

18 March. A West German–Greek agreement, signed in Bonn, provides for the payment of DM115 million to Greek victims of Nazi persecution.

8 April. West Germany and the Netherlands sign a treaty after three years of negotiation, including a frontier settlement which broadly restores the border of 1939 with some 20 minor amendments, and returns three villages to German administration. It also provides for the payment of DM125 million to Dutch victims of Nazi persecution.

15 July. A West German–French agreement, signed in Bonn, provides for the payment of DM400 million to French victims of Nazi persecution.

26 August. West Germany initials an agreement with Belgium to pay DM80 million to Belgian victims of Nazi persecution.

14 December. West Germany participates in the establishment of the Organisation for Economic Co-operation and Development (OECD).

1961

20–22 June. President Lübke of West Germany makes the first state visit to France by a German head of state since German unification in 1871. Although only the French Communists are openly hostile, one right-wing national newspaper comments that it could not be expected that 'we should welcome [the visit] with the same feelings as [we welcome] that of others who have always been our friends'. (Hitler had paid a triumphal visit to Paris after the fall of France in 1940.)

19 July. The British Labour Party abstains in the House of Commons' vote permitting the West German army to exercise in Wales. The beginning of the exercises prompts a protest march on 9 September.

1962

2–8 July. Chancellor Adenauer pays a state visit to France. His reception becomes increasingly cordial as the visit progresses.

8 July. Chancellor Adenauer and President de Gaulle take the salute at the first joint parade ever held by the French and German armies, at Mourmelon in Champagne, site of some of the fiercest Franco-German fighting in the First World War. They then attend a High Mass in Rheims Cathedral dedicated to the theme of Christian reconciliation. President de Gaulle describes the visit as a 'resounding success', the Chancellor returns to Germany 'deeply happy'.

4–9 September. President de Gaulle pays a triumphal return state visit to West Germany. He is enthusiastically received by crowds, whom he addresses in German, in a number of cities and is considered to have received the greatest welcome ever given in Germany to a visiting statesman.

19 October. The WEU increases the limit under the Brussels Treaty of 350 tons for submarines built by West Germany to 450 tons so that West Germany may 'fulfil NATO requirements'.

1963

22 January. Chancellor Adenauer and President de Gaulle sign a Franco-German Treaty of Co-operation in Paris. It provides for the co-ordination of their policies in the fields of foreign affairs, defence, information and cultural matters. The treaty envisages that the heads of state and government will meet for consultation whenever necessary and in principle at least twice every year.

16 May. The Bundestag and the Bundesrat ratify the Franco-German Treaty of Co-operation, but with a preamble to the ratification bill to the effect that the treaty will be so implemented as to strengthen the partnership between Europe and the United States, realisation of the German right to self-determination and reunification, common defence within NATO, European unification with the integration of further countries including Great Britain, and the reduction of trade barriers generally within the framework of GATT.

4–5 July. The first meeting of French and German cabinet ministers is held in Bonn pursuant to the terms of the Franco-German Treaty of Co-operation.

5 July. The ministers agree to establish a Franco-German Youth Office with its headquarters in Bonn. The aim is to promote exchanges of 500,000 young people annually.

1964

26 May. President Lübke of Germany, President de Gaulle of France and the Grand Duchess Charlotte of Luxembourg inaugurate the 168-mile canalisation of the River Mosel(le) between Thionville, France, and Koblenz, Germany, agreed in 1956.

9 June. West Germany agrees after seven years of negotiation to provide DM11.2 million for distribution to British victims of Nazi persecution.

1965

18–28 May. Queen Elizabeth II makes the first state visit to Germany by a British monarch since 1913. Her reception is particularly warm in Bavaria.

8 July. West Germany and France agree to establish a joint very high flux nuclear research reactor at Grenoble.

1967

26 September. West Germany signs a memorandum of understanding with Britain and France on the first phase of a joint 'airbus' project.

1968

17 July. West Germany signs a memorandum of understanding with Britain, Italy and the Netherlands on the first phase of a joint advanced military aircraft project. It is envisaged that the new aircraft will replace the American F-104 *Starfighter*, in service with all the air services but the British.

1977

18 October. Chancellor Schmidt and James Callaghan, the British prime minister, sign an agreement in Bonn to terminate in 1980 West German payments to offset British foreign exchange costs from the stationing of troops in West Germany.

1979

5 July. The approved West German budget provides for a first tranche of DM50 million in indemnity payments to inhabitants of Alsace-Lorraine conscripted into the German Army following the region's incorporation into Germany in 1940.

1980

21 July. The Council of the Western European Union, of which West Germany is a member, unanimously abolishes all restrictions on the size of West German warships under the protocol to the Paris Agreements of 1954. The protocol restrictions on the manufacture of nuclear, biological or chemical weapons, long-range and guided missiles, strategic bombers and nuclear powered warships remain.

1982

15 April. Hans-Dietrich Genscher, the West German foreign minister, and Dr Arthur Burns, the American ambassador, sign a Wartime Host Nations Agreement. Under its terms, West Germany will provide greater military and civilian support for the six additional American divisions to be despatched in an emergency. The estimated cost of $570 million is to be borne equally.

1984

6 June. Germany is not invited to the commemorations of the Normandy D-Day landings attended by western heads of state and government.

22 September. The 'hereditary enmity' between Germany and France is again ceremonially declared over by the 'Verdun handshake'. Chancellor Kohl and President Mitterand hold hands before the memorial to the hundreds of thousands of men who died in the fruitless battle for Verdun in the First World War.

1987

12–13 November. Chancellor Kohl and President Mitterand meet in Karlsruhe for the 50th in the regular series of Franco-West German consultative meetings. They agree in principle to establish the joint troop brigade originally suggested by Chancellor Kohl in June 1987. The proposed brigade is likely to comprise 3,000–4,000 troops, and be stationed at Böblingen near Stuttgart. They also agree to set up joint councils on economic and financial issues, education and telecommunications.

The French and West German defence ministers on the same occasion sign a DM5 billion agreement on the joint development of an anti-tank helicopter.

1989

6 December. President Mitterand maintains in Kiev that West Germany should make its priority strengthening the EC, not German unification.

3.3 East Germany and the east

1949

7 October. East Germany gains the power to conduct its own foreign relations on its proclamation as a state. (See sections 1.2 and 2.3 for fuller particulars.) The exchange of diplomatic missions with the Soviet Union is followed by diplomatic recognition from Bulgaria, Czechoslovakia, Hungary, Poland and Romania.

25 October. The new People's Republic of China recognises East Germany.

1950

23 June. Walter Ulbricht, as deputy prime minister, signs cultural, scientific and technical, and financial agreements in Prague with Antonin Zapotocky, the Czechoslovak prime minister. They also declare that their countries have no territorial claims on each other and that the resettlement of Germans from Czechoslovakia has been settled in an unalterable, just and permanent manner.

24 June. Ulbricht signs parallel agreements in Budapest with István Dobi, the Hungarian prime minister. They also make a formal declaration of friendship, in which they assure each other of their permanent loyalty to the great Soviet Union, to which they both owe their liberation.

6 July. East Germany and Poland sign a treaty in Görlitz recognising the Oder-Neisse line as their joint frontier.

23 September. Ulbricht signs parallel agreements in Bucharest with Dr Petru Groza, the Romanian prime minister.

26 September. Ulbricht signs parallel agreements in Sofia with Vulko Chervenkov, the Bulgarian prime minister.

1 October. East Germany becomes a member of the Council of Mutual Economic Assistance (COMECON). The Council had been created in January 1949 by Albania, Bulgaria, Czechoslovakia, Hungary, Poland, Romania and the Soviet Union.

1953

20–22 August. East German–Soviet talks at the highest level result in agreement on a number of measures to aid the development of the East German economy and to improve the standard of living, following the demonstrations of June 1953. They include the termination of reparations payments and the return of all Soviet enterprises there (see sections 1.2

and 7.3 for fuller particulars), together with a reduction in the costs of the Soviet occupation forces to not more than 5 per cent of the East German budget and the writing off of any arrears, as well as the payment of postwar state debts. East Germany is to receive from the Soviet Union during the year goods valued at US$147.5 million (590 million roubles) and two-year credits of 485 million roubles at 2 per cent per annum from 1955. War criminals are to be released except for the worst offenders.

1955

11–13 May. East Germany signs 20-year treaties of friendship, co-operation and mutual assistance with Albania, Bulgaria, Czechoslovakia, Hungary, Poland, Romania and the Soviet Union, in Warsaw. A unified military command is created for all of the signatories bar East Germany whose participation is to be examined later. It follows on 27–28 January 1956.

14 May. East Germany signs the Warsaw Treaty of Friendship, Co-operation and Mutual Assistance (the Warsaw Pact) with the other countries of the Soviet bloc.

6 July. East Germany and Poland confirm on the fifth anniversary of the Görlitz agreement that the Oder-Neisse line has been fixed as their joint frontier 'definitely and irrevocably'.

8 November. East Germany and Poland reach an agreement whereby the eastern part of the city of Görlitz (Zgorzelec) on the Polish bank of the Neisse is returned to East Germany on the basis that it will be resettled by Germans from elsewhere in Poland, and a joint commission is to plan for the administration of the port of Szczecin (Stettin), now Polish but on the German bank of the Oder. East Germany thereby gains a deep-water harbour for its new merchant marine, pending the later development of Rostock. Agreement is also reached on the establishment of five Polish consulates in East Germany and two East German ones in Poland.

25 December. Otto Grotewohl and Chou En-lai (Zhou-Enlai) sign an East German–Chinese friendship pact.

1957

22 August. East Germany signs a treaty of friendship with Mongolia.

15 October. East Germany and Yugoslavia agree to establish diplomatic relations. Pursuant to the Hallstein Doctrine, West Germany breaks off relations with Yugoslavia on 19 October. (See 'Hallstein Doctrine' in *Glossary* for fuller particulars.)

1958

17 November. East Germany concludes trade and cultural agreements with Guinea. They are the first international agreements to be made by the newly independent African state.

1959

1 April. East Germany signs a cultural and scientific agreement with Iraq.

25 September. The government of the United Arab Republic (Egypt) emphasises that the establishment of an East German consulate-general in Cairo does not imply recognition of the East German regime.

1960

12 February. East Germany approves the creation of the 'Intervision' television network linking it with Czechoslovakia, Hungary and Poland.

21 July. East Germany announces that it will build fifteen complete factories for Cuba, which will allegedly eliminate Cuban dependence on western imports in several significant fields. It will also train Cuban technicians.

1961

22 April. East Germany signs a trade agreement with Ceylon (Sri Lanka) in Colombo.

19 December. East Germany announces that it has decided to recall its ambassador from Tirana, as Albania is making normal diplomatic activity impossible.

1962

16 June. East Germany opens a consulate-general in Baghdad, Iraq.

2 July. Laos announces that it intends to recognise East Germany.

7 July. East Germany opens a consulate-general in Phnom Penh. The Cambodian (Kampuchean) government contends that it does not imply recognition of East Germany under international law, just as the opening of consular relations by the UAR (Egypt and Syria) and Burma had not implied such recognition.

1963

12 January. East Germany and Cuba agree to open full diplomatic relations and to upgrade their existing missions to full embassy status. Pursuant to the Hallstein Doctrine, West Germany breaks off diplomatic relations with Cuba.

1964

14 February. East Germany and Ceylon agree to convert the East German trade mission in Colombo into a consulate-general and to establish a Ceylonese consulate-general in East Berlin.

21 February. West Germany announces that its programme of development aid for Ceylon is discontinued in consequence. West German capital loans to Ceylon in the previous ten years had totalled some DM40 million.

17 May. East Germany signs a Treaty of Friendship, Mutual Assistance and increased Co-operation with the new United Republic of Tanzania. An accompanying agreement provides for development credits and aid in housing, public health and education. (Tanzania was created by an Act of Union between Tanganyika and Zanzibar signed by Zanzibar on 23 April 1964.)

12 June. East Germany and the Soviet Union sign a 20-year Treaty of Friendship, Co-operation and Mutual Assistance in Moscow. An accompanying statement declares that the two countries, with the other members of the Warsaw Pact, will ensure their own security if West Germany acquires nuclear weapons within the framework of NATO.

1965

27 January. It is announced in East Berlin that Ulbricht is to make an official visit to Egypt at the end of February at the invitation of President Nasser. Nasser maintains that the secret West German arms supplies to Israel are a source of concern to the whole Arab world.

19 February. East Germany is permitted to open a consulate-general in Tanzania, although that country does not extend full diplomatic recognition. West Germany expresses regret and announces that it will terminate all military aid.

24 February–2 March. Ulbricht pays a state visit to Egypt. Economic and industrial aid agreements are signed, but he does not secure recognition for East Germany. The West German government spokesman describes his reception as 'a provocation to all Germans'.

8 June. President Tito of Yugoslavia pays his first official visit to East Germany. He maintains that German unification can only be achieved by the establishment of contacts between the two parts of Germany. West Germany maintains that Yugoslavia has forfeited any claim to be regarded as uncommitted.

30 December. East Germany signs an economic aid agreement with North Vietnam, which is suffering from American bombing.

1966

24 March. The new government of Ghana breaks off relations with East Germany and closes the East German trade mission. It does not take as radical a step with any other Communist country.

1967

15 March. Walter Ulbricht signs a 20-year Treaty of Friendship, Co-operation and Mutual Assistance with Poland in Warsaw.

17 March. Ulbricht signs a parallel Treaty with Czechoslovakia in Prague. It declares in addition that the 1938 Munich Agreement was invalid from the very beginning.

17–18 May. Ulbricht signs a parallel Treaty with Hungary in Budapest.

7 September. Ulbricht signs a parallel Treaty with Todor Zhivkov of Bulgaria in Sofia.

1968

8 May. East Germany, as a member of the 'Group of Five', attends discussions in Moscow with Bulgaria, Hungary, Poland and the Soviet Union on Dubček's liberalisation in Czechoslovakia, 'the Prague Spring'.

14–15 July. The East German leadership (Walter Ulbricht, Willi Stoph, and Hermann Axen) meets the other members of the 'Group of Five' in Warsaw to prepare a joint letter to the Czechoslovak Communist Party.

17 July. East Germany is a co-signatory of the letter, which criticises the liberal reforms.

3 August. East Germany participates in the Bratislava meeting with the Czechoslovaks. Ulbricht, accompanied by Stoph, Axen, Erich Honecker and Günter Mittag, is believed to have taken a 'hard' line both here and earlier in Warsaw.

12 August. Ulbricht follows up the letter by meeting Dubček in Karlovy Vary. He receives a cool reception from the Czech crowds.

20 August. East Germany participates in the invasion of Czechoslovakia by the 'Group of Five'.

12 September. Willi Stoph signs a 20-year Treaty of Friendship, Co-operation and Mutual Assistance with Marshal Zebendal of Mongolia in Ulan Bator. It supersedes the Treaty concluded in 1957.

1969

30 April. Iraq is the first Arab country to decide to give full diplomatic recognition to East Germany. (An Iraqi consulate-general had been maintained in East Berlin since 1965.) West Germany describes the Iraqi decision as 'an unfriendly act' on 1 May.

8 May. East Germany and Cambodia (Kampuchea) establish full diplomatic relations at ambassadorial level. West Germany describes the action as 'an unfriendly act' and Cambodia formally breaks off diplomatic relations with West Germany on 11 June.

27 May. The new Sudanese government announces that it will recognise East Germany and establish diplomatic relations as soon as possible, because of East Germany's positive approach to the Arabs. West Germany describes the decision as 'an unfriendly act'.

4 June. Syria announces that it also has decided to recognise East Germany, and to open full diplomatic relations. West Germany again describes the decision as 'an unfriendly act' on 15 June and adds that it will not support any new projects for economic development in Syria, including projects like the Euphrates dam which are subject to multilateral agreements.

9 July. Egypt also decides to open full diplomatic relations. A number of smaller third world nations are to follow suit in the next twelve months.
9 September. East Germany and Cambodia conclude an economic and technical co-operation agreement.

1970
20 May. East Germany and Algeria agree to establish diplomatic relations. West Germany 'regrets' the Algerian decision.
22 June. Ceylon announces that it has extended full diplomatic recognition to East Germany with effect from 16 June.
3 August. India and East Germany agree to establish diplomatic relations at consular level.

1972
13–21 June. Fidel Castro, the Cuban leader, visits East Germany.

1975
7 October. Erich Honecker signs a 25-year Treaty of Friendship, Co-operation and Mutual Assistance with Leonid Brezhnev of the Soviet Union in Moscow.

1977
7 December. Egypt orders the closure of the East German cultural centre in Cairo and its consulate in Alexandria. It alleges that the cultural centres of the Soviet Bloc had been disseminating Marxist propaganda. Relations had deteriorated with the Soviet condemnation of President Sadat's visit to Israel the preceding month.

1978
26 August. Lt-Col. Sigmund Jähn becomes the first East German cosmonaut by participating in the Soviet Soyuz 31 space mission.

1979
8–12 January. Erich Honecker pays a state visit to India. Its fruits include a six-year economic co-operation agreement.
15 February. Erich Honecker commences a tour of Libya, Angola, Zambia and Mozambique accompanied by Willi Stoph, prime minister, and Oskar Fischer, foreign minister.
19 February. Erich Honecker signs a 20-year Treaty of Friendship and Co-operation with President Agostinho Neto of Angola. It is East Germany's first such treaty with an African country.
24 February. Erich Honecker signs a similar treaty with President Machel of Mozambique. It envisages 'co-operation in the military sector through bilateral agreements'.

1980

1 June. East Germany and Cuba sign a 25-year Treaty of Friendship and Co-operation at the end of an official visit there by Erich Honecker. It makes no reference to military co-operation.

8 October. Erich Honecker claims in an East German television interview that Poland 'belongs inseparably to the world of socialism, and no one can turn back the wheel of history. . . . Together with our friends in the socialist camp, we will see to that'.

3 December. East Germany and Czechoslovakia sign a 'joint border treaty' which promotes economic co-operation in the context of economic and political uncertainty in Poland.

1981

9–13 September. Erich Honecker visits Mexico and signs economic, scientific and technical co-operation agreements. He briefly breaks his return journey to visit Cuba.

1982

19–23 May. East Germany and President Karmal of Afghanistan sign a 20-year Treaty of Friendship and Co-operation in East Berlin.

22 September. East Germany and Laos sign a 25-year Treaty of Friendship and Co-operation. It envisages greater East German help in the mechanisation of Laotian agriculture.

1984

11–13 September. Erich Honecker attends the tenth anniversary celebrations of the Ethiopian revolution in Addis Ababa.

22–23 August. Erich Honecker is the only party leader from eastern Europe to attend the 40th anniversary celebrations of the Romanian Revolution in Bucharest.

3.4 Unified Germany and the world

1990

9 October. Germany and the Soviet Union sign a treaty on Soviet troop withdrawals from Germany.

9 November. Chancellor Kohl and President Gorbachev sign a treaty of good neighbourliness between Germany and the Soviet Union. They also sign a treaty on economic co-operation.

14 November. Hans-Dietrich Genscher and Krzystof Skubiszewski, German and Polish foreign ministers, sign a treaty confirming the Oder-Neisse line as their joint border.

1991

23 December. Germany, having intimated that it does not feel bound by an EU compromise plan, recognises Slovenia and Croatia. The rest of the EU reluctantly follow suit on 15 January 1992.

1992

27 February. Chancellor Kohl and President Havel sign a treaty of good neighbourliness and co-operation between Germany and Czechoslovakia in Prague.

29 March. The declaration by Hans-Dietrich Genscher, German foreign minister, on 26 March, that 'the persecution of the Turkish civilian population by military units was unacceptable' provokes President Özal of Turkey to maintain that Germany since 1990 had tried 'to intervene everywhere . . . to prove that it was a major power' and that 'in the past Hitler's Germany had tried to do the same thing, although in other ways'.

22 May. Germany and France agree to create a joint army corps of at least 35,000 soldiers to be operational by October 1995. The European Corps is to operate under the WEU for the defence of western Europe and for humanitarian and peacekeeping operations, and is envisaged as the core of a European army.

15 July. A destroyer and three reconnaissance aircraft join the UN force monitoring the sanctions imposed on Serbia and Montenegro. Volker Rühe, defence minister, maintains that although it is not a full military deployment, the move represents 'more than a gesture, more than symbol – it is a serious step'.

1993

11 January. Boutros Boutros-Ghali, UN secretary-general, urges Germany, as the UN's third largest financial contributor, to contribute also 'real participation on the ground'.

13 April. Volker Rühe and Marshal Pavel Grachev sign a German–Russian defence co-operation agreement.

21 April. The government decides to send 1,600 troops to Somalia to help the UN relief effort there.

1994

8 June. The government bans all exports of anti-personnel land mines for an initial period of three years.

11–12 July. President Clinton of America, on a state visit to Germany, speaks of the 'truly unique relationship' between Germany and America and maintains that it reflects the fact that 'so many of our challenges are just to Germany's east'.

22 July. The Bundestag retrospectively approves German participation in military operations in the former Yugoslavia. (See section 2.8 for fuller particulars.)

20 December. The German government agrees in principle to a NATO request for military participation, if UN peacekeeping forces leave Bosnia.

1995

30 June. The Bundestag approves the deployment of aircraft and more than 1,000 support troops as part of the rapid reaction force in Bosnia.

6 December. The Bundestag approves the despatch of 4,000 troops to Bosnia as part of the Implementation Force under the Dayton peace accord.

1996

4 December. The German government authorises, subject to Bundestag approval, the stationing of 3,000 troops in Bosnia. It is the first deployment of federal German active combat troops since 1945.

1997

21 January. Germany and the Czech Republic sign a declaration of reconciliation covering the German annexations under the Munich Agreement and the Czechoslovak postwar expulsion of 3 million Germans.

7 April. Germany's advocacy of 'critical dialogue' with Iran's religious government is put into question by a Berlin court's verdict that it was deeply implicated in the murder of Iranian Kurdish dissident leaders in Berlin in 1992. (German–Iranian trade is rooted in the friendship treaty between Persia and Prussia of 1857.)

SECTION FOUR

Germany and the EU

4.1 Commentary

The evolution of the EU into a supranational body with Germany as its most influential single arbiter can appear from the perspective of 1998 as an inevitable, indeed irresistible, phenomenon. Historians have suggested on a number of occasions that Germany would have been the arbiter of Europe by 1919–20 if only the First World War had been confined to its direct Balkan origins. Many in the 1930s, particularly in Britain, were as much concerned at Germany's economic expansion into eastern Europe as they were at its growing military power.

The evolution of the EU which we tend to take for granted was nevertheless rooted in developments between 1945 and 1957 which were far from inevitable at the time. De Gaulle's initial concept was not of a Franco-German partnership, in the sense familiar from more recent history, but rather a co-operation between Belgians, French, Dutch and Rhinelanders whose geographical proximity made co-operation essential. In de Gaulle's view, outlined in a press conference in 1945, Western Europe was bounded to the east by the Rhine basin, and he appeared readier to envisage cultural and economic co-operation by that core with Britain, Italy, Spain and Portugal than with the much larger proportion of Germany east of the Rhineland. This was a reinterpretation of well-established French ambitions and perspectives. Louis XIV had sought to extend the French national territory to its 'natural frontiers' on the Rhine, and France had occupied the Rhineland after the First World War. De Gaulle was now maintaining that the border region south from Cologne to the Swiss border was essential to French security. The border region to the north was similarly essential to the security of Belgium, the Netherlands and Britain, and should be permanently detached from Germany. This again had a degree of historical resonance. The British had been desperately anxious to keep the Belgian ports out of German control during the First World War. In earlier centuries they had been equally anxious to keep them out of the hands of the French.

The French did, however, have an additional argument in 1945. They could point out that the Potsdam Conference had amputated Germany in the east but not in the west. As Georges Bidault, the French foreign minister, bluntly said on 4 November,

> No French government could survive which accepted that a German government set up in Berlin or anywhere else should give

orders in territory a few miles from the French frontiers, and that French orders would no longer be obeyed there, while on the eastern side of Germany the German writ no longer ran in towns like Königsberg (Kaliningrad). . . .
[*Source*: Keesing's Contemporary Archives, p. 7593]

Germany west of the Rhine was not, however, France's sole or perhaps even greatest concern. It was the Ruhr, the historic focus of German heavy industry, which was seen as the key to any future German military threat. De Gaulle's answer was internationalisation, but internationalisation with a positive rather than a negative purpose – 'If the nations whose welfare depends on the Ruhr had the boldness to impose an international regime on that territory, they would have a common stake, the existence of which would lead the whole of Europe to co-operation. . . .' The internationalisation proposed would have included the Soviet Union as a partner and was in many respects closer to the concept of a Europe running from the Atlantic to the Urals promulgated by de Gaulle after 1958 than to the western European integration to be promoted by the Treaty of Rome in 1957. Nevertheless the vision of co-operation is there; a remarkable advance on the 'beggar my neighbour' policies pursued by the European powers up to 1939.

That was no consolation to the Germans. Having lost East Prussia, most of Pomerania and Silesia to the east, they were now faced with the loss of at least the Saar, the Rhineland and the Ruhr to the west. In the absence of a German government, the four main parties appealed to the Allied Control Council in April 1946 not to permit the separation of the Rhineland and the Ruhr, arguing that Germany could not survive without those areas' resources.

These initial pressures for co-operation on the basis of dismemberment came to nought basically because the economic situation in the western zones grew so adverse that interzonal fusion to facilitate recovery was agreed to be vital by both the Americans and the British. The French followed suit because of their own economic weakness and because of growing unease over the intentions of the Soviet Union. The nearest they came to fruition was in the Saar, where a despairing and hungry population accepted economic union with France in 1947. The decision led to considerable Franco-German acrimony in the following years prior to the Saar's final reunification with Germany at the end of 1956. It seems most unlikely in retrospect, even if internationalisation of the Rhineland and the Ruhr had been practicable, that they would have promoted long-term peace. They flew too obviously in the face of even the most liberal national sentiment. The Six-Power agreement on the statute of an International Authority for the Ruhr reached in December

1948 had succeeded in uniting the whole spectrum of West German politics in total opposition.

The French vision was, however, to bear more positive fruit. Dr Adenauer, German Chancellor since 1949 and himself a Rhinelander, was attuned to the Gaullist sense of Europe, sharing its markedly Roman Catholic cultural roots. Above all he shared the desire to orientate Germany towards the west, and accepted that a policy of integration was the only basis on which Germany could regain the trust of its western neighbours. He was fortunate in that Robert Schuman, the French foreign minister, was able to reinterpret the concept of internationalisation of key German resources at Germany's expense into the much more lasting concept of pooling the mineral resources of the Rhine corridor to mutual benefit, but Schuman was equally fortunate in dealing with a Chancellor whose vision was compatible with his own. It was a vision over which many Germans had considerable reservations. Both the left and the far right feared that an orientation towards the west would damage the prospects for German unification. Many on the right who favoured the orientation towards the west still feared that rapprochement with France would inhibit relations with America, now seen almost universally as the key protecting power. The left, including the SPD leader, Kurt Schumacher, wanted any economic links with France to be paralleled by comparable links with Britain. The SPD was to remain a determined advocate of British membership of the later European Economic Community until Britain secured entry in 1973.

Many of these fears were to be proved by events to have had considerable justification. Britain was still hesitant about the process of integration 25 years after joining the EEC and was simply not available as a complementary partner to France. Whether or not a policy of German neutrality would have led to unification cannot be known, but growing economic integration with the west was paralleled by a degree of military integration which spelled the end of any chance of unification before the collapse of Soviet will in 1989–90. The surprise is that West Germany was able to grow steadily closer to France and the other members of the EEC while developing ever warmer relations with America, even after the French withdrawal from NATO's command structure, and at the same time to cultivate relations with the Soviet Union.

West Germany's signature of the Treaty of Rome in 1957 started it on the path to European integration which has since led to the creation of the single market and the proposed creation of a single currency under economic and monetary union (EMU) with effect from 1999. German participation in the Community was enthusiastic from the very beginning for a number of reasons, some of which are no less important for being conjectural. The former West Germany, however, seemed to lack a sense of completeness which perhaps acquired a measure of satisfaction from integration in a wider whole. It has also increasingly tended to see the emerging European Union as a development of its own federal structure writ large. It may also be worth remembering that Germany was only united in 1871 and that its greatest poet, Goethe, was treating the concept of Germany as a political, as distinct from a cultural, entity as ridiculous only some 50 years before that. Not least, German history in the twentieth century has made the concept of nationalism highly suspect. Few Germans would agree with Baroness Thatcher that the nation state has been the guarantor of personal liberty. Above all, incorporation in a wider whole has been seen as reassuring Germany's neighbours that she can be trusted as a partner and that anxieties as to her latent aggressiveness, anxieties which Chancellor Kohl himself occasionally seems to share, are quite misplaced. Integration has been the path back to acceptance by the wider world.

European integration has also been profitable. The original tacit bargain between Germany and France, whereby the industrial interests of the former were traded for the agricultural interests of the latter, has been subsumed in a Europe-wide elimination of trading barriers. In 1995 Germany exported to its five original partners in the European Economic Community (France, Italy and the Benelux) goods valued at DM239.973 billion, compared with total exports of DM727.732 billion. Exports to Britain alone in the same year at DM58.136 billion were higher than to the United States at DM54.603 billion. Such totals have to be set against Germany's net contribution to the EU of DM25.5 billion in 1995, some 50 per cent of all national net contributions.

Such a scale of contribution reinforces the powerful political influence Germany has always enjoyed through the EU. Chancellor Schmidt and President Valéry Giscard d'Estaing are normally seen as the architects of the European Monetary System. The first, and one of the most successful, presidents of the European Commission was Dr Walter Hallstein, who effectively raised the profile of the position to head of government level, much to the fury of General de Gaulle. Although Hallstein's successors have been more circumspect, the more effective among them have built upon the foundations he laid. Germany has provided its quota of commissioners, but the most significant may be Martin Bangemann, a former chair of the FDP and candidate for the Commission presidency, who has been a commissioner since 1989 and currently holds the key portfolio of industry, information technology and telecommunications.

The key policy issues for Germany in more recent years have been the expansion of the EU to the east and economic and monetary union, with the latter being identified to a remarkable degree with Chancellor Kohl personally.

Expansion to the east confronts Germany with both opportunities and problems. On the credit side it would provide a framework for Germany to renew its historic links with eastern Europe without appearing economically or politically threatening. This is easier on the economic than the political front. The Czech Republic and Poland are already the recipients of major German investment and are anxious to attract more, despite the risk that Germany will see them primarily as a source of cheap labour and a base for essentially secondary functions. At the political level relations remain sensitive, particularly with the Czech Republic. If the press reports of December 1996, that Theo Waigel, the German finance minister, was trying to link Czech admission to the EU with concessions to Germany over the Sudeten issue, were correct, it is an initiative which could easily misfire. On the negative side, Germany is highly nervous of the impact on eastern Germany in particular of an ingress of Polish workers. The earlier rioting against asylum applicants and guest workers could be only a foretaste of something much more serious. Germany's comparatively inefficient agricultural sector is equally nervous of the impact of imports of cheap Polish foodstuffs.

The more immediate issue, however, is economic and monetary union, with Chancellor Kohl and President Chirac of France reaffirming in April 1997 their 'entire determination' to introduce the European single currency on schedule on 1 January 1999. The single currency project is one with which Chancellor Kohl has been associated for many years, but it was conceived in the context of West German conditions prior to unification. The cost of unification, however, has been such as to place a heavy burden even on an economy as powerful as Germany's and the government has sought to compensate by reducing other public expenditure, much of it of a social nature, and by strictly controlling inflationary pressures. These challenges have been aggravated by obligations imposed under the Maastricht Treaty, laying down the conditions under which economic and monetary union is to be achieved. The treaty specifically restricts government deficits to 3 per cent of GNP and determinedly pursues anti-inflationary objectives. The total effect has been deflationary and the high existing levels of unemployment – particularly in East Germany – resulting from restructuring have been worsened across the country by the constraints of meeting the Maastricht Treaty criteria for admission to the single currency. This has, not surprisingly, led to calls by the trade unions and other interests for the planned entry into the single currency to be postponed.

Such calls have been resisted for several reasons. One is the likely damage to the Chancellor's personal prestige. Another is that for historical reasons Germans probably fear inflation even more than they fear unemployment. They are apprehensive that the new single currency, the euro, will be less trustworthy than the Deutsche Mark, and many instinctively prefer the concept of an equally 'hard' euro to a 'soft' euro, comparable to the French franc or the Italian lira. Public opinion by the end of December 1997 appeared from surveys to be increasingly ready to accept the new euro, and the SPD, which had earlier opposed its scheduled introduction, seemed far less likely to make it a party political issue in the 1998 elections. Germany nevertheless thought it prudent in the final negotiations for the 1997 Amsterdam Treaty, which updated Maastricht, to drop its earlier objections to an 'employment chapter' in return for French agreement to a monetary stability pact setting stern budgetary rules for the management of monetary union.

4.2 European Parliament

European Parliament elections

* 1st direct elections 10 June 1979
(Turn-out 65.7%)

	%	Seats
CDU	39.1	32
CSU	10.2	8
SPD	40.8	34
FDP	6.0	4
Greens	3.2	—

* West Germany, excluding West Berlin, only

* 2nd elections 17 June 1984
(Turn-out 56.8%)

	%	Seats
CDU	37.5	32
CSU	8.5	7
SPD	37.4	32
FDP	4.8	—
Greens	8.2	7

* West Germany, excluding West Berlin, only

* 3rd elections 18 June 1989
(Turn-out 62.3%)

	%	Seats
CDU	29.5	24
CSU	8.2	7
SPD	37.3	30
FDP	5.6	4
Greens	8.4	7
Die Republikaner	7.1	6

* West Germany, excluding West Berlin, only

4th elections 12 June 1994
(Turn-out 60.0%)

	%	Seats
CDU	32.0	39
CSU	6.8	8
SPD	32.2	40
FDP	4.1	—
Greens	10.1	12

German membership of the political groups in the European Parliament

	1979	1984	1989	1994
Socialist Group	35	33	31	40
	(122)	(132)	(180)	(193)
European People's Party Group	42	41	32	47
(CDU Group)	(116)	(110)	(121)	(157)
Liberal and Democratic Group	4	—	4	—
	(40)	(31)	(49)	(43)
Greens	—	7	8	12
	(11)	(19)	(30)	(23)
European Right Group	—	—	6	—
	(—)	(—)	(17)	(—)

Total group size in each Parliament in brackets. Indirectly elected West Berlin members included 1979–89.

SECTION FIVE

Berlin

5.1 Introduction

The history of Berlin since 1945 has been a saga of extremes. From a starting point of devastation probably greater than that of any other German conurbation, and division into four sectors, it became by 1948 the focus of distrust and hostility between the Soviet Union and the western Allies. The inevitable corollary was that it spearheaded growing co-operation between the two sides with 'their' Germans.

As time advanced, Berlin was rebuilt as essentially two separate cities, with West Berlin focused on the Kurfürstendamm and East Berlin on the Alexanderplatz. Areas too close to the dividing line to be attractive for development, particularly in the centre, were widely abandoned, most strikingly perhaps at the Potsdamer Platz, which had been the 'Piccadilly Circus' of prewar Berlin. The division became even starker with the erection of the Wall in 1961.

Desperately serious as the division was for Berliners and other Germans, it also reflected an element of shadow-boxing between the Allies themselves. Both sides were seeking to win a war of nerves, rather than risk their military strength. Even at the height of the Berlin blockade, the Soviet Union refrained from cutting the sewerage system, which might have made West Berlin uninhabitable. Through every subsequent crisis, both sides insisted upon and were awarded the formal rights which had been agreed in 1945. The daily Four-Power military tours of the city continued and the Soviet guard on duty at the Soviet war memorial in West Berlin was left unmolested. Spandau prison was manned on a Four-Power rota to guard the diminishing number of convicted war criminals, and for 21 years to guard just one man, Rudolf Hess.

Away from these crises and posturings, East and West Berlin slowly returned to a semblance of normality. East Berlin had the easier task in that it could become East Germany's leading industrial city and the East German capital. West Berlin, isolated from the west, was increasingly dependent on West German subsidies, but still saw the departure of many of its traditional strengths such as fashion and film making. Nevertheless, it emerged as a city of congresses and fairs. Both halves of the city were seen as the show windows of their respective systems and were promoted somewhat ruthlessly accordingly.

Unification in 1990 saw the final irony of Germany being deeply uncertain as to whether it actually wanted Berlin as its working capital again, and a tug of wills with Bonn as to the future seat of government. The victory which Berlin ultimately secured was far from a foregone conclusion.

5.2 Chronology

1945

2 May. The Battle of Berlin ends with the surrender of the Berlin garrison to Soviet forces. The war had caused the total destruction of more than 600,000 dwellings and the 1939 population of 4.3 million had fallen to 2.8 million.

8 May. The Allies agree that Berlin shall be administered jointly and as a unit and that it shall accordingly be divided into four sectors, each with its own commandant. Air Marshal Tedder, signatory of the surrender in Berlin on behalf of the Allied Expeditionary Force declares:

> Berlin as a city has been utterly destroyed. The ruins that were Berlin should be preserved as a modern Babylon or Carthage – a monument to Prussian militarism and the evil Nazi regime. The city is completely dead. One drives for miles through desolate and smoking ruins and finds nothing habitable. It can never be reconstructed.
>
> [*Source*: Keesing's Contemporary Archives, p. 7180]

19 May. The commandant of Greater Berlin, Col.-General Nikolai Berzarin, appoints a governing council of eighteen members headed by a former city engineer without party affiliations, Dr Arthur Werner, as chief mayor. The council comprises Communists (about half of the total), Social Democrats and middle-class opponents of Hitler. A famous surgeon, Professor Ferdinand Sauerbruch, is responsible for public health and the architect, Professor Hans Scharoun, for housing and rebuilding. Dr Andreas Hermes, a former minister in the Weimar Republic, is in charge of organising food supplies.

21 May. First issue of *Berliner Zeitung*, the first postwar German-language Berlin newspaper.

end May. Anastas Mikoyan, Soviet deputy prime minister, is sent to assess the city's needs, following which Soviet foodstocks are made available.

1 June. The new Berlin police are established under Paul Markgraf, an army colonel before his capture by Soviet forces at Stalingrad in 1943.

5 June. The 'Allied Representatives' formally declare that the area of Greater Berlin will be occupied by forces of each of the Four Powers. An inter-Allied governing authority (in Russian, *komendatura*) consisting of four commandants, appointed by their respective Commanders-in-Chief, will be established to direct jointly its administration.

7 August. It is reported that despite Marshal Zhukov's order that no refugees be allowed to enter Berlin, they are arriving at the rate of 25,000–30,000 daily. They are being accommodated in 50 camps, but only permitted to remain for 24 hours.

2 October. Field-Marshal Montgomery claims in London that 'Conditions in Berlin are dreadful, far graver than anything in our zone. The population there is already showing signs of starvation.'

25 October. The Allied *Kommandatura* raises rations for children of up to eight years to 1,550 calories a day and for those up to sixteen to 1,543 calories, involving increases in cereal, fat, sugar, bread, potato, meat, coffee and salt rations. (1,500 is the barest subsistence minimum.)

25 October. The British sector authorities launch 'Operation Stork' featuring the voluntary evacuation from Berlin to the countryside for the winter of 50,000 children aged four to fourteen accompanied by 10,000 mothers and teachers, so as to guard them against the anticipated hardships.

1946

20 October. Elections are held throughout Berlin for a municipal assembly. The SPD wins decisively with 43.6 per cent of the vote as against 29.8 per cent for the SED in the Soviet sector, and with over 50 per cent of the vote in the other sectors.

1947

17 April. Dr Otto Ostrowski (SPD), who had succeeded Dr Werner as chief mayor in December 1946, resigns following criticism from within the SPD that he is too conciliatory to the SED.

22 April. Major-General Kotikov, the Soviet commandant, refuses to accept Dr Ostrowski's resignation and alleges that opposition to him has been fermented by certain American officers.

24 June. The Berlin Assembly elects Professor Ernst Reuter as chief mayor. Major-General Kotikov refuses to approve his appointment and it is referred to the Allied Control Council for future decision.

1948

1 April. The Soviet Union disputes the proposed introduction of the western currency reform in West Berlin and begins to disrupt land traffic into Berlin on a regular basis.

24 June. The Soviet Union blockades all rail, road and water routes across its zone into West Berlin.

26 June. The western Allies launch the Berlin airlift with flights to Tempelhof in West Berlin.

1 July. The Soviet chief of staff in the Berlin *Kommandatura* announces that Soviet representatives will no longer attend any meetings. He cites the behaviour of the American commandant at the previous meeting and the introduction of the western currency reform.

6 September. The non-SED majority of the Berlin municipal assembly moves to West Berlin and dismisses Paul Markgraf for partiality in the discharge of his duties.

9 September. Ernst Reuter appeals to the 'peoples of the world' at a freedom rally before the Reichstag building.

30 November. The SED calls a meeting in the Admiralspalast Theatre to establish a separate East Berlin city administration. Friedrich Ebert, son of the first president of the Weimar Republic and a former member of the SPD, is elected mayor. Berlin is thereby divided politically.

5 December. Elections for the Berlin assembly are held in West Berlin, but not in East Berlin where they are banned. The SPD wins. Ernst Reuter is elected mayor of West Berlin.

1949

18 February. Supplies transported by the Berlin airlift reach one million tons.

20 March. The western Allies declare that the reformed West Mark is the sole legal tender in West Berlin (although some shops are to continue to accept East Marks).

12 May. The Soviet Union lifts its land blockade of West Berlin, and the airlift ends, with a total loss throughout of 65 lives.

20 June. The Soviet Union assumes an 'obligation', under the Four-Power agreement ending the blockade, to guarantee the normal operation of transport and communications between Berlin and the western zones of Germany.

8 October. The West Berlin City Assembly calls on the western Allies to agree to the incorporation of Berlin as West Germany's twelfth *Land* and to recognise it as the German capital.

1950

29 August. The commandants of the western Allies approve the new constitution for Berlin, but express reservations over the declaration that Berlin is West Germany's twelfth *Land*.

1951

18 January. Professor Ernst Reuter is re-elected as governing mayor of West Berlin.

1952

26 May. The memorandum on principles governing the relationship between the Allied *Kommandatura* and Greater Berlin, which forms part of the wider contractual arrangements signed on that day (see section 1.2 for fuller particulars), 'grants the (West) Berlin authorities the maximum liberty compatible with the special situation of Berlin'.

1953
16 June. The East Berlin strikers also demonstrate in West Berlin.
17 June. The East Berlin demonstrations are suppressed with some loss of life. (See section 1.2 for fuller particulars.)

1955
27 April. Agreement is reached between the West German government and the West Berlin Senate on federal aid of DM1.6 billion for a four-year reconstruction plan to run from 1955–59.
20 September. East Germany signs an agreement with the Soviet government whereby responsibility for the control of the western Allies' lines of communication to West Berlin remain 'for the time being' with the Soviet military.

1957
6 October. Willy Brandt (SPD) is elected governing mayor of West Berlin, following the death of Dr Otto Suhr on 30 August.

1958
27 October. Ulbricht maintains that the whole of Berlin belongs to the area under East German sovereignty and that the authority of the occupying western Allies no longer has any legal basis in Berlin.
10 November. A second Berlin crisis is threatened by Khrushchev's declaration that the western Allies should leave Berlin, and that the Soviet Union proposes to transfer responsibility for East Berlin to the East Germans.
21 November. America promises to uphold its rights in Berlin.
27 November. The Soviet Union proposes 'free city' status for West Berlin and advises the western Allies that it proposes to transfer its control powers in East Germany, including access to West Berlin, to the East German government on 27 May 1959, if a Four-Power agreement on Berlin is not reached by that date.

Willy Brandt, as governing mayor of West Berlin, describes the Soviet proposals for 'free city' status as 'unbearable'.
25 December. Andrei Gromyko, the Soviet foreign minister, says in a speech to the Supreme Soviet in Moscow that there is a danger of West Berlin becoming 'a second Sarajevo'.
31 December. The American, British and French ambassadors in Moscow convey the rejection by their respective foreign ministers, who had met in Paris on 14 December, of the Soviet note of 27 November.

1959

5 January. West Germany submits its own note in response to the Soviet proposals of 27 November. It specifically rejects any concept of a confederal relationship between the two parts of Germany and forcefully denies that West Berlin is a centre for spying by the western Allies.

12 January. Willy Brandt is re-elected governing mayor of West Berlin.

27 March. The first incident occurs of the 'buzzing' by Soviet fighters of western aircraft flying at more than 10,000-feet in the air corridors linking West Berlin and West Germany. The western Allies refute the Soviet claim of a 10,000-foot ceiling, and both sides maintain that the incidents show a determination by the other to poison the atmosphere at the forthcoming Summit conference. (See section 1.2 for fuller particulars.) The dispute fades away.

3 July. Dr Gerhard Schröder, West German minister of the interior, contradicts the view of Dr Gerstenmaier, president of the Bundestag, that, as West Berlin is a West German *Land* and subject to the Basic Law, its representatives have full voting rights in the Federal Assembly. He maintains that they have no voting rights.

6 October. The flying of the new East German flag on West Berlin *S-Bahn* stations operated by East Germany leads to fighting between West Berlin police seeking to take down the flags and East German railwaymen. Two policeman are seriously injured. The flags had been hoisted to mark the tenth anniversary of the foundation of the East German state.

1960

3–4 January. Police raid the homes of members of two extreme right-wing student organisations in a determined attempt by the West Berlin authorities to 'smash' anti-semitism and neo-Nazism. Chancellor Adenauer hopes that their vigorous response will be a precedent for all the *Länder*.

30 June. The Soviet Union protests against the alleged recruitment of West Berliners to the *Bundeswehr* and the West German law of 8 January allowing military orders to be placed with West Berlin firms. The charge of recruitment is denied, although it is admitted that any West Berliner is free to volunteer for military service.

30 August. East Germany bans West Germans (but not West Berliners) without residence visas from entering East Berlin until midnight on 4/5 September, the duration of planned rallies in West Berlin by the German Association of ex-Prisoners of War and Missing Persons' Relatives and the German Federal Refugees' Association. East Germany describes the planned rallies as militaristic and revanchist.

5 September. An East German News Agency statement draws attention to Ulbricht's earlier pronouncement that no representative of the West German government has 'any business to be in Berlin'.

8 September. The East German Council of Ministers approves regulations requiring West Germans to obtain an entry permit to visit East Berlin with effect from midnight that day.

13 September. East Germany ceases to recognise the validity of West Berlin passports. West Berliners wishing to visit East Germany, as distinct from those in transit to West Germany, must in future carry an identity card together with an East German permit.

1961

15 February. East Germany withdraws the requirement, imposed in August 1960, that West Germans hold special visas to enter East Berlin.

13 March. Willy Brandt visits America and discusses the Berlin issue with President Kennedy. He states afterwards that Kennedy had 'reiterated the determination of the United States, in co-operation with its Allies, to preserve and maintain the freedom of West Berlin, to which it is committed, and to defend the Allied position in the city, upon which the preservation of that freedom in large measure depends'.

3–4 June. Khrushchev meets the new American president at a Summit in Vienna. He tells Kennedy that he wishes 'to tranquillise the situation in the most dangerous spot in the world . . . to excise this thorn, this ulcer – without prejudicing interests on either side . . .' He seeks the demilitarisation of the city and adds that once responsibilities have been transferred to the East Germans, 'any infringement of the sovereignty of East Germany would be regarded as open aggression with all its consequences'.

8 June. The Soviet government protests to America, Britain and France at the holding of committee sessions of the Bundestag in West Berlin during June and at the planned Bundesrat meeting there on 16 June. It describes them as a new and major provocation against itself and East Germany.

15 June. Khrushchev maintains on Soviet television following his Summit meeting in Vienna with President Kennedy that a peaceful settlement of the questions of Germany and Berlin 'must be attained this year.'

Ulbricht expresses his confidence at a press conference that the Berlin question will be resolved within twelve months and adds that 'a peace treaty will come and West Berlin will be a free city with its neutrality guaranteed'.

6 July. Kennedy declares at a press conference that it is 'of the greatest importance that the American people understand the basic issues involved and the threats to the peace and security of Europe and of ourselves posed by the Soviet announcements that they intend to change unilaterally the existing arrangements in Berlin'.

7 July. East Berlin enforces an earlier ordinance requiring about one half of the 50,000 East Berliners working in West Berlin to register with the East Berlin authorities.

17 July. The western Allies reject Khrushchev's proposals for a demilitarised free city.

23 July. East Germany imposes new travel restrictions in an attempt to stem the flow of refugees to West Berlin.

25 July. President Kennedy in a broadcast to the American people reaffirms the right of the western Allies to be in Berlin and to enjoy free access to it. He insists that 'we cannot permit the Communists to drive us out of Berlin, either gradually or by force', and adds that the freedom of West Berlin is 'not negotiable'. He announces planned additional defence expenditure of more than $3 billion in the current year and an increase in the size of the defence budget 'to meet a worldwide threat, on a basis which stretches far beyond the present Berlin crisis'.

4 August. East Germany imposes tighter restrictions on the 53,000 East Berliners working daily in West Berlin (*Grenzgänger*).

13 August. East Germany seals the borders between East and West Berlin and between West Berlin and East Germany, leaving open thirteen official crossing-points. West Berliners can still with some exceptions enter East Berlin and the transit corridors to West Berlin are unaffected.

East Berlin begins to evacuate families from along the sector border.

14 August. The Brandenburg Gate, one of the thirteen crossing-points, is closed 'temporarily'.

16 August. Willy Brandt tells a gathering of almost 300,000 West Berliners outside the Schöneberg Town Hall that the protest at the East German action by the western commandants was 'good but not good enough' and that he has written to President Kennedy that 'Berlin expects not merely words but political action'. He adds that, 'What has happened in the past few days in Berlin is a new edition of the occupation of the Rhineland by Hitler; in the coming weeks and months Berlin must not become another Munich'.

19–20 August. American Vice-President Lyndon Johnson visits West Berlin to demonstrate 'American interest'. He is welcomed by some half million West Berliners, but agrees with Chancellor Adenauer that the crisis must be resolved by negotiation.

19–22 August. East Germany erects the concrete Berlin Wall between the eastern and western halves of the city.

22 August. East Germany announces a no-man's-land, 100 metres wide, on each side of the border and warns West Berliners not to enter it 'in the interests of their own safety'. The number of crossing-points is reduced to six, with three for West Berliners, two for West Germans and one for foreigners and diplomats. West Berliners are barred from East Berlin unless holding special visas.

23 August. The commandants of the western Allies describe the no-man's-land declaration as an 'effrontery' and some 1,000 American,

British and French troops with tanks and other armoured vehicles patrol right up to the sector boundaries.

26 August. The western Allies protest to the Soviet Union over the threats to the Berlin air corridors contained in the Soviet notes of three days earlier and warn that any interference with free access to the city would have the most serious consequences.

30 August. President Kennedy appoints General Lucius Clay as his personal representative in Berlin, with the rank of ambassador.

6 October. President Kennedy and Andrei Gromyko, the Soviet foreign minister, meeting in Washington, fail to agree on Berlin.

27–28 October. American and Soviet tanks confront each other at the Friedrichstrasse crossing-point ('Checkpoint Charlie').

1963

26 June. President Kennedy visits West Berlin where he receives a delirious welcome from an estimated 1.25 million people and delivers the celebrated '*Ich bin ein Berliner*' speech. (See 'Kennedy speech in Berlin' in *Glossary* for fuller particulars.)

25 December–5 January 1964. Following an agreement between East Germany and the West Berlin Senate, more than 1.2 million day-visits to the East are made by West Berliners over the Christmas/New Year holiday. It is the first time they have been able to visit East Berlin since the erection of the Wall.

1964

14 February. West Germany and the West Berlin Senate reject the East German proposal of a similar arrangement for Easter 1964, because East Germany requires the necessary passes to be distributed by East German postal officials in West Berlin.

23 September. West Germany approves a permanent 'technical agreement' between East Germany and West Berlin permitting West Berliners to visit relations in East Berlin during four periods of 14–16 days annually. Extra visits are permitted in cases of hardship.

1 November. Elderly East Germans are allowed to visit relatives in West Berlin and West Germany for the first time since the erection of the Wall.

1965

25 November. East Germany and the West Berlin Senate, with the approval of the West German government, reach a new agreement similar to that of 1964 allowing West Berliners to make two visits to relatives in East Berlin over the Christmas and New Year period. The new agreement, valid only until 31 March 1966, also allows for additional visits in cases of hardship.

1966

7 March. East Germany and the West Berlin Senate, with the approval of the West German government, reach a further agreement permitting West Berliners to visit relatives in East Berlin over the Easter and Whitsun holidays. In the absence of further agreements, the Wall is then to remain closed for most West Berliners until 1971.

14 December. Pastor Heinrich Albertz (SPD) becomes governing mayor of West Berlin following Willy Brandt's appointment as Vice-Chancellor and foreign minister in the 'grand coalition'.

1967

2 June. Benno Ohnesorg is shot by police in West Berlin during demonstrations against the visit of the Shah of Iran. The date gives its name to a subsequent terrorist movement and marks the beginning of a long period of student unrest in universities across West Germany and in West Berlin in particular.

5 July. Friedrich Ebert resigns as mayor of East Berlin and is succeeded by Herbert Fechner. Both men had been members of the SPD before the creation of the SED in 1946.

26 September. Pastor Heinrich Albertz resigns as governing mayor of West Berlin as a result of the continuing student unrest.

1968

6 February. Rudi Dutschke, the left-wing student leader, leads a demonstration in West Berlin against the Vietnam War.

11 April. Rudi Dutschke is shot and gravely wounded as he leaves the SDS headquarters. (See *Biographies* and 'SDS' in *Glossary* for fuller particulars.) The Springer building is attacked by demonstrators in protest.

12 April. The protest demonstrations across West Germany are at their most violent in West Berlin.

17 October. The NPD in West Berlin decides to disband in view of the threat of a ban by the Allied commandants. The West Berlin Senate had requested such a ban by the commandants, in whom the power was vested, on 3 October. The Senate was mindful of its image in eastern Europe.

1969

6 February. The East German ministry for foreign affairs sends a teletyped message to the West German foreign ministry denouncing the proposal to hold the 1969 West German presidential election in West Berlin as a 'deliberate, serious provocation'.

8 February. The East German ministry of the interior issues a directive barring all members of the West German Federal Assembly (the presidential elective body) and all members of the West German armed forces and of the Bundestag's defence committee from crossing East Germany to or from West Berlin until further notice. The directive maintains that the proposal is fresh evidence of West Germany's intention to 'continue its aggressive actions to annex the independent political entity of West Berlin to the West German state'.

10 February. The ambassadors of the western Allies in Bonn point out that three previous presidential elections had been conducted in West Berlin 'without causing any difficulty'.

13 February. The Soviet ambassador to West Germany presents a statement of protest to Chancellor Kiesinger. It claims that 'No state in the world elects its president on the territory of other states.'

21 February. Ulbricht writes to Willy Brandt as chairman of the SPD stating that if the Federal Assembly were to meet elsewhere than Berlin the West Berlin Senate might approach the East German government about permitting West Berliners to visit East Berlin at Easter 1969. The East German government would be 'willing to examine such a proposal in a positive manner'.

25 February. Brandt replies that no discussions are possible between the SPD and Ulbricht about the Federal Assembly, but that the SPD supports efforts to solve the problems of West Berlin.

28 February. The Soviet ambassador to East Germany presents a note to the East German foreign minister accusing the West Germans of 'flagrant abuse of the communications routes' between Berlin and West Germany and asking the East Germans to 'examine the possibilities of taking the necessary measures' to curtail such 'unlawful activities', in which they can count on Soviet bloc support. The note maintains that as part of West Germany's 'revanchist military preparations', young West Berliners are being illegally recruited into the West German army and that several thousand have already received military training, that 'dozens' of West Berlin industrial enterprises are manufacturing military and other strategic goods, and that they are being secretly transported to West Germany by the communication routes through East Germany.

1 March. The three western Allies dismiss the Soviet allegations as 'groundless'.

1 and 2 March. East German troops and border guards close the Helmstedt/Marienborn border point on the Berlin autobahn for two hours each day, as large concentrations of Soviet and East German troops assemble near the border for manoeuvres.

2 March. The chief controller of the Soviet section of the Four-Power Berlin Air Security Centre warns that the Soviet authorities cannot guarantee the safety of the three air corridors to Berlin from the west, if they are used by members of the Federal Assembly. He repeats the earlier Soviet objection that it includes members of the neo-Nazi NPD.

4 March. The Berlin autobahn is sealed at both ends for two hours even to Allied military traffic.

5 March. The Helmstedt/Marienborn border point is closed for periods of three hours and four hours. Dr Gustav Heinemann is elected West German president in West Berlin.

10 July. Andrei Gromyko, Soviet foreign minister, tells the Supreme Soviet in Moscow that the Soviet Union is ready to respond to an approach from the western Allies on the subject of Berlin, so as to 'eliminate now and for ever complications around West Berlin'.

7 August. The ambassadors of the western Allies, after consulting the West German government, propose talks with the Soviet Union on improving the situation in Berlin.

12 September. The Soviet Union agrees on talks but suggests neither time nor place, nor an agenda.

13 November. The three western commandants protest against the extension of conscription to East Berliners.

16 December. The western ambassadors in identical notes repeat their proposal of 7 August.

1970

26 March. The western Allies and the Soviet Union open talks on the future status of Berlin.

31 July. East Germany and West Berlin agree to restore the telephone links between East and West Berlin severed since May 1952. The links become operational on 31 January 1971.

28 November–2 December. East Germany disrupts civilian transit traffic on the Berlin autobahn in protest against meetings of CDU/CSU Bundestag members in West Berlin.

19–22 December. Autobahn traffic is again disrupted in protest against meetings of SPD Bundestag and Landtag members in West Berlin.

1971

27 January–1 February. Six days of autobahn disruption in protest against visits to West Berlin by President Heinemann and Chancellor Brandt, and at a meeting there of FDP Bundestag leaders.

24 February. Willi Stoph proposes direct talks between the East German government and the West Berlin Senate on visits by West Berliners to East Germany.

3 March. Further autobahn disruption follows the rejection by the western Allies of a Soviet protest against another meeting of CDU Bundestag members in West Berlin.

6 March. Talks open between East German and West Berlin representatives.

18 March. The three western commandants describe as illegal and contrary to Berlin's Four-Power status an East German decree extending military service obligations on East Berliners.

20 April. Klaus Schütz is re-elected as governing mayor of West Berlin.

3 September. The western Allies and the Soviet Union sign the Four-Power Berlin Agreement. Under the first part of the agreement, the signatories commit themselves to not using the threat of force in the city and to resolving their differences by peaceful means alone. The rights and responsibilities of all signatories are confirmed and respected. Under the second part, the western Allies confirm that their sectors do not form part of West Germany and do not fall under its jurisdiction. The Soviet Union promises that surface traffic between West Germany and West Berlin will not be interrupted and that West Berliners will have the right to visit East Germany. The Soviet Union acquires the right to a consulate in West Berlin and West Berlin may have its own representation abroad. The Soviet Union is to argue subsequently that the agreement relates only to West Berlin, as the Four-Power status of Berlin as a whole lapsed in 1948.

17 December. East and West Germany sign an Agreement on the Transit Traffic of Civilian Persons and Goods between West Germany and West Berlin. It gives permanent residents of West Berlin the right to visit East Berlin and East Germany for a total of 30 days annually.

1972

10 April. West Berlin announces that 449,597 West Berliners have visited East Berlin or East Germany during the Easter period. They are the first visits they have been able to make to East Berlin for six years and to East Germany for more than 20 years.

1974

30 August. David Klein, US deputy commander in Berlin, bans the NPD from participating in the 1975 Berlin elections.

1975

7 January. The Berlin election commission permits two Communist parties to participate in the 1975 Berlin elections. They are the Maoist DKP and the KBW. (The DKP had already taken part in Landtag elections in Hesse and Bavaria, and the KBW in Hesse.)

10 November. The Soviet convoy to the Soviet war memorial in West Berlin, for the annual commemoration there of the Russian Revolution, contains two East German soldiers in uniform. An immediate protest by the western Allies at the breach of the city's demilitarised status receives an acceptable reply.

1976
13 August. East Germany denies access to West Berlin to eleven out of eighteen buses chartered by the youth branch of the CDU.

26 August. The ambassadors of the western Allies protest formally to the Soviet Union at the perceived breach of the Four-Power Agreement.

31 December. East Germany removes all control points between itself and East Berlin.

1977
2 May. Klaus Schütz and the SPD Senate in its entirety resign after a series of financial scandals, although Klaus Schütz is not personally implicated. Dietrich Stobbe (SPD) is elected as governing mayor. His revised Senate is approved ten days later.

1978
16 July. East Germany delays transit traffic by up to fourteen hours in a presumed protest against President Carter's visit to West Berlin.

10 November. East and West Germany sign an important agreement on the improvement of transit routes between West Germany and West Berlin. (See section 3.1 for fuller particulars.)

1979
28 June. The Volkskammer votes unanimously to give its 66 representatives from East Berlin full voting rights and to amend the electoral law of 1967 to allow their direct election to the chamber.

The ambassadors of the western Allies protest that the unilateral action is contrary to the 1971 Four-Power Agreement.

5 July. The East German foreign ministry maintains that the Volkskammer's decision is of an internal nature.

1983
20 May. SPD members of the West Berlin city council meet members of the East Berlin council and city government in the first official contact between the two halves of the city since 1948.

30 December. The East German Railways (*Deutsche Reichsbahn*) and the West Berlin government agree to transfer to West Berlin the running of the western part of the Berlin suburban railway (*S-Bahn*), hitherto run by the *Reichsbahn*. West Berlin agrees to pay an annual rental of DM9.5 million and the *Reichsbahn* remains responsible for the tracks used by long distance trains to West Germany in Berlin.

1984
5 February. Eberhard Diepgen (CDU) is elected governing mayor of West Berlin.

1985
26–27 January. The ruling committee of the Greens, meeting in Freiburg, dissolve the party's West Berlin branch, which has allegedly been infiltrated by neo-Nazi elements. Branch members are advised to support the Alternative List (*Alternative Liste – A.L.*).

1986
8 October. East Germany invites Eberhard Diepgen to attend the 1987 East Berlin celebrations to mark the 750th anniversary of the foundation of Berlin.

1987
3 March. Eberhard Diepgen announces that America, Britain and France have agreed to his acceptance of the East German invitation.

8 March. Eberhard Diepgen invites Erich Honecker to attend the West Berlin celebrations.

13 April. Erich Honecker rejects the invitation, citing a letter written by Eberhard Diepgen the previous July urging West German *Ministerpräsidenten* not to attend the East Berlin celebrations as their presence might prejudice West Berlin's special status.

30 April. The Soviet Union objects to the presence of Chancellor Kohl and other West German government figures in West Berlin for its 750th anniversary. The Chancellor declares that 'The German question will remain open for as long as Germans are denied their freedom, and for as long as basic human rights are violated in the heart of Germany. Berlin symbolises the open German question. We will never acquiesce in the existence of the Wall and barbed wire.'

5 May. East Germany cancels the planned first official contacts between the boroughs comprising East and West Berlin since 1948.

6 May. East Germany withdraws its October 1986 invitation to Eberhard Diepgen.

11 May. President Mitterand of France visits West Berlin.

26–27 May. Queen Elizabeth II of Great Britain visits West Berlin.

28–29 May. Mikhail Gorbachev, General Secretary of the Soviet Communist Party, attends a summit meeting of the Warsaw Pact in East Berlin.

11 June. 20–30,000 demonstrators protest, about 1,000 violently, against the following day's visit by President Reagan of America.

12 June. President Reagan visits West Berlin, completing the trio of visits by the heads of state of the western Allies. He suggests a number of initiatives for both parts of the city, including the hosting of international conferences, the expansion of its air transport role, and the organisation ultimately of an East–West Olympics. In a separate speech delivered close to the Wall near the Brandenburg Gate, he insists 'Mr Gorbachev, open this gate. Mr Gorbachev, tear down this wall.'

18 June. Eduard Shevardnadze, the Soviet foreign minister, describes the demand as inflammatory and melodramatic and insists that barriers 'would best be overcome by acts in favour of peace, security and co-operation'.

2 July. Jacques Chirac, French prime minister and mayor of Paris, visits West Berlin and signs a friendship treaty between West Berlin and Paris.

17 August. Rudolf Hess, Hitler's deputy until 1941, dies in Spandau Prison, Berlin, of which he was the only occupant. His death is followed by the prison's demolition, leaving the Air Safety Centre as the only tangible expression of Four-Power co-operation in Berlin.

23 October. East Germany celebrates the 750th anniversary of the foundation of Berlin. The *Ministerpräsidenten* of Bremen, Hamburg and the Saarland are present, but not the ambassadors of any of the NATO countries or the permanent representative of West Germany.

1988

31 March. East Germany and West Berlin sign a treaty transferring 97 hectares including the Lenne Triangle (the Potsdamer Platz) to West Berlin and an 87-hectare enclave at Prenzlauer Berg to East Berlin. The exchange is effected on 1 July with a West Berlin compensatory payment of DM76 million.

27 June. America, Britain and France agree to lift the prohibition on Lufthansa from operating its own flights to West Berlin. The initial flight by EuroBerlin France, in which Lufthansa has a 49 per cent stake, follows on 7 November.

25 October. The Soviet Union protests that the decision violates Four-Power agreements, the grounds on which the western Allies have hitherto maintained their prohibition.

31 October. The East German air traffic authorities at Schönefeld airport demand with Soviet support that they be included in Berlin air traffic control arrangements. The western Allies refuse on the grounds that it would damage the city's Four-Power status.

10 November. Restoration commences of the East Berlin synagogue, a victim of the Nazis' *Kristallnacht* of 1938.

1989

29 January. *Die Republikaner* secure their most successful result to date with 7.5 per cent of the vote in inconclusive West Berlin elections. Their success is attributed in part to housing shortages in the city and to the large number of immigrants, including ethnic Germans from eastern Europe.

6 February. Chris Gueffroy is the last person to be killed trying to cross the Berlin Wall.

16 March. Walter Momper becomes governing mayor. His coalition includes three representatives of the *Alternative Liste* (*A.L.*), the Berlin Green grouping. They accept the continued Allied presence, but want it reduced to a token level, the validity of West German legislation in West Berlin, and the right of the police to use force, although they want the riot police to be disbanded.

1 May. Rioting engendered by a 'revolutionary May Day' rally in Kreuzberg puts the West Berlin coalition under pressure. The anarchist element of the Alternative List is opposed to the List's participation in government.

9 November. The Berlin Wall is opened.

10 November. Tens of thousands of East Berliners visit West Berlin.

11 December. The ambassadors of the western Allies to West Germany and the Soviet ambassador to East Germany meet at Soviet request at the Allied Control Council building in West Berlin for the first time since 1971. They announce 'common understanding of the importance of stability . . . in and around Berlin'.

22 December. A 'Provisional Regional Committee' is established in the Schöneberg City Hall, the seat of the West Berlin City Council. Led by the head of the Senate chancellery, it comprises representatives of the specialised administrations in East and West Berlin, the federal government, the East German government until unification in October 1990 and the East German *Bezirke* (districts) of Potsdam and Frankfurt/Oder subsequently subsumed in the *Land* of Brandenburg.

23 December. The Brandenburg Gate is reopened.

1990

6 May. City elections held in East Berlin. The results are contrary to the East German trend, with support for the SPD at 34 per cent, the PDS at 30 per cent, the CDU at 17.7 per cent, Alliance 90 at 9.9 per cent and the Greens at 2.7 per cent. The SPD and CDU form a coalition government with Tino Schwierzina of the SPD as mayor. East Berlin gains the *Land* prerogative of control of the police from East Germany. The elections are followed the next month by the first joint meeting of the East and West Berlin city councils in the *Rotes Rathaus* in East Berlin, the traditional seat of the Berlin Council.

29 June. The federal president, Dr Richard von Weizsäcker, supports the vision of Berlin as the future seat of government by publicly declaring 'Here is the place for a responsible leadership of Germany.'

4 October. The Bundestag at its ceremonial initial session in the Reichstag formally declares Berlin the national capital, but leaves open the question of the future seat of government.

15 November. The West Berlin coalition government between the SPD and the Alternative List (primarily Greens), led by Walter Momper, collapses when the List withdraws its support because of the violent eviction with more than 100 injuries of several hundred, mainly West Berlin, squatters from thirteen apartment blocks in the Friedrichshain district of East Berlin.

2 December. Berlin for the first time directly elects its members to the Bundestag. (West Berlin's voters had previously voted only indirectly in view of the city's special status). Berlin also holds the first citywide elections to the city council since national unification. The CDU with 40.3 per cent of the vote becomes the largest party on the council.

1991

11 January. The city council elects the first Senate for the whole of Berlin. The 1950 *Land* constitution becomes valid throughout the city, and the East Berlin constitution of July 1990 lapses. Tino Schwierzina resigns as mayor of East Berlin.

24 January. Eberhard Diepgen (CDU) becomes governing mayor of Berlin.

20 June. The Bundestag decides by a majority of just seventeen votes and after lengthy debate to move both itself and the seat of government from Bonn to Berlin.

29 September. A commission of enquiry is established, under Article 88 of the 1950 constitution, to review the constitution and to propose parliamentary reform.

1 October. The seats of the governing mayor and of the Senate are transferred from the Schöneberg Rathaus, their provisional home for more than 40 years, to the Berliner Rathaus (known as the *Rotes Rathaus* because of the red colour of its bricks, not because of its politics) in the Mitte district in the heart of Berlin.

1992

25 August. Chancellor Kohl, the *Ministerpräsident* of Brandenburg, Manfred Stolpe, and the governing mayor of Berlin, Eberhard Diepgen, sign the Capital Treaty.

1993

April. The Berlin council (parliament) moves into the restored building of the former Prussian provincial parliament (*Landtag*).

12 October. The federal cabinet decides to move the government to Berlin in stages up to the year 2000.

1994

January. The presidency moves to Berlin.

10 March. The Bundestag decides to move to Berlin by the summer break, 2000, at the latest.

18 May. The commission of enquiry appointed on 29 September 1991 submits its final report to the Berlin parliament.

31 August. President Yeltsin of Russia comes to Berlin for the formal withdrawal of Russian troops, in a gesture of reconciliation. The last military parade had been held on 25 June.

8 September. Chancellor Kohl takes leave of the three western protecting powers, whose last military parade had been held on 18 June, and thanks them for their commitment to the freedom of Berlin over five decades.

26 October. Enactment of the Berlin–Bonn law, effecting a compromise whereby 7,300 new jobs will be created in Bonn by the direction there of new functions and institutions of national significance, to compensate for those jobs being lost to Berlin.

1995

6 February. The joint commission established under the Capital Treaty announces its proposals for the transfer of the seat of the federal government to Berlin. Parliament and administration will be concentrated in three areas: the Spree bend, around the Spree island, and in the vicinity of the prewar government quarter at the crossing of the Wilhelmstrasse and the Leipziger Strasse.

The ministry of finance is to occupy the 'Detlev-Rohwedder-Haus', first built in 1936 as the Reichs Air Ministry, later the East German 'House of Ministries', and from 1990–94 used by the Treuhandanstalt. The foreign ministry is to occupy the former Reichsbank building of 1940, which was the seat of the Central Committee of the SED from 1959–89.

Six ministries will remain in Bonn: education and science; environment; health; food, agriculture and forests; economic co-operation; and defence.

27 September. The Bundesrat reverses an earlier decision by agreeing to move to Berlin in 1999. It will occupy the building of the former Prussian upper house (*Landrat*).

22 October. A new constitution is approved in a referendum with 75.1 per cent of the votes cast in favour and 24.9 per cent against. It extends the objectives of the 'state' to the explicit support of marriage, family and other partnerships, female equality, environmental protection and enhanced rights of citizen participation (citizens' initiatives). The parliament is to be elected every four years and the minimum number of members is reduced to 150.

1996

5 May. The electorate rejects in a referendum the merger of the *Länder* of Berlin and Brandenburg, recommended by their governments. Although supported in Berlin, it is rejected in Brandenburg by a majority of two to one.

29 November. It is announced that, although plenary sessions of the Bundestag will be held in Berlin, as agreed, from the spring of 1999, Bundestag committees will continue to meet in Bonn until at least 2000.

SECTION SIX

Germany as a federal state

6.1 Distinctive approaches

In retrospect, the discretion given to the *Länder* under the Basic Law has had two particular interrelated effects. It has permitted parties with a more localised appeal to become established or alternatively to survive, if only for a time, when they might not have been able to nationally, and it has opened the possibility of those parties influencing the thrust of important *Land* policies with implications for federal policy.

The parties with more localised appeal have fallen since 1945 into four broad categories. The first and rather exceptional case is the CSU, which is the sister party of the CDU, and organises solely in Bavaria. Although the CSU is therefore in one sense a national party supplying key ministers to government (of whom Franz-Josef Strauss and currently Theo Waigel have probably been the most important), it also has a powerful regional flavour. Strongly Catholic and still influenced by expellees and their dependents, it was well to the right of CDU-led federal coalitions with the FDP on relations with the Soviet bloc prior to 1990 and a bitter opponent of Brandt's Ostpolitik. Less nervous than other large parties of proclaiming German national policies, it is still viewed with some caution in the Czech Republic. Slightly paradoxically, the CSU under the Bavarian *Ministerpräsident*, Edmund Stoiber, has emerged more recently as one of the centres of reserve within Germany as to the benefits of EU economic and monetary union, much to the discomfiture of Theo Waigel, its chairman and federal finance minister.

The second category comprises the almost exclusively right-wing parties, favoured first by the expellees and then later by groups resentful of immigrants and the influence of foreign powers, notably the Soviet Union. Although the philosophies of such groups have been national, usually by definition, they have thrived and gained a foothold in conditions of more localised resentment. This was initially the case in those *Länder*, such as Schleswig-Holstein, where the proportion of expellees was particularly high, and where their party gained representation in the *Land* assemblies. Such parties lost influence, however, as expellees and refugees were absorbed into the burgeoning West German economy, and the parties had been similarly absorbed by the mainstream groups by the early 1960s.

The 1960s, however, also saw the public emergence of neo-Nazi groups, which, like their forebear, were adept at securing publicity, however small and fragmented they might actually be. Total membership of far-right groups was estimated by the Federal Office for the Protection of the Constitution in 1992 at 39,800 the previous year, with some 6,000 members of specifically neo-Nazi groups. These again thrived, and have continued to thrive, in conditions of localised resentment. The best-known such party, *die Republikaner*, succeeded in obtaining eleven seats in the West Berlin elections of 1989, allegedly because of housing shortages and the high number of immigrants, both Turks and ethnic Germans from eastern Europe. Similar pressures have led to a number of attacks on Turkish and refugee hostels in East German cities such as Rostock, but had less strictly political impact. Nevertheless, Chancellor Kohl has on several occasions, as over the replacement of Heiner Geissler as CDU general secretary, tilted the CDU to the right to reduce the appeal of *die Republikaner*.

The third category, the Greens, is in many ways the most obvious type of party to have been helped by the federal nature of the German system. Public environmental concern was initially stimulated to a large degree by the evidence of widespread tree death (*Waldsterben*) attributable to acid rain, but the incidence of tree death was much more marked in those areas of Germany where sulphur deposition was high. The ability of the Greens to obtain representation in those same areas, and to exercise influence at *Land* as well as at city or *Kreis* level, was a key element in their ability to become an effective national party and to enter the Bundestag in 1983. Their influence has been keenly felt, most obviously perhaps over nuclear issues, where they have inspired reducing reliance on nuclear power and particular hostility to nuclear reprocessing facilities, notably at Gorleben. In the cities, they have promoted numerous green transport initiatives, associated in particular with Joschka Fischer.

A fourth category, and an intriguing one, may be represented by the PDS. Written off by many observers in 1990 as a historical relic, it has shown unexpected resilience, particularly in East Berlin. It may well wither away or be absorbed by the SPD in due course, in practice if not in name, or even spread to western Germany as a party fundamentally critical of global capital and market orthodoxies. On the other hand, its proposal of an East German committee to represent the interests of former East German nationals could bear fruit if the psychological barrier between the two populations remains a serious problem. If not a *Land* party, it could become an eastern German regional party with a local base no less strong than that of the CSU.

6.2 Basic data on the *Länder*

Baden-Württemberg

Capital	Stuttgart
Population (1995)	10,319,367
Origin	Created as the 'south-west state' from the *Länder* of South Baden, Württemberg-Baden and Württemberg-Hohenzollern by a plebiscite of 9 December 1951. It has emerged as the focus of Germany's most high-tech industries.

Bavaria (*Bayern*)

Capital	Munich
Population (1995)	11,993,484
Origin	A kingdom within Imperial Germany until 1918, it was proclaimed a *Land* by the American military government on 27 September 1945. A traditional centre of strong German national sentiment, it is also the nearest Germany has to 'a country within a country': a dichotomy which shows no sign of weakening.

Berlin

Population (1995)	3,471,418
Origin	Greater Berlin was established within its present boundaries in 1920, but between 1948 and 1990 East Berlin and West Berlin were separate units, the former being the capital of East Germany. Administration was again united in 1991.

Brandenburg

Capital	Potsdam
Population (1995)	2,542,042
Origin	The core of Prussia, and the hinterland of Berlin, it lost about a third of its territory to Poland when it was established within its present

boundaries by the Soviet military government in May 1945. A provincial government was set up by the Soviet authorities on 5 July 1945. Abolished as a *Land* in 1952, it was re-established on 22 July 1990. A proposed merger with Berlin was rejected in a referendum in May 1996.

Bremen (*Freie Hansestadt Bremen*)

Population (1995)   679,757

Origin   Like Hamburg a trading city with a long history of autonomy, its emergence as a modern *Land* was almost accidental. As the supply port for the American occupation forces it was an enclave within the British Zone, and was declared the American Zone's fourth *Land* on 22 January 1947.

Hamburg (*Freie und Hansestadt Hamburg*)

Population (1995)   1,705,900

Origin   A great trading port with a long autonomous history as a free city and a member of the medieval Hanseatic League, which linked leading trading cities along the Baltic. It was established as a *Land* by the British military government on 23 October 1946.

Hesse (*Hessen*)

Capital   Wiesbaden

Population (1995)   6,009,913

Origin   An amalgamation of the Prussian province of Hesse-Nassau, the northern part of the former State of Hesse (*Oberhessen*), and Rhinehesse (*Rheinhessen*), it was proclaimed a *Land* by the American military government on 27 September 1945. It includes Frankfurt, Germany's financial capital and seat of the European Monetary Institute, the precursor of the European central bank.

Lower Saxony (*Niedersachsen*)

Capital   Hannover

Population (1995)   7,780,422

Origin   Formed by the British military government on
                              1 November 1946 by merging the former
                              Prussian province of Hannover with the
                              traditional *Länder* of Brunswick (*Braunschweig*),
                              Oldenburg, and Schaumburg-Lippe.

Mecklenburg-West Pomerania (*Mecklenburg-Vorpommern*)

Capital   Schwerin
Population (1995)   1,823,084
Origin   The former *Land* Mecklenburg and that part
                              of the former province of Pomerania not
                              transferred to Poland in 1945. Traditionally,
                              one of the poorest and most backward parts
                              of Germany. A provincial government was
                              established by the Soviet authorities on 5 July
                              1945. Abolished as a *Land* in 1952, it was re-
                              established on 22 July 1990.

North Rhine-Westphalia (*Nordrhein-Westfalen*)

Capital   Düsseldorf
Population (1995)   17,893,045
Origin   Created by the British military government on
                              23 October 1946 from the former Prussian
                              province of Westphalia, the governmental
                              districts of Aachen, Cologne and Düsseldorf,
                              and the *Land* Lippe.

Rhineland-Palatinate (*Rheinland-Pfalz*)

Capital   Mainz
Population (1995)   3,983,282
Origin   Created by the French military government
                              in 1946 by the amalgamation of the historic
                              Palatinate and the Rhine districts of Koblenz,
                              Mainz, Montabaur and Trier.

Saarland

Capital   Saarbrücken
Population (1995)   1,084,370
Origin   A region which had been under League of
                              Nations control 1919–35 and which the French
                              sought to detach from Germany after 1945.

Policies of international status and economic union with France failed to retain popular support and the Saar returned to Germany on 1 January 1957.

Saxony (*Freistaat Sachsen*)

Capital	Dresden
Population (1995)	4,566,603
Origin	The former *Land* Saxony and part of the former province of Silesia. Like Bavaria, Saxony had been a kingdom within Imperial Germany until 1918. It was the historical home of the German labour movement. A provincial government was established by the Soviet authorities on 5 July 1945. Abolished as a *Land* in 1952, it was re-established on 22 July 1990.

Saxony-Anhalt (*Sachsen-Anhalt*)

Capital	Magdeburg
Population (1995)	2,738,928
Origin	The former Prussian province of Saxony, excluding the governmental district of Erfurt, and the *Land* Anhalt. Abolished as a *Land* in 1952, it was re-established on 22 July 1990.

Schleswig-Holstein

Capital	Kiel
Population (1995)	2,725,461
Origin	A former Prussian province.

Thuringia (*Thüringen*)

Capital	Erfurt
Population (1995)	2,503,785
Origin	The former *Land* Thuringia and the Erfurt governmental district of the former Prussian province of Saxony. Abolished as a *Land* in 1952, it was re-established on 22 July 1990.

6.3 *Land Ministerpräsidenten*

Baden-Württemberg

Dr Reinhold Maier (FDP) (1951–53)
Dr Gebhard Müller (CDU) (1953–58)
Dr Kurt Georg Kiesinger (CDU) (1958–66)
Dr Hans Filbinger (CDU) (1966–78)
Dr Lothar Späth (CDU) (1978–91)
Erwin Teufel (CDU) (1991–)

Bavaria

Dr Friedrich Schäffer (1945)
Dr Wilhelm Högner (SPD) (1945–46)
Dr Hans Ehard (CSU) (1946–54)
Dr Wilhelm Högner (SPD) (1954–57)
Dr Hans Seidel (CSU) (1957–60)
Dr Hans Ehard (CSU) (1960–62)
Alfons Goppel (CSU) (1963–78)
Franz-Josef Strauss (CSU) (1978–88)
Max Streibl (CSU) (1988–93)
Edmund Stoiber (CSU) (1993–)

Berlin (West 1948–90) (Governing mayor)

Dr Arthur Werner (1945–46)
Dr Otto Ostrowski (SPD) (1946–47)
Louise Schröder (SPD) (1947–48)
Professor Ernst Reuter (SPD) (1948–53)
Dr Walther Schreiber (CDU) (1953–55)
Dr Otto Suhr (SPD) (1955–57)
Willy Brandt (SPD) (1957–66)
Pastor Heinrich Albertz (SPD) (1966–67)
Klaus Schütz (SPD) (1967–77)
Dietrich Stobbe (SPD) (1977–81)
Dr Hans-Jochen Vogel (SPD) (Jan–June 1981)
Dr Richard von Weizsäcker (CDU) (June 1981–1984)

Eberhard Diepgen (CDU) (1984–89)
Walter Momper (SPD) (1989–90)
Eberhard Diepgen (CDU) (1991–)

Brandenburg

Dr Manfred Stolpe (SPD) (1990–)

Bremen (Mayor)

Wilhelm Kaisen (SPD) (1945–65)
Willy Dehnkamp (SPD) (1965–67)
Hans Koschnik (SPD) (1967–85)
Klaus Wedemeier (SPD) (1985–95)
Dr Henning Scherf (SPD) (1995–)

Hamburg (Governing Mayor)

Max Brauer (SPD) (1946–53)
Dr Kurt Sieveking (SPD) (1953–57)
Max Brauer (SPD) (1957–61)
Dr Paul Nevermann (SPD) (1962–65)
Professor Herbert Weichmann (SPD) (1965–71)
Peter Schultz (SPD) (1971–74)
Hans-Ulrich Klose (SPD) (1974–81)
Dr Klaus von Dohnanyi (SPD) (1981–88)
Henning Voscherau (SPD) (1988–)

Hesse

Dr Karl Geiler (1945–46)
Christian Stock (SPD) (1947–50)
Dr Georg August Zinn (SPD) (1950–69)
Albert Osswald (SPD) (1969–76)
Holger Börner (SPD) (1976–87)
Walter Wallmann (CDU) (1987–91)
Hans Eichel (SPD) (1991–)

Lower Saxony

Dr Hinrich Kopf (SPD) (1945–55)
Heinrich Hellwege (DP) (1955–59)
Dr Hinrich Kopf (SPD) (1959–61)

Dr Georg Diederichs (SPD) (1962–70)
Dr Alfred Kubel (SPD) (1970–76)
Dr Ernst Albrecht (CDU) (1976–90)
Gerhard Schröder (SPD) (1990–)

Mecklenburg-West Pomerania

Alfred Gomolka (CDU) (1990–92)
Berndt Seite (CDU) (1992–)

North Rhine-Westphalia

Dr Amelunxen (CDU) (1946–47)
Karl Arnold (CDU) (1947–56)
Fritz Steinhoff (SPD) (1956–58)
Dr Franz Meyers (CDU) (1958–66)
Heinz Kühn (SPD) (1966–78)
Johannes Rau (SPD) (1978–98)
Wolfgang Clement (SPD) (1998–)

Rhineland Palatinate

Dr Peter Altmaier (CDU) (1947–69)
Dr Helmut Kohl (CDU) (1969–76)
Bernhard Vogel (CDU) (1976–88)
Carl-Ludwig Wagner (CDU) (1988–91)
Rudolf Scharping (SPD) (1991–94)
Kurt Beck (SPD) (1994–)

Saarland

Dr Johannes Hoffmann (Saar Christian People's Party) (1952–55)
Dr Heinrich Welsch (non-party) (1955–56)
Dr Hubert Ney (CDU) (January–March 1957)
Egon Reinert (CDU) (1957–59)
Dr Franz Josef Röder (CDU) (1959–79)
Werner Zeyer (CDU) (1979–85)
Oskar Lafontaine (SPD) (1985–)

Saxony

Dr Kurt Biedenkopf (CDU) (1990–)

Saxony-Anhalt

Gerd Gies (CDU) (1990–91)
Dr Werner Münch (CDU) (1991–93)
Christoph Bergner (CDU) (1993–94)
Dr Manfred Höppner (SPD) (1994–)

Schleswig-Holstein

Hermann Ludemann (SPD) (1947–50)
Dr Walter Bartram (CDU) (1950–51)
Friedrich-Wilhelm Lübke (CDU) (1951–54)
Kai-Uwe von Hassel (CDU) (1954–62)
Dr Helmut Lemke (CDU) (1962–71)
Dr Gerhard Stoltenberg (CDU) (1979–82)
Uwe Barschel (CDU) (1982–87)
Henning Schwarz (CDU) (1987–88)
Björn Engholm (SPD) (1988–93)
Heide Simonis (SPD) (1993–)

Thuringia

Josef Duchac (CDU) (1990–92)
Bernhard Vogel (CDU) (1992–)

SECTION SEVEN

The economy

7.1 Defeat and recovery

The dislocation of the German economy by the time of the final surrender in May 1945 was virtually total, but the actual degree of physical destruction of its industrial installations is harder to calculate. The impact of Allied bombing on production was assessed in retrospect as having been appreciably less than thought at the time, but victors and defeated alike had far more pressing priorities in 1945 than producing comparable and reliable statistics on a factory-by-factory basis. Such base data as were available were also soon subject to selective presentation as east and west each sought to demonstrate how well its economic model was performing compared with its rival. An assertion that 20 per cent of industry was destroyed in the western zones but 45 per cent in the Soviet Zone should therefore be treated with caution. A very broad assessment of severe damage or destruction of, perhaps, one third overall may be a better guide. The destruction of agriculture is an even more imprecise concept, but it was the most pressing consideration at the time. The Allies were shipping food in to avoid mass starvation at the same time as they were shipping industrial plant out as reparations.

The obligation to pay reparations had been placed on Germany under the Potsdam Conference agreements, as had the loss of its arms industry. Factories were soon being dismantled in all zones and shipped to a wide range of countries which had been at war with Germany. Thirty plants valued at more than US$92 million were allocated in December 1945 alone. Their arrival obviously had the greatest impact in those countries such as Poland whose industries had been largely eliminated. This dismantling of industry was accompanied by a number of restrictions on the levels of output of a range of products and of steel, then a bedrock of any industrial economy. The export of coal to the liberated countries was, however, a priority from the very beginning.

The Allied thinking behind the inspiration of the predictable spiral of decline contained a number of threads. Sheer necessity for some countries was one, primitive revenge another. The fate of Germany and of the Germans as a whole elicited scant sympathy among any of the combatants. More profoundly, there was no agreed vision of Germany's economic future. The Potsdam Conference decisions, to which France was not a party, envisaged a unitary democratic state with a living standard equivalent to that of Europe as a whole, excluding Britain and the

Soviet Union. By March 1946 the Allied Control Council was envisaging industrial output of 50 per cent of the 1938 level and living standards at 70 per cent of the 1938 level. The Morgenthau Plan, named after the American treasury secretary, Henry J. Morgenthau, and which had been American and British official policy from September 1944 to the spring of 1945, had envisaged the permanent partition of Germany and the destruction and future prohibition of all its heavy industry. The French were harking back to prewar policy and sought to detach the Rhineland as a separate state, internationalise the Ruhr, and economically absorb the Saar, a combination which in the circumstances of the time would have made Germany an economic eunuch.

The catalyst for a change in outlook was the growing realisation throughout Europe that the full price of victory as much as of defeat was yet to be paid. The discernible optimism of 1946, in countries as diverse as Britain and Czechoslovakia, that the worst was over and that conditions would now steadily improve, succumbed to alarm at the consequences of indebtedness and vulnerability to extreme weather conditions. The social cleavages in France which had made a major contribution to the collapse of will in 1940 opened up again in 1947 with fears of a communist seizure of power. Relations between the western Allies and the Soviet Union steadily deteriorated. It is no denial of the generosity of the concept of Marshall Aid to remember that it was launched by the Americans to stave off the fear of a total European collapse and of a power vacuum which would be filled by the Soviet Union. It must also be said that Marshall Aid did not favour Germany. US$332.9 billion were allocated to the three western zones in 1949–50, as against $919.8 billion to Britain and $673.1 billion to France.

European economic prosperity was, however, seen as a necessity and as such it was indivisible. The energies which had been devoted to dismantling Germany were now converted to recreating it as an economic power, an exercise in which the Germans themselves were, needless to say, all too ready to co-operate. Ludwig Erhard, as director of the bizonal economic council from 1948, had already formulated the basic principles of the social market economy on which West Germany's later 'economic miracle' was to be built. East Germany's first Two-Year Plan covered the period 1949–51.

The restoration of West Germany's economic power was, however, to be pursued within a framework very different from that of the prewar years. Just as political sovereignty was restored on the basis of integration within NATO, economic sovereignty was restored on the basis of integration within the evolving institutions for economic co-operation which have become the European Union. It was Adenauer's particular genius to achieve reconciliation with both America and France on the basis of this twin approach without compromising the triangular relationship.

Developments in the Soviet Zone were much more halting but nevertheless advanced in a comparable direction. The demonstrations of June 1953 in what had become East Germany persuaded the Soviet and East German governments alike that East Germany could no longer be treated simply as a pool of resources for the Soviet bloc. With effect from 1 January 1954 both the Soviet Union and Poland waived their claims to reparations in August of that year. The Soviet Union announced at the same time that it would relinquish the German companies which had been operating as Soviet concerns (SAGs) since 1945 and which were valued on transfer back at MDN2.7 billion. Political integration was promoted through adherence to the Warsaw Pact in 1955 and economic integration through membership of COMECON from October 1950, although the degree of integration achieved by the latter was appreciably less than that secured by the European Union.

Significant differences nevertheless remained. West Germany clearly had the potential from at least the mid-1950s to become western Europe's predominant economy. The corollary of western European integration was that West Germany would be its economic leader, a prospect to which the British have really never been able to reconcile themselves. East Germany was not only much smaller than West Germany but it had less than a tenth the population of the Soviet Union. However important its science and technology might be to the Soviet bloc, it was bound to remain a subordinate partner.

There was an element of compromise. East Germany was to enjoy a much higher standard of living throughout most of its existence than the Soviet Union. Nevertheless, economic agreements were normally in what the Soviet Union perceived at the time as its interest. This could lead its planners to despair. Erich Apel was to commit suicide in December 1965 allegedly because the economic agreement about to be signed with the Soviet Union directed East Germany's trade links eastwards. He percipiently saw that if the East German economy was not exposed to the stimulus of the west, it would slowly become technologically obsolescent, even if output continued to increase: a vision which had largely become a reality by 1990.

7.2 West Germany

The rebirth of the West German economy was preceded by the arguments over ownership which had resulted in extensive nationalisation in most western European countries, although not in America, in the immediate postwar period. The fledgling German political parties had approved a similar approach in Berlin in June–July 1945 (see section 2.4 for fuller particulars), and some utilities, notably the railways, had in any event been state undertakings since their initial construction. In the absence of a national government, any German political pressure could only be expressed at *Land* level and Hesse did vote in December 1946 in favour of transferring its key industries into communal ownership. However, action was reserved to the western Allied military governments, and none acted to that end. Despite the imprisonment of a number of industrialists such as Krupp and Thyssen as war criminals (76 were arrested in November–December 1945 alone) and the confiscation of their holdings, these were returned to them within a few years. The British attempt to nationalise the Ruhr mines was vetoed by the Americans, who argued that such a move was the preserve of a future national government. The underlying structures in the western zones thus remained in place, with the partial exception of banking. The assets of the former *Reichsbank* were transferred on 1 January 1947 to a new Central Bank in each *Land* and the commercial banks were totally decentralised at the same time. The *Bank Deutscher Länder* was established in Frankfurt on 14 February 1948 as West Germany's central bank of issue and as the central reserve bank of the new *Land* Central Banks. The *Bank Deutscher Länder* became the *Bundesbank* on 1 August 1957, but a *Land* structure remains in its decision-making council, although it was streamlined in 1991 by a merger of some of the smaller units. In eastern Germany, Saxony alone has a *Land* bank.

West German business and industry were nevertheless to be rebuilt on western capitalist lines, subject to the concept of the social market economy (see *Glossary* for fuller particulars) and subject also to the growing impact of EU competition policy, which forbade the recreation of the cartels which had been a feature of prewar German industry.

Gross National Product

Year	DM millions
1950	98 100
1955	181 400
1961	331 400
1965	458 200
1970	679 000
1975	1 034 900
1980	1 485 700
1985	1 844 300
1989	2 260 400

Exchange rates

	£		DM		US$
1950	1	=	11.76	=	4.20
1958	1	=	11.76	=	4.20
1968	1	=	9.60	=	4.00
1969	1	=	8.78	=	3.66
1990	1	=	2.91	=	1.54

7.3 East Germany

Economic activity in the east resumed within a context of what might perhaps be described as 'conditional capitalism'. Progress was slow. Gross industrial output was 43 per cent of the 1936 level in 1946, 54.4 per cent in 1947 and 68 per cent in 1948, with labour productivity being about half the prewar level by 1948. As in the west, the largest concerns had been confiscated and much heavy industry shipped as reparations to Poland and the Soviet Union. The transformation of perhaps a quarter of industrial capacity into Soviet concerns (*Sowjetische Aktiengesellschaften – SAGs*) working directly for the Soviet economy was yet a further handicap. The greater part of what remained was nevertheless in private hands. Indeed, the confiscation and redistribution of what remained of the great estates associated in particular with the Junker Prussian landlords had increased the number of landowning farmers.

Heavy emphasis was, however, placed from the beginning on planning, as was also the case in France, and a two-year economic plan was launched covering the years 1949–51. The same period saw serious moves towards remodelling the economy, like the political system, on Soviet lines. The power and prestige of the Soviet Union were such that pressures within the communist movement for a distinctively German road to socialism were overruled as early as 1948 amongst fears of Titoism. This was somewhat ironic when both Marx and Engels were Germans and Lenin had always assumed that the worldwide communist revolution would break out in Germany. The adoption of the model devised by Stalin to meet specifically Soviet circumstances was arguably the earliest and the greatest of the mistakes to be enforced on the leaders of East Germany and, for that matter, on the leaders of other eastern European countries as well. Public ownership increasingly replaced private ownership, and by mid-1950 68 per cent of industrial production came from the public sector. Agriculture, however, remained for the time being in private hands.

The subsequent economic history of East Germany was essentially to be the history and comparative success or failure of its successive Soviet-style Five-Year Plans and their aims, targets, means and assessed level of achievement are summarised below. The leadership appears to have genuinely believed its own claims that East Germany was on the way to overtaking West Germany, with Ulbricht claiming at the 5th SED Congress in July 1958 that the per capita consumption of the main foods and of consumer goods would overtake the West German figure within a few years. This was partly the result of insulation from the reality of the outside world, partly an unquestioning faith in the predictions of 'scientific socialism'. That particular claim by Ulbricht was put forward in the presence of the ebullient Khruschev whose world-view was coloured by the inexhaustible resources of the Soviet Union. It could even have become a reality if East Germany had been able to use for itself, and to sell at world prices, its one great natural resource – the uranium deposits of Saxony and Thuringia. However, Soviet friendship for East Germany was never to extend that far.

First Five-Year Plan, for the period 1951–55

Launched at:	The 3rd SED Congress, 20–24 July 1950.
Aim	To raise the level of production to double that of 1936 within the period of the Plan.
Targets	To produce 1.8 million tons of iron ore, 1.5 million tons of brown coal (lignite), 205 million tons of ordinary coal and 4 million tons of hard coal. The creation of a merchant marine of 22 ocean-going vessels.
Means	The opening of new coal mines, the construction of a large ironworks on the Oder, and the exploitation of oil deposits. The collectivisation of agriculture.
Level of achievement	The Plan was conceived when east–west tension was at its height, focused on the Korean War, and the Stalinist orthodoxy of the development of heavy industry at the expense of any other consideration was unquestioned. It was therefore thrown off course by the more relaxed atmosphere following the death of Stalin in 1953, which contributed to the East German demonstrations of June 1953. Following Soviet precedent as usual, the East German government announced that consumer goods would enjoy higher priority in the plan for the latter half of the year and that food rationing would be ended in 1954, so as to reduce two of the more obvious sources of public discontent.

Second Five-Year Plan, for the period 1956–60

Launched at:	The 3rd SED party conference, 24–30 March 1956.
Aim	To place more emphasis on consumer goods.
Targets	To introduce a 40-hour working week in some industries, to increase pensions, and to permit the abolition of rationing.

Means   An acceleration of the collectivisation of agriculture.
Level of   Like its predecessor, the Second Plan underwent
achievement   significant amendment within its period of
                   application. The 5th SED Congress in July 1958 saw
                   an announcement of greater industrial specialisation,
                   particularly in chemicals, specialist machine tools,
                   optics and electronics.

The collectivisation of agriculture, which still extended to only 29 per cent of the agricultural land area in June 1958, was indeed accelerated, with the process being completed by April 1960. It was, however, counter-productive in that it stimulated a further wave of agricultural emigration to the west, and shortages of butter and vegetables had to be officially announced in October 1959.

The Plan was abandoned in 1959 in favour of the Seven-Year Plan below.

First Seven-Year Plan, for the period 1959–65

Launched by: The law of the Seven-Year Plan approved by the
                   Volkskammer on 1 October 1959.
Aims   To achieve as rapidly as possible maximum
                   productivity and world levels of production and
                   technology, so as to equal and then surpass West
                   Germany and prove the economic superiority of
                   the socialist system.

To integrate more closely the economies of East Germany and the Soviet Union. It had been agreed under a co-ordinated COMECON 'division of work' of 1956 that East Germany would concentrate on the production of brown coal (lignite), chemicals, high quality steels, potash and fertilisers.

Targets   To raise gross production to 188 per cent of the
                   1958 level by 1965, with particular emphasis on the
                   electricity, chemical, electro-technical and machine
                   building industries.

To increase foreign trade turnover from MDN14.5 billion in 1958 to a minimum of MDN25 billion by 1965.

Means   To increase lignite production to 278 million metric
                   tons by 1965 and to raise electrical output to
                   63 billion kwh, as against 34.9 billion in 1958.

To increase the output of iron ore to 2.1 million metric tons and of raw steel to 4.6 million metric tons, equivalent to increases of 121 and 152 per cent respectively.

To double the output from the chemicals industry on the basis of investment of MDN11 billion, with particular emphasis on plastics and synthetic fibres which are to increase by 334 and 581 per cent respectively.

To expand the merchant marine from 140,000 to 480,000 tons.

Level of achievement   The execution of the Plan was significantly affected by the introduction in 1963 of the 'New Economic System of Planning and Managing the Economy', an adaptation by Erich Apel and Dr Günter Mittag of the Liberman reforms in the Soviet Union. Its focus on a degree of decentralisation in economic decision making and on better management training significantly improved management morale, but its parallel emphasis on international competitiveness was still-born. The trade treaty with the Soviet Union of 3 December 1965 confirmed a pattern of more exports at low prices and negated the premise of the 'New System' that competitiveness was to be promoted by increased trade with the west. The suicide of Erich Apel, chairman of the State Planning Commission and a deputy chairman of the Council of Ministers, was believed to be a direct consequence.

The Plan period nevertheless saw real advances in output, even if quantity was not always matched by quality. Industrial production by 1965 was 43 per cent more than in 1958.

Five-Year Plan for the period 1966–70

Launched by: The law of the Five-Year Plan approved by the Volkskammer in May 1967.

Aim   To move the economy from extensive to intensive forms of production, so as to cope with the problems provoked by the unfavourable age structure of the population.

Targets   An overall annual growth rate of 6 per cent. The rebuilding of the centres of Berlin, Dresden, Leipzig and Karl-Marx-Stadt (Chemnitz).

Means	The rationalisation of production at individual plant level. Concentration on the petrochemical and electronics industries and on the manufacture of scientific instruments and machine tools.
Level of achievement	Although considerable progress was made, not least because the benefits were being felt of trained labour not being able to go to the west, considerable imbalances arose between supply and demand in the different sectors, and urban rebuilding made a disproportionate demand on the resources available.

Five-Year Plan for the period 1971–75

Launched at:	The 8th SED Congress, May 1971.
Aims	To enhance the integration of the East German economy with those of the other COMECON countries. (COMECON adopted a complex programme for greater economic integration in July 1971.) To achieve a more balanced pattern of production.
Targets	To secure continuity in the economy, and eliminate breakdowns and excessive overtime working. To achieve crop production of 4,400 kilograms per hectare by 1975.
Means	Investment of some M180 billion. Nationalisation of the remaining small businesses.
Level of achievement	The Plan was a success in that national income grew by 30 per cent from M108.3 billion in 1970 to M141 billion in 1975 and industrial production grew from M172 billion to M235 billion over the same period. The agricultural target was exceeded for fat-stock cattle, milk and eggs, making East Germany self-sufficient in basic foods other than sugar, fruit, vegetables and some bread grain.
	The nationalisation of the remaining small service businesses was not a success and the policy was reversed by a decree of 12 February 1976.

Five-Year Plan for the period 1976–80

Launched at:	The 9th SED Congress, 18–22 May 1976.
Aim	To ensure stable economic and social development by greater economic integration with the Soviet Union and other COMECON countries.

Targets   To raise national income during the Plan period by
                  some M200 billion to M830 billion and industrial
                  production over the five years by M400 billion to
                  M1,400 billion. To increase labour productivity in
                  industry by at least 30 per cent.

Means   Investment of M240 billion. An average annual
                  reduction of 2.8–3.0 per cent in the consumption
                  of energy and materials.

Level of   National income increased by 25.4 per cent over the
achievement   1971–75 Plan level but, at M812.5 billion, missed
                  the target of M830 billion. Industrial production
                  increased by 32.2 per cent and building production
                  by 27.7 per cent. Foreign trade turnover increased by
                  61 per cent, with 70 per cent of trade being with the
                  communist world. The volume of trade with the
                  capitalist world increased by 82 per cent.

                  By 1980 labour productivity had increased by
                  53.6 per cent overall compared with 1970 levels and
                  industrial productivity by 68 per cent over the same
                  period.

                  Agriculture performed less satisfactorily, with grain
                  being a particular problem. The difficulties were
                  attributed to overspecialisation by the agricultural
                  collectives.

Five-Year Plan for the period 1981–85

Launched at: The 10th SED Congress, 14 April 1981.

Aims   To promote scientific development with particular
                  regard to microelectronics, automation systems and
                  chemicals. To reduce the level of hard currency debt.

Targets   To increase national income, industrial production
                  and labour productivity by 28–30 per cent. To
                  increase the yield of arable farming by 6.9–8.1 per
                  cent.

Means   An increase in labour productivity, and more
                  efficient use of energy and raw materials. The
                  particular development of heavy industry and the
                  faster completion of investment projects. An increase
                  in the output of lignite both to reduce the level of
                  use of Soviet oil and to act as a substitute for East
                  Germany's exhausted hard coal reserves.

Level of   Aspects of Plan fulfilment were distorted during its
achievement   term by the urgency of paying off immediate hard

currency debts. Imports from western countries were reduced by some 30 per cent in 1982, and food shortages were caused by the dual burdens of exporting meat to West Germany, to obtain hard currency, and providing emergency food aid to Poland.

Overall underperformance in 1982 was, however, balanced by overperformance in 1983 and 1984, and longer-term hard currency loans of more than DM2 billion were successfully raised by consortia of West German banks, and further loans by other western consortia.

Both national income, at M1.087 billion for the five years, and gains in industrial productivity exceeded the set targets.

Five-Year Plan for the period 1986–90

Launched at:	The 11th SED Congress, 17–21 April 1986.
Aim	To introduce as chief priority advanced technology and automated systems into the production process.
Targets	To increase national income over five years by 24–26 per cent to more than M1.3 billion. To end the national housing shortage by 1990 through the construction or modernisation of 1,064,000 homes.
Means	Ever reducing unit consumption of raw materials, enhanced quality control, and higher investment. Increased productivity in the industrial sector of some 50 per cent and in the construction sector of some 30 per cent.
Level of achievement	The Plan was overtaken by the events of 1989–90, but there is no reason to believe that its overall objectives would not have been achieved. The essential economic problems were that quality (with some important exceptions) did not match quantity, that however much East Germany progressed West Germany progressed even more, particularly in the application of information technology, and that belated recognition of environmental constraints was undermining basic natural resources.

7.4 Economic data

Inter-German trade turnover

Year	East German Valuta-Mark (millions)
1960	1 585.9
1965	1 781.1
1970	3 428.6
1975	4 989.5
1980	7 305.6
1985	11 422.1
1986	10 703.0
1987	10 063.5
1988	10 118.0

Unemployment

Average annual unemployment in West(ern) Germany

Year	Total	%
1980	888 900	3.8
1984	2 265 559	9.1
1988	2 241 556	8.7
1990	1 883 147	7.2
1992	1 808 310	6.6
1993	2 270 349	8.2
1994	2 555 967	9.2
1995	2 564 906	9.3
1996	2 796 243	10.1

Average annual unemployment in East(ern) Germany

Year	Total	%
1992	1 170 261	14.8
1993	1 148 792	15.8
1994	1 142 090	16.0
1995	1 047 015	14.9
1996	1 168 821	16.7

SECTION EIGHT

Human statistics for East, West and united Germany

8.1 Population statistics

Population levels

Population levels – West and East Germany

Year	West Germany	East Germany
1946	46 190 000*	18 388 000**
1961	56 175 000*	17 125 000
1970	60 651 000*	17 058 000
1987	61 077 000*	16 641 000

* Census years
** 1950 figure

Population levels – united Germany

Year	United Germany
1990	79 365 000
1991	79 984 000
1992	80 594 000
1993	81 179 000
1994	81 422 000
1995	81 661 000
1996	81 896 000

Birth and death rates

Year	per 1000 population
Birth rate 1994	9.5
Death rate 1994	10.9

Foreign residents

Foreign residents by country of origin

Country of origin		Number at 31 December 1996
EU member states		1 839 900
including: Italy	599 400	
Greece	362 500	
Austria	184 900	
Portugal	130 800	
Spain	132 500	
Bosnia-Hercegovina		340 500
Yugoslavia (Serbia and Montenegro)		754 300
Croatia		201 900
Poland		283 400
Romania		100 700
Turkey		2 049 100
Morocco		82 900
United States		109 600
Iran		111 100

Total of all foreign residents including those from countries not listed above: 7 314 000.

8.2 Immigration

Chronology

1945

4 September. The German Red Cross estimates the overall number of refugees coming into the Soviet Zone from the east at some 13 million, a figure in line with Allied estimates of 12–14 million. Of these perhaps 2 million are from prewar Poland, including hundreds of thousands of *Volksdeutsche* resettled there by Hitler from as far as Estonia and Romania; 3 million from the Sudetenland; 4.5 million from Silesia; 2 million from East Prussia: and 1 million from East Pomerania. Saxony alone, with a population of 5 million, has 5 million extra refugees. Dr Arthur Werner, Berlin's chief mayor, tells them:

> You have been experiencing only a small part of what the Russians, Poles, Czechs and other peoples, as well as anti-Fascist Germans, have had to suffer for years under Hitler. There is no intention of returning evil for evil. We are doing everything possible to help you. You cannot remain in Berlin, and after staying here overnight, you must go into the countryside, which is ready for you . . .

7 October. The German refugee administration announces in Berlin that by agreement with Marshal Zhukov a further 4.5 million Germans will be evicted, from Poland 1.5 million (at the rate of 20,000 daily), from Czechoslovakia 2.25 million (at the rate of 6,000 daily), and 500,000 from Hungary. They will be distributed over the Soviet Zone.

It is announced on the same day that 2 million refugees each will be received in the British and the American Zones, a report which is denied in the House of Commons on 10 October.

19 October. The Polish ambassador in London doubts whether the movement of Germans out of Poland can be stopped by any human agency.

25 October. The city president of Wroclaw, formerly Breslau, announces that the 250,000 Germans still in Wroclaw will be evicted to Germany at the rate of 4,000 a week, and that within six months it will be the second city in Poland.

by the end of 1945. 623 resettlement camps have been established for some half a million people in the Soviet Zone.

by January 1947. 11.6 million people have arrived in the four zones, 4.3 million in the Soviet Zone, the largest proportion, where they make up a quarter of the population. The largest proportion is in Mecklenburg, where they represent 43 per cent of the population.

1950

4 March. The Allied High Commission directs the West German government to take all necessary steps to prevent the admission of any further German expellees from Poland.

23 June. Walter Ulbricht, deputy prime minister of East Germany, and Antonin Zapotocky, the Czechoslovak prime minister, declare in Prague that the resettlement of Germans from Czechoslovakia has been effected in an unalterable, just and permanent manner.

1959

2 January. The West German minister for refugees and expellees announces that some 400,000 refugees and repatriates are still in camps, including 215,000 in transit camps.

1970

18 November. The initialling of the Treaty of Warsaw is accompanied by a Polish government statement on 'measures for a solution of humanitarian problems'. It relates to the position of ethnic Germans still resident in Poland and indicates a more sympathetic approach to mixed and separated families.

1978

7 January. It is announced in Bucharest during an official visit by Chancellor Schmidt that over the following five years Romania will allow some 11,000 ethnic Germans to leave Romania annually.

1988

31 August. West Germany makes DM2.3 billion available over the next two years to build temporary housing for immigrants from the Soviet bloc and to organise resettlement programmes.

1989

27 April. Chancellor Kohl announces that ethnic Germans resident abroad will in future be discouraged from emigrating to West Germany and be encouraged to stay in their own countries.

1990

28 March. The cabinet decides to require ethnic Germans from Eastern Europe to apply for West German citizenship in their country of residence before coming to West Germany.

1991
21–23 November. President Yeltsin of Russia enters into a firm commitment while visiting Germany to create an autonomous republic for ethnic Germans near Volgograd, within the Russian Federation. It is a means of discouraging the 2 million ethnic Germans in the Soviet Union from emigrating to Germany.

Repatriates to West Germany from eastern Europe

Total repatriates
1957   114 000
1958   132 000

Repatriates from the Soviet Union
1957   1 078
1958   5 340

Ethnic Germans from eastern Europe settling in West Germany

From Poland
1986   27 188

From Romania
1986   13 130

From the Soviet Union
1976   9 700
1985   430
1986   753
1987   14 000 (approx)
1990   147 950

From all countries
1987   78 000 (approx)
1988   200 000 (approx)
1989   377 055
1990   397 095
1991   221 995
1992   220 530

East Germans registering as refugees in West Germany (including West Berlin)

1949	125 245
1950	197 788
1951	165 648
1952	182 393
1953	331 390
1954	184 198
1955	252 807
1956	279 189
1957	261 622
1958	204 061
1959	143 917
1960	199 188
1961	155 402 (before the erection of the Berlin Wall)
	51 624 (after the erection of the Berlin Wall)

Note: Some 177,204 East Germans took refuge via third countries between the erection of the Wall and the end of 1977.

East Germans permitted to emigrate permanently to West Germany

1962	21 500
1963	47 100
1964	39 300
1965	29 500
1966	24 300
1967	20 700
1968	18 600
1969	20 600
1983	7 729
1984	34 982
1985	18 752
1986	19 982
1987	11 459

Short-term visits by East Germans to West Germany

1980–84	Some 40 000 annually.
1985	66 000
1986	573 000
1987	1 290 000 together with more than 2 000 pensioners.

(*Note*: East German pensioners enjoyed much greater freedom to visit relatives in the West than did those of working age.)

Asylum seekers (principally from the former Yugoslavia, Romania and Turkey)

1989	121 000
1990	193 063
1991	256 112
1992	438 000
1993	322 599
1994	127 210
1995	127 937

SECTION NINE

Social statistics for East, West and united Germany

9.1 Social statistics

Living standards

East Germany – Real income per head, as a percentage of the 1950 level

Year	%
1949	91
1950	100
1955	170
1960	238
1965	272
1970	334
1975	439
1980	542
1985	666
1988	766

East Germany – Availability of selected consumer goods per 100 households

	Cars	Refrigerators	Washing machines	Televisions
1955	0.2	0.4	0.5	1.2
1960	3.2	6.1	6.2	18.5
1965	8.2	25.9	27.7	53.7
1970	15.6	56.4	53.6	73.6
1975	26.2	84.7	73.0	87.9
1980	38.1	108.8	84.4	105.0
1985	48.2	137.5	99.3	117.6
1988	54.7	159.6	107.3	125.2

West Germany – Average gross annual figures for income per head and wage per employed person

Year	Income per head DM	Wage per employed person DM
1950	1 588	2 911
1955	2 795	4 391
1960	4 252	6 150
1965	6 020	9 300
1970	8 725	13 773
1975	13 045	22 426
1980	18 669	29 922
1985	23 177	35 820
1987	25 634	38 299

Education

West Germany (1989–90)

	Schools	Pupils/students
Kindergärten	3 199	66 559
Primary	13 595	2 363 178
Post-primary	7 118	1 289 387
Special	2 770	247 965
Secondary modern	2 580	875 049
Grammar	2 460	1 562 966
Comprehensive	407	257 593
Vocational	7 543	2 401 090*
Universities	49	1 004 755

* Includes part-time students

East Germany (1988)

	Schools	Pupils/students/trainees
Pre-school	13 402	764 423
10-year comprehensive	5 207	1 953 012
12-year comprehensive	700	101 805
Vocational	955	359 308
Technical	237	157 513
Universities	9 ⎱	132 423
Higher education institutes	44 ⎰	

United Germany (1994–95)

	Schools	Pupils/students
Kindergärten	4 170	86 468
Primary	17 895	3 558 906
Post-primary	8 585	1 488 341
Special	3 390	382 946
Secondary modern	3 503	1 141 326
Grammar	3 152	2 148 702
Comprehensive	957	550 099
Vocational	9 178	2 427 751*
Universities	83	1 213 773

* Includes part-time students
(See also section 10.1 Education and re-education.)

Health

East Germany
Doctors: 13,268 (1950); 27,255 (1970); 33,894 (1980); 40,840 (1989)
Dentists: 7,176 (1950); 7,349 (1970); 9,709 (1980); 12,288 (1989)
Hospital beds: 187,219 (1950); 190,025 (1970); 171,895 (1980); 163,305 (1989)

West Germany
Doctors: 135,711 (1979); 188,225 (1989)
Dentists: 32,958 (1979); 40,805 (1989)
Hospitals: 3,286 (1979); 3,585 (1989)
Hospital beds: 712,055 (1979); 833,055 (1989)

United Germany (1995)
Doctors: 273,880
Dentists: 60,616
Hospitals: 2,325
Hospital beds: 609,123

Tourism

East Germany
Trade union holiday homes: 1,373 with 84,838 beds (1955); 1,260 with 89,522 beds (1970); 1,178 with 126,101 beds (1980); 1,166 with 137,078 beds (1985)

Enterprise-owned holiday homes: 72,242* with 839,545 visitors (1981)
Contracted private lodgings: 40,368 with 361,686 visitors (1981)
* 49,363 available throughout the year

West Germany (1989)
Accommodation sites: 48,000 with 1.8m beds
including hotels: 10,168 with 570,541 beds

United Germany (1995)
Accommodation sites: 51,635 with 2.23m beds
including hotels: 12,611 with 806,953 beds

9.2 The environment

Environmental concern appeared in Germany at a slightly earlier date than in many other European countries for several interrelated reasons. One was that the very division of Germany and the rearming of both states had generated a counter-current of pacifist, anti-nuclear sentiment in both East and West Germany during the 1970s, which provided an organisational base for the first environmental campaigners. Another was that the decentralised political structure of West Germany and its distinctive form of proportional representation permitted environmental groups to gain a political foothold in those areas where local conditions were generating serious environmental anxiety. Initially, that meant those where acid rain was clearly contributing to the death of whole forests (*Waldsterben*). The forests were themselves a third reason, because they are considered by very many Germans to be a key element of Germany's physical identity. To damage Germany's forests was to damage Germany itself. A fourth reason was that Germany, like the Nordic countries, had a tradition of the outdoors, manifested in such differing ways as naturism, vegetarianism and the youth hostelling movement, which was alien to the more Mediterranean countries.

For all these potential advantages, the environmentalists of the late 1970s and very early 1980s had an uphill task. Chancellor Schmidt was unsympathetic, fearing the implications for jobs, and in East Germany environmental data were state secrets. The growing intimacy of inter-German relations was causing its own problems, with West Germany exporting mountains of its waste to polluting East German tips such as Schöneberg, Rotehof, Deetz, Vorketzin and Schöneiche in return for hard currency.

The environmentalists' response was to unite as a political party, the Greens, in 1980 and they surprised many observers, including probably themselves, by securing 5.6 per cent of the vote and 27 seats in the 1983 Bundestag elections, compared with just 1.5 per cent in 1980. This level of success provoked both the CDU and the SPD to absorb the environment into their philosophies to a striking degree. The CDU gave it a specifically Christian flavour by arguing that care for the environment was an integral element of caring for God's creation, of which man himself was part. More controversially, it drew parallels between the care for life which endorsed environmentalism and the care for life which opposed abortion. The SPD, on the other hand, linked the environment with its traditional stress on solidarity, by extending worker solidarity to solidarity between generations and solidarity with the wider world.

Parallel with these philosophical adjustments there have been others of a structural nature. East Germany created a state environmental inspectorate within its existing ministry of environmental protection and water management with effect from September 1985 and West Germany created a specific environment ministry in 1986. The Bundestag went appreciably further on 30 June 1994 by amending the Basic Law so as to make it a state duty to protect the environment for future generations.

The environment is also a dimension of state policy in which first West Germany and now the united Germany have felt able to be assertive without the risk of being feared as aggressive. The first and most important expression of this was Willy Brandt's chairmanship of the Independent Commission on International Development Issues (the Brandt Commission), which contributed significantly to the Brundtland Commission concept of sustainable development. A similar level of international commitment was shown by the long-serving CDU environment minister, Dr Klaus Töpfer, and is being continued by his successor, Dr Angela Merkel. High priority has also been given to improving the European environment, not least through conventions with Germany's neighbours. The improvement of the Rhine was followed by that of the North Sea and, consequent to unification, by that of the Elbe. Even before unification, co-operation was growing with East Germany and Czechoslovakia on the restoration of the Elbe, but more widely, and with Poland as well, on mitigating the consequences of the intensive burning of lignite and sulphurous coals which was poisoning the countryside of all four countries.

In EU councils, Germany has consistently urged that policy be based on the twin pillars of the precautionary principle (*Vorsorgeprinzip*) and the principle that the polluter pays, which underlie domestic policy. The precautionary principle has often been resisted by countries such as Britain, who are reluctant to act in the absence of proof of harm.

The SPD is, however, more radical in its approach than the CDU. As early as the Bundestag elections of 1990 it endorsed the principle of environmental taxation, meaning not just the taxation of pollution but a switch in the whole burden of taxation from income and labour to resource consumption. It also supports, at least in principle, the pursuit of environmental goals through the internalisation of externalities, which means including the cost of a product to the environment in the cost of the product to the consumer, an initiative consonant with the environmental accounting initiatives of the European Parliament.

The SPD also sides with the Greens in calling for the phasing out of nuclear power. Green activism in this direction has been at its most intense in opposing nuclear reprocessing and the use of German sites for nuclear waste disposal, notably Gorleben. Localised opposition has led to the delay or cancellation of a number of nuclear projects over the years, including Brokdorf in Schleswig-Holstein, Kalkar near the Dutch border and Wackersdorff in Bavaria.

Germany has been a leader, nationally and in the EU, in the drive to reduce waste. Inspired originally by the shortage of disposal sites, it has increasingly put its weight behind a hierarchy of waste avoidance, reuse, recycling and only then disposal, culminating in the circular economy law (*Kreislaufwirtschaftsgesetz*), effective from October 1996, which has as its ultimate ideal the reduction of waste to zero. Such initiatives have often been controversial. The 'green dot' (*der grüne Punkt*) scheme to promote recycling initially prompted such a flood of material that it threatened to bankrupt the recycling industries in other member states. The maintenance of a 72 per cent quota for refillable drinks packaging under the EU packaging directive is bitterly opposed by the paper and board industries and Scandinavian governments, who see it as a barrier to trade within the EU single market. Similar objections were raised in 1984, when the German government made lead-free petrol obligatory for new cars from 1989, earlier than the EU target date.

Germany has similarly been a leader in the drive to reduce the emissions of greenhouse gases associated with global warming, strongly urging more demanding targets than those proposed by countries such as America. Delivering the target may, however, prove unexpectedly demanding. The contribution of transport to such emissions is growing as a proportion everywhere, and German unification has provided a considerable boost to the proportion of goods carried by road. Moreover, the CDU has always maintained that the autobahn speed limits which would reduce emissions – of nitric oxide by almost a fifth and of carbon dioxide by more than 420,000 tons a year – are politically unacceptable. In the industrial sector, reductions have been achieved in part through unification and the subsequent recession. Lastly, if public opinion prevents the construction of new nuclear power stations when present plant becomes obsolescent, the renewed reliance on coal will lead to a substantial increase in emissions from power stations.

SECTION TEN

Culture and the media

10.1 Education and re-education

Considering the condition of Germany in 1945, education was restored with quite remarkable speed in all zones. Most children returned to school in October of that year. The quality of the education initially received must, however, have been immensely variable. Very large numbers of teachers were dismissed because of their Nazi associations, with 28,000 out of a total of 39,000 going in the Soviet Zone alone. They were replaced by 40,000 'new teachers' drawn primarily from the working class, who profited from crash courses but essentially learned on the job.

The universities reopened one by one, but again with remarkable rapidity. Similarly again, large numbers of lecturers were dismissed, particularly in the Soviet Zone. The University of Leipzig lost 170 out of 222.

New textbooks were issued to schools to replace those issued under the Nazi regime, but elements of their content remained controversial for many years to come. As late as 12 February 1981, the West German council of culture ministers reaffirmed that Germany should be held to comprise all territories within the frontiers of 31 December 1937, despite a state treaty to the contrary signed by Chancellor Brandt in 1970. They also maintained that maps of West Germany should include maps of Berlin with the sectors differentiated, although the 1971 Four-Power Agreement had confirmed that West Berlin did not form part of West Germany. The decisions sparked protests in Czechoslovakia, East Germany, Poland and the Soviet Union.

Some Allied decisions were perhaps arbitrary. The use of Gothic text was banned for normal purposes, and the *Kaiser Wilhelm Gesellschaft zur Förderung der Wissenschaft*, formerly one of the world's largest scientific research organisations, whose presidents had included Einstein and Planck, was closed down in July 1946. It was to be reborn as the Max Planck Society for the Advancement of Science in February 1948.

Inevitably, education could not be divorced from politics, even in the west. The ten *Ministerpräsidenten* decided in January 1960, for example, that the history of the Nazi period should be taught more fully in schools in an attempt, unsuccessful as it turned out, to eradicate anti-semitism. Political considerations, however, were much to the forefront in the east, where education was seen as the key to producing a new type of human being. Tensions with the church inevitably resulted, although they never reached the intensity of those between the governments of Czechoslovakia, Hungary and Poland and the Roman Catholic Church. Some smaller religious groups such as the Jehovah's Witnesses and the Christian Scientists were banned in 1950 and 1951, but a church–state agreement with the mainstream churches was signed on 10 June 1953. It matured into an equilibrium with the protestant church under the slogan 'Not the Church against, nor the Church next to, but the Church in Socialism'.

The tensions, however, were always present. Some of the more significant centred on the Central Committee for the Consecration of Youth. Directed, as was the Society for the Promotion of Scientific Knowledge, by Johannes Becher, the culture minister (q.v.), it aimed to prepare 14-year-olds for a secular confirmation ceremony which would ultimately replace religious confirmation. Not surprisingly, it was declared incompatible with Christianity by the evangelical and catholic bishops, led by Dr Dibelius, the evangelical bishop of Berlin-Brandenburg. Nevertheless the church–state relationship endured in a way that it did not in, say, the Soviet Union between 1928 and 1942, partly perhaps because it was seen by the state as a necessary safety valve. The protestant churches certainly acted as a haven for, but also as a moderating influence on, the protest movements which began to gather force during the 1980s.

The corollary of renewed education and of re-education was the renewal of cultural links and cultural agreements, and these were signed by the two Germanys as the years advanced. Some were a screen for essentially political initiatives. The Society for the Study of the Culture of the Soviet Union established in 1947 had become the German–Soviet Friendship Society by 1949. The truly difficult one was the cultural agreement between East and West Germany, not signed until May 1986 after thirteen years of negotiation.

10.2 The arts

The goal of denazification was pursued by the Allies in the arts as vigorously as in any other sphere, but with very uncertain benefits or justification. The best known case is that of Wilhelm Furtwängler, the celebrated orchestral conductor who was accused of Nazi sympathies and banned from performing by the Americans in the autumn of 1945. His arguments that music was above politics and in any event a civilising influence on all who heard it have perhaps been more widely accepted since, and he was acquitted by a Berlin 'Denazification Court of Creative Artists' on 11 December 1946. Similar bans were placed on his fellow conductor, Hans Knappertsbusch, the pianist Walter Gieseking, the actor Emil Jannings and the author Friedrich Sieburg.

Such bans were progressively lifted in the west, where the state was not directly involved in artistic questions as such, but for the increasingly dominant Communists in the east, the arts not only had to be transformed like the rest of German society but were themselves an instrument of that transformation. The very title of 'The Cultural League for the Democratic Renewal of Germany', founded in the summer of 1945, made that purpose very clear. German artists and writers were themselves divided. Both Hermann Hesse and Thomas Mann (q.v.) had left Germany in self-imposed exile before the War, but were now old men. The Communists, however, enjoyed the support of a number of younger figures including Johannes R. Becher, the poet and first president of the Cultural League, Anna Seghers, the novelist, and most famously, Bert Brecht, the dramatist, who returned from the United States in 1947 and 1948 respectively.

Their role was never officially in question, although Brecht was a rebel by nature, and a successful one as well. The very first SED party conference in 1949 laid down that all cultural activity in East Germany was to be based on Marxism-Leninism and that the arts had an essential role in the achievement of the country's Two-Year Plan.

Their discretion was to be yet further limited by a resolution of the SED Central Committee in March 1951 which reflected the socialist realist principles already enunciated in the Soviet Union in 1948 in the so-called 'Zhdanov decree'. Under the terms of the resolution, entitled 'Against formalism in Art and Literature, for a Progressive German Culture', all artistic work should correspond to the Stalinist formula of 'national in form and socialist in content'. The pressure was, however, somewhat relaxed following the death of Stalin, with Ulbricht calling for greater tolerance in the arts in the autumn of 1953. Nevertheless, Erich Honecker was stressing at the 10th SED Congress in 1981 the need for 'partisanship' in literature and opposing 'all attempts to spread, in the guise of art, hostile ideologies directed against real socialism'. It is far from clear whether such constraints actually restrained or even stimulated the better writers, such as Christa Wolf (q.v.).

The paradox was that both the resolution and East German cultural policy in general also laid great stress on the German classics, as East Germany claimed to be the true inheritor of Germany's national ideals. This had some strange consequences. The guarded relationship between church and state did not prevent East Germany from celebrating the 500th anniversary of Martin Luther in some style. No more did the city's militaristic traditions prevent a major celebration of Berlin's 750th anniversary in 1987. Indeed, by 1984, both Frederick the Great of Prussia and Otto von Bismarck, the creator of a united Germany in the nineteenth century, had been rehabilitated.

Artists in the west had fewer problems, but were perhaps less prominent after the death of the masters of the earlier generation led by Thomas Mann. First Heinrich Böll and then Günther Grass (q.v.) emerged, however, as major novelists from younger generations, with the latter probably now being considered as Germany's most important living novelist. The best of his writing compares favourably with that of novelists in any other language in the same period.

Musical composition has been less persuasive. The steady flow of genius from Beethoven onward appeared to falter with the death of Richard Strauss, and both Paul Hindemith, who acquired American nationality, and Carl Orff (q.v.), were too individual in their approach to stimulate direct successors. The music of Stockhausen (q.v.) is so experimental that a lasting assessment of its artistic merit is unlikely for an appreciable time. Musical performance has, however, remained at an exceptionally high level. Wilhelm Furtwängler, together with Otto Klemperer and Bruno Walter, who had left Germany in 1933, kept tradition alive, but it was Herbert von Karajan, himself an Austrian, who progressively made the Berlin Philharmonic one of the world's most important orchestras, following his appointment as permanent artistic director on the death of Furtwängler in 1956. He was probably the most successful conductor on record the world has yet seen. A discerning albeit ruthless judge of talent, his protégés include the violinist, Annie-Sophie Mutter, and the Northern Irish flautist, James Galway.

The *Leipzig Gewandhaus*, for many years under the direction of Kurt Masur, was comparably pre-eminent in East Germany and could be counted the Berlin Philharmonic's nearest rival in Germany as a whole.

The legacy of the War has not yet been fully settled in the field of fine art. Although the Soviet Union decided as long ago as 1955 to return to the Zwinger Art Gallery in Dresden its outstanding collection of paintings, removed to the Soviet Union after the War, the return of other works of art has been slow and widely contested in what is now the CIS. Many in Russia consider that they represent an appropriate form of reparations for some of the suffering caused by German forces between 1942 and 1945, and should stay in Russia permanently as of right.

10.3 Press, radio and television

The media, like education, emerged from the ruins with considerable speed. The first German-edited newspaper in the western zones, *Frankfurter Rundschau*, came out on 31 July 1945. All the Allies were nevertheless mindful of the potential power of propaganda, in which Dr Goebbels had proved such a master, and applied a new framework to discourage any future successor.

In the western zones, the control of broadcasting was made a *Land* responsibility and kept away from any putative central government. In the Soviet Zone, the media were seen as instruments in the necessary transformation of society rather than as transmitters of public opinion, a role it must be said not totally alien to the free press of the west. The largest newspaper in East Germany was thus to be *Neues Deutschland*, the organ of the SED, just as the largest paper in the Soviet Union was *Pravda*, the organ of the Soviet Communist Party.

The free exchange of information and opinion was to remain restricted in the media as in the political sphere, and for the same reasons. As comparatively late as June 1979, the Volkskammer was making yet stricter the legal penalties for infringement of the already tight guidelines as to what was permitted.

The West German problem was of a different nature, and it was not a specifically German one. Although the control of broadcasting was the responsibility of the *Länder*, there was no constitutional bar on the concentration of press ownership, and the Axel Springer group in particular came to own in the 1960s a high proportion of popular titles. There was reason to believe that the bellicose tone of some of them contributed to the attempted murder of Rudi Dutschke (q.v.), and that was certainly the opinion of the protesters who targeted the Springer press and its premises. The group divested itself of part of its holding in the face of a degree of public concern which extended well beyond the student protest movement.

10.4 Restoration, rebuilding and new construction

The built environment was self-evidently a major victim of the Second World War, and German architecture suffered catastrophic losses. Outside the small towns and villages and a handful of larger places like Erfurt and Heidelberg, almost all the apparently historic buildings are heavy restorations or replicas of the original. Ironically, the major exceptions, at least proportionately, are the great Gothic cathedrals such as Cologne, Magdeburg and Ulm, which were allegedly valued by the Allied bomber crews as navigation marks. Destruction did not even finish at the end of the War, as the Soviet Union demolished the ruins of the Prussian royal palaces in Berlin and in the city of Potsdam, alleging that they were beyond restoration, but more plausibly because they represented a tradition which was both feared and hated.

Other priorities were so pressing that restoration did not start seriously for some ten years, which may well have been a blessing, as when work did start it was on an exceptionally painstaking basis. In the author's purely personal opinion, the reconstruction of the city centre of Münster, Westphalia, and of the cathedral in particular, alone fail to carry conviction. Successful examples are too numerous to mention, in East Germany as much as West, although progress there was appreciably slower. Particular reference, though, must be made to the city of Dresden. Known before the War as the Florence of the North, the city centre was totally devastated in the notorious raids of April 1945 and the ruins have been, and are still being, restored one by one with extraordinary attention to detail. The first, such as the Zwinger palace and art gallery, stood out as solitary landmarks in a wasteland, but a city centre has been recreated, albeit with a number of conspicuous gaps. The bombing was commemorated on 13 February 1985 by the reopening of the state opera house, which had been under restoration and reconstruction since the middle of 1977. The East German government never failed to emphasise that the bombing had been carried out by the British and American air forces. More recent controversies have also arisen. It was decided in the face of much opposition to reconstruct totally the great *Frauenkirche* (Church of Our Lady) which was known as the St Peter's of Protestant Christianity and which stood as nothing but a pile of rubble for some 50 years. Work started in 1993. Opponents of reconstruction maintained that the pile should be retained as a permanent war memorial more telling than the standing ruins of, say, the preserved *Kaiser-Wilhelm-Gedächtniskirche* in West Berlin.

Restoration in East Germany also revealed some of the same paradoxes as were noted in the section above on the arts. The restoration of Frederick the Great's palace of Sans Souci on the outskirts of Potsdam was arguably obligatory for any regime claiming to be the torchbearer of German cultural traditions, but its decision to restore the nineteenth-century palace in Schwerin of the Dukes of Mecklenburg, who exercised absolute power until 1918, was a much less obvious choice.

Unification in 1990 brought its own changes and controversies. Karl-Marx-Stadt quickly reverted to its old name of Chemnitz, and the traditional street names were gradually restored to those which had been renamed in honour of Marx, Engels, Grotewohl, Pieck and other members of the Communist pantheon. The progressive removal of the memorials to Marx, Engels and to East German workers' achievements has, however, met a measure of resistance, with a significant strand of opinion arguing that they are an integral part of the German heritage and cannot simply be wished away. Similar arguments may be raised over the future of East Germany's Palace of the Republic, which was constructed on the commanding site in East Berlin formerly occupied by the Prussian royal palace demolished after the War. A cultural as well as a political centre, it was closed after unification, allegedly because of danger from the asbestos contained in its cavity walling. Whether the erection of a mock-up of the original palace facade by the French artist, Catherine Feff, in 1993–94 is a hint of future plans remains to be seen.

Important as the restoration of Germany's architectural heritage has been, it has obviously been quantitively overshadowed by the volume of new building, necessitated as much by German development and growth as by the legacy of the War. The subject is too large to be discussed in any depth here, but any visitor to Germany will be aware of certain characteristics.

Early construction in what were to become East and West Germany was strongly influenced by the styles of the relevant occupying power. Frankfurt soon strongly resembled an American city such as Chicago, whereas Berlin, Magdeburg and other cities in the east acquired examples of the massive 'wedding cake' style of development associated with Stalin's Moscow. *Stalinallee* in East Berlin was the most publicised example. More realistic approaches emerged with the death of Stalin, and in the west the growth in German self-confidence helped to keep Frankfurt something of an exception. West Berlin emerged as an amalgam of some very high quality development such as Hans Scharoun's *Philarmonie am Kemperplatz*, opened in 1963, and Ludwig Mies van der Rohe's New National Gallery, opened in 1968 and also situated in the Tiergarten, and a great deal of brash commercial development which has worn comparatively poorly.

It proved a considerable disappointment to many East Berliners when the Wall was finally opened in 1989.

Of much wider relevance was the determined separation of pedestrians and traffic in an ever greater number of towns and cities. This was achieved much more successfully than has often been the case in Britain, although the main protagonist of the approach, Professor Colin Buchanan, was actually British. It has provoked an increasing acceptance that the car has no place in city centres and that a 30 km/hr speed limit is appropriate for residential areas.

The number of good new buildings is again too large to discuss here, but it is worth noting that the contribution of foreign, and not least British, architects has been substantial. Examples of the latter include Sir James Stirling's New State Gallery in Stuttgart of the mid-1980s and Sir Norman Foster's current reconstruction and restoration of the Reichstag building in Berlin as the future home of the Bundestag. The master plan for the whole new government quarter in Berlin is, however, the work of Axel Schultes, a German architect. The redevelopment of the Potsdamer Platz area, long symbolic of the division of Berlin and perhaps the new Berlin's prime commercial development site, is proceeding in accordance with a master plan prepared by the Munich architects, Hilmer and Sattler. Individual elements are in different hands, including those of Helmut Jahn for the Sony headquarters and of the Italian Renzo Piano, co-architect of the Pompidou Centre in Paris, for the Daimler Benz building.

SECTION ELEVEN

Biographies

The following list aims to be comprehensive, but cannot pretend to be complete. It does, however, normally exclude Austrians, German-speaking Swiss, and those Germans who relinquished German nationality as a result of the Nazi regime and the War. The latter group includes (with their adopted nationality in brackets): Marlene Dietrich (American), Albert Einstein (Israeli), Hermann Hesse (Swiss) and Paul Hindemith (American).

Adenauer, Dr Konrad: Born Cologne, 5 January 1876. Studied law at the Universities of Freiburg and Bonn. Joined the Centre (Catholic) Party, and was active in local government, becoming chief mayor of Cologne, 1917–33, when he was dismissed by the Nazis for refusing to fly the swastika from the city hall. As mayor, he was associated with the revival of the University of Cologne and the building between Cologne and Bonn of Germany's first autobahn. He lived in retirement throughout the Nazi period except for brief periods of arrest in 1934 and 1944.

Reappointed as chief mayor by the Americans in June 1945, he was summarily dismissed by the British four months later. He was one of the founders of the postwar CDU, becoming its chairman until 1966, and was particularly responsible for its pragmatism and openness to protestants which were to keep it in power for so long. In foreign policy he led West Germany along the path of integration with the west and, most significantly, of rapprochement with France, cemented by a warm personal relationship with General de Gaulle. He argued that a strong West Germany tied to the west was the best guarantor of German unification, but unification was not to come about until the very different world circumstances of 1989–90.

His warmth towards the west was never matched by a comparable sensitivity towards the peoples of central and eastern Europe, although he developed a working relationship with the Soviet Union. The SPD and the far right both argued against Adenauer at the time, maintaining that his policy of integration was fast making unification impossible. The argument re-opened in 1989–90 when the CDU maintained that Adenauer's determination had finally borne fruit, while the SPD argued that their policy of dialogue had made a key contribution to undermining the East German regime.

At the time of his resignation it was pointed out by the president of the Bundestag that he was the only head of government for the past 100 years to have stepped down after a long period in office, in peace and undefeated. It was a remarkable achievement, but due in part to a determination to hang on to power which in his last years was far from edifying and helped to undermine his successor, Erhard's, position as Chancellor. Intensely autocratic in his personal style, Adenauer generated adulation but also bitterness and hostility. His readiness to accept former Nazis back into German public life was one topic of particular contention. Died Rhöndorf, 19 April 1967.

Bangemann, Dr Martin: Born Wanzleben/Magdeburg, 15 November 1934. Educated at the Universities of Tübingen and Munich. A lawyer. Joined the FDP, 1963, and a member of the Bundestag, 1972–80 and 1986–89. Chairman of the FDP, 1985–88. A member of the European Parliament, 1973–84. West German economics minister, 1984–88. Member of the European Commission with responsibility for industrial affairs, and a vice-president, 1989–93. Responsible for industry, information technology and telecommunications in the Santer Commission, 1994–.

Becher, Johannes R: Born Munich, 22 May 1891. A founder member of the KPD who emigrated to the Soviet Union during the Nazi period. A significant poet, he was the author of the East German national anthem, *Auferstanden aus Ruinen,* to music by Hans Eisler. East German minister of culture from 1954 until his death. Died East Berlin, 11 October 1958.

Biedenkopf, Professor Dr Kurt: Born Ludwigshafen, 28 January 1930. Studied political science in the United States before entering the Universities of Munich and Frankfurt. Lecturer in law at the University of the Ruhr in Bochum, 1964–67, when he became rector. Joined the CDU, 1965, becoming general secretary, 1973–77. A one-time close associate of Franz-Josef Strauss. CDU *Land* chairman and Landtag leader in North Rhine-Westphalia on the death of Heinrich Köppler, 1980, serving as chairman until 1987.

Ministerpräsident of Saxony since 1990, he takes an independent line within the CDU. He is one of those who question the logic of introducing the single currency on schedule on 1 January 1999. He has often been seen as a possible successor to Chancellor Kohl, whom he treats with less than the usual deference (they were born in the same town in the same year!). He urged him in 1997 to think again about standing for election in 1998.

Böll, Heinrich: Born Cologne, 21 December 1917. Served on the eastern front in the Second World War, an experience which was to prove central to his art as a novelist. His most important novels include: *Das Brot der frühen Jahre* (*The Bread of our Early Years*) (1955); *Billard um halb zehn* (*Billiards at Half-Past Nine*) (1959); *Ansichten eines Clowns* (*The Clown*) (1963); *Gruppenbild mit Dame* (*Group Portrait with Lady*) (1971) and *Die verlorene Ehre der Katharina Blum* (*The Lost Honour of Katharina Blum*) (1974).

A Christian, a humanist and a pacifist, with an austere style tinged by satire, he forms an interesting contrast to his younger contemporary, Günter Grass (q.v.). Awarded the Nobel Prize for Literature, 1972. Died near Bonn, 16 July 1985.

Brandt, Willy: Born illegitimate as Herbert Ernst Karl Frahm, Lübeck, 18 December 1913. Joined the SPD at the age of nineteen. Fled to Norway in 1933 to escape the Gestapo and assumed the name Willy Brandt. Studied history at the University of Oslo, and practised journalism in Norway until the German invasion of 1940, and then in Sweden. A correspondent in Berlin for the Scandinavian press immediately after the War. Entered the Bundestag, 1949, and the West Berlin House of Representatives, 1950, becoming governing mayor of West Berlin, 1957–66. Chairman of the SPD, 1964–87, and honorary chair for life thereafter. Vice-Chancellor and foreign minister in the grand coalition, 1966–69, and Chancellor, 1969–74, when he resigned over the Guillaume affair. Awarded the Nobel Peace Prize for his Ostpolitik, October 1971. Elected president of the Socialist International, November 1976, holding office until his death. Chairman of the Independent Commission on International Development Issues (the 'Brandt Commission') from 1979, and, as such, one of the few German politicians and statesmen since 1945 to have played a major role on the non-German scene.

Widely admired in Germany and abroad, and indeed idolised by many in the SPD, he was nevertheless never really forgiven by many on the right for relinquishing German nationality during the Second World War. His real failing, however, was a certain weakness of personal judgement on individuals, most notably in the case of Günter Guillaume (q.v.) and then in that of Dr Margarita Mathiopoulos, whom he chose to replace Günter Verheugen as party spokesperson in March 1987, although she was neither a German citizen nor a member of the SPD. She subsequently declined the post.

Died Unkel, near Bonn, 8/9 October 1992.

Brecht, Bertolt: Born Augsburg, 10 February 1898. Generally considered Germany's greatest twentieth-century dramatist, his most important works were written before 1945. The most widely known, *Die Dreigroschenoper* (*The Threepenny Opera*) of 1928 is indelibly associated with the brittle atmosphere of interwar Berlin. A dedicated Communist who had fled Germany in 1933, he returned to East Berlin from the United States, where he had been investigated by the House of Representatives' 'Un-American Activities Committee' in 1948. His best known postwar play is *Der Kaukasische Kreidekreis* (*The Caucasian Chalk Circle*) written 1943–45 but not performed professionally until 1954. His company, the Berliner Ensemble, was given a permanent home in the *Theater am Schiffbauerdamm* in the same year and he received the Stalin Peace Prize in 1955.

His famed theatrical technique of *'Verfremdungseffekt'* (alienation effect) sat uneasily with the canons of socialist realism, just as his irreverent personality and satirical style frequently irked the East German government. His standing, nationally and internationally, however, was so high and his propaganda value so great that he was effectively untouchable. Died East Berlin, 14 August 1956.

Brentano, Dr Heinrich von: Born Offenbach, 20 June 1904. A member of the same family as Clemens von Brentano and his sister, Bettina von Arnim, the celebrated nineteenth-century Romantic writers. A lawyer. An opponent of the Nazi regime and arrested on a number of occasions, particularly in connection with the 1944 plot against Hitler. A founder member of the CDU in Hesse after the War. Entered the Bundestag, 1949, and was leader of its CDU group, 1949–55 and 1961–64. President of the Schuman Plan committee established to draft the constitution of what became the EEC, 1952–53. West German foreign minister, 1955–61, during which period he was an active exponent of European political unity and British membership of the EEC. Declined to be reappointed in 1961, fearing that his freedom of action would be circumscribed in coalition with the FDP. Died Darmstadt, 14 November 1964.

Carstens, Professor Karl: Born Bremen, 14 December 1914. Studied jurisprudence in Germany, France and America. A member of the Nazi storm troopers, 1933–35, and briefly of the Nazi Party, 1940. A wartime artillery officer. Nazi Party membership assessed as 'nominal' in 1945. Professor of constitutional and international law, University of Cologne 1969–73. State secretary in the ministry of foreign affairs, 1960–66, in the ministry of defence, 1966–67, and in the Chancellor's office, 1968–69. Entered the Bundestag, 1972, and elected chairman of the CDU/CSU Bundestag group, 1973. His candidacy as West German president provoked considerable opposition on the Left, not least from Chancellor Schmidt. President of West Germany, 1979–84. Died Meckenheim, near Bonn, 30 May 1992.

Dutschke, Rudolf (Rudi): Born Schönefeld, Luckenwalde, 7 March 1940. An active member of the Evangelical Church as a youth. Refused to serve in the East German army and was, therefore, denied a university education. Trained initially as an industrial salesman. Left East Germany, 1960. Entered the Free University of Berlin to study sociology, becoming the chief ideological spokesman of the *Sozialistischer Deutscher Studentenbund* (*SDS*), the radical student group. (See 'SDS' in *Glossary* for fuller particulars.) In his own terms he was a 'professional revolutionary' and a 'Marxist', basing his ideology on Marx, Engels, Lenin, Rosa Luxembourg, Mao Zhe Dong, and Herbert Marcuse. Equally opposed to what he saw as the corrupt capitalism of the west and the dictatorial authoritarianism of the east, he favoured a new sort of communism achieved through public awareness of past manipulation. Despite his espousal of 'active opposition', he never personally endorsed violence.

His attempted murder in West Berlin by Josef Bachmann, an alleged admirer of Hitler with a criminal record, in April 1968 provoked widespread protests and rioting in a large number of West German cities. Died Aarhus, Denmark, 24 December 1979.

Ebert, Friedrich: Born Bremen, 12 September 1894. Son of the first President of the Weimar Republic. An SPD official and then an SPD member of the Reichstag, 1928–33. Interned in three concentration camps during the Nazi period. Member of the SED executive committee, 1946, and the Politbüro, 1949. Mayor of East Berlin, 1948–67. Elected to the Council of State on its foundation in 1960 and Deputy Chairman, 1971. Deputy president of the Volkskammer, 1971. Died in East Berlin on 4 December 1979.

Erhard, Professor Ludwig: Born Fürth, Bavaria, 4 February 1897. Educated in Nuremberg and the University of Frankfurt. An economist. Staff member and then head of the *Institut für Wirtschaftsbeobachtung* in Nuremberg, 1928–42, and head of the *Institut für Industrieforschung* there, 1943–45. Untainted by Nazi associations. Bavarian minister for economic affairs, October 1945–December 1946. Chairman of the agency charged with currency reform in the western zones before the establishment of West Germany (*Sonderstelle Geld und Kredit*) and director of the bizonal economic council, 1948–49. Entered the Bundestag, 1949, becoming minister of economics in the first West German government and holding the post until 1963. He is credited with West Germany's postwar economic miracle and the concept of the social market economy. German representative on the board of governers of the World Bank. Elected to succeed Adenauer as Chancellor, October 1963, to the dissatisfaction of Adenauer, who allegedly sought subsequently to undermine his position. His coalition government collapsed in October 1966 with the resignation of its four FDP ministers over taxation questions. CDU chairman, 1966–67, and honorary chair thereafter. Died Bonn, 5 May 1977.

Fuchs, Dr Klaus: Born Rüsselsheim, 29 December 1911. Studied at the Universities of Leipzig and Kiel. Joined the KPD, 1930. Fled the Nazis and completed his studies in Britain, at the University of Edinburgh. A nuclear scientist. Briefly interned by the British at the beginning of the Second World War. Released to conduct research on the atomic bomb at the University of Birmingham, and acquired British nationality, 1942. Sent to America to work on the atom bomb project at Los Alamos, 1943.

Arrested and sentenced to fourteen years' imprisonment in 1950 for passing British atomic secrets to the Soviet Union. Stripped of British nationality, 1951. Released in June 1959, he travelled immediately to East Berlin and was granted East German nationality on 25 June. He was appointed deputy director of the East German Central Institute for Nuclear Physics, near Dresden, on 31 August. Died East Germany, 28 January 1988.

Genscher, Hans-Dietrich: Born Reideburg/Saalkreis, East Germany, 21 March 1927. Studied at the Universities of Halle and Leipzig. Emigrated to the west, 1952. Secretary-general of the FDP parliamentary group, 1959–65. FDP deputy chairman, 1969–74, and chairman, 1974–85. Minister of the interior, 1969–74, and Vice-Chancellor and minister of foreign affairs, 1974–92.

As foreign minister he successfully pursued the difficult balancing act of not only maintaining good relations with America and NATO, while drawing closer to France, but also of developing warmer relations with eastern Europe and the Soviet Union. Although he was frequently criticised by the CDU for departing from American policy in that respect, he was also sustained by West German anxieties that West Germany was the most likely site for any super-power conflict involving battlefield nuclear weapons.

Unerring for years, Genscher's first and greatest mistake was arguably to have urged the premature recognition of Croatia. In the opinion of many, though by no means all, the misjudgement precipitated, although it did not cause, the Yugoslav civil wars.

Gerlach, Manfred: Born Leipzig, 8 May 1928. Joined the LDPD, 1945, and member of the Saxony *Land* executive committee, 1947–52. Member of the Volkskammer, 1949–90. Mayor of Leipzig, 1950–53. Deputy chairman LDPD, 1951–53. Secretary-general of the LDPD, 1954–67. Chair of the LDPD, 1967–90. Chairman of the Council of State, 1989–90.

Graf, Steffi: Born Brühl/Mannheim 14 June 1969. Internationally famous tennis player and winner of Wimbledon 1988–89, 1991–93, and 1995–96. Olympic Gold Medal, Seoul, 1988, and Olympic Silver Medal, Barcelona, 1992. Beneficiary of an intensity of national pride, which Germans since 1945 have felt anxious about expressing in political form.

Grass, Günter: Born Gdansk (Danzig), 16 October 1927. Wounded in the Second World War and a prisoner of war. Shot to fame in 1959 with the publication of his first novel, *Die Blechtrommel* (*The Tin Drum*). It was followed by *Katz und Maus* (*Cat and Mouse*) in 1961 and *Hundejahre* (*Dog Years*) in 1963, completing a Danzig trilogy. Later novels include *Der Butt* (*The Flounder*) (1977); *Das Treffen in Telgte* (*The Meeting at Telgte*) (1979); *Kopfgeburten: oder die Deutschen sterben aus* (*Headbirths, or, the Germans are Dying Out*) (1980) and *Unkenrufe* (*The Call of the Toad*) (1992). He uses legend and fantasy, humour and absurdity, blended with the very different strands of the German postwar experience to create highly entertaining novels which are at the same time of considerable moral and political weight. Opposed Germany's rapid unification in 1990. He was an active member of the SPD but terminated his membership in disagreement with Party policy on asylum applicants after unification.

Günter Grass and Heinrich Böll (q.v.) are by common consent the two greatest novelists to have emerged from West Germany, but his works since the Danzig trilogy have nevertheless met with very varied critical acclaim. That is particularly true of his last, *Ein weites Feld* (*A Wide Field*) (1995).

Grotewohl, Otto: Born Brunswick, 11 March 1894. A printer by trade. Joined the trade union movement and the SPD in 1912. Active in the province of Brunswick after 1918 as a journalist, deputy, minister and regional chairman of the SPD. Elected to the Reichstag, 1925. Persecuted and imprisoned by the Nazis on several occasions. Chairman of the SPD Central Committee after the War. Joint chairman of the SED, 1946–54. Head of the constitutional committee of the German People's Council, 1947, a member of the SED Politbüro and Chairman of the East German Council of Ministers (prime minister), 1949–64. Signatory of the 1950 Görlitz agreement between East Germany and Poland, recognising the Oder-Neisse line as their mutual frontier. Intelligent and a good speaker, he probably anticipated that the SPD element in the SED would play a more positive role than proved possible in the Cold War climate of the late forties and the fifties. Died East Berlin, 21 September 1964.

Guillaume, Günter: A Berliner. Joined the SED, 1950, and employed in the East German publishing firm *Volk und Wissen*, 1951–55. Supposedly fled to West Germany, 1956, and then worked as a photographer. He became the leader of a spy ring at that time in Frankfurt. Joined the SPD, 1957, and was a district official, 1964–68. Attached to the Chancellery, 1970, and personal assistant to Willy Brandt, autumn 1972. In that capacity he dealt with Brandt's party correspondence. Attracted suspicion as early as 1956, but denied allegations that he was an East German agent as late as December 1972, and was not arrested for espionage until 24 April 1974. Brandt's resignation as Chancellor followed on 6 May. He was convicted of aggravated treason and sentenced to thirteen years' imprisonment at Düsseldorf on 15 December 1975. His wife, Christel, was imprisoned for eight years for aiding and abetting him.

The case gave rise to both independent and Bundestag commissions of inquiry which identified a lack of co-operation between the various security services and the extent to which the SPD had earlier been the victim of illegal counter-espionage activities.

Gysi, Gregor: Born East Berlin, 16 January 1948. Of Jewish origin, and son of Klaus Gysi, East German state secretary for religious affairs until 1988. President of the national lawyers' association and defence counsel for several well-known dissidents, including Rudolf Bahro and Robert Havemann (q.v.).

Elected leader of the SED, soon to change its name to the SED–PDS, on 8 December 1989. The Party under his leadership secured some unexpected electoral successes, and he handed it on to his successor, Lothar Bisky, in 1993 in much more robust form than might have been expected four years previously.

Hahn, Otto: Born Frankfurt am Main, 8 March 1879. Credited with the discovery of nuclear fission, and awarded the Nobel Prize for Chemistry in 1944. Taken to Britain in 1945, he returned to Germany, becoming president of the former Kaiser Wilhelm Society, now the Max Planck Society for the Advancement of Science. An outspoken opponent of nuclear weapons in postwar Germany, he signed the letter to Adenauer of 12 April 1957 (see section 1.2 for fuller particulars). Joint beneficiary of the Enrico Fermi Award, 1966. A friend of President Heuss. Died Göttingen, 28 July 1968.

Havemann, Professor Robert: Born Munich, 11 March 1910. Distinguished East German writer and scientist. Joined the KPD, 1932. Imprisoned by the Nazis in the same prison as Erich Honecker. A founder member of the SED, but his criticisms of Party policy given during university lectures resulted in his expulsion from both the university and the Party. Defended by Gregor Gysi. He nevertheless remained a Communist and wrote to President Brezhnev in October 1981 calling for the withdrawal of both Soviet and American forces from Germany. Died East Berlin, 9 April 1982.

Heidegger, Martin: Born Messkirch, Schwarzwald, 26 September 1889. Educated at the University of Freiburg. One of the leading exponents of existentialist philosophy. Actively pro-Nazi in the early 1930s, his enthusiasm grew more conditional, but he was forbidden from lecturing officially by the Allies in 1945. The ban was lifted and he gave a number of influential lectures, 1951–58, and produced a number of major works in the period up to 1962. Died Messkirch, 26 May 1976.

Heinemann, Dr Gustav: Born Schwelm, Ruhr, 23 July 1899. Studied at the Universities of Marburg and Münster, graduating from the latter as Doctor in Law, 1929. Legal adviser and subsequently company director in the steel industry, and lecturer in law at the University of Cologne,

1933–39. An opponent of the Nazis for religious reasons. A postwar founder of the CDU in Essen, where he was mayor, 1946–49. Minister of justice in North Rhine-Westphalia, 1947–48, and minister of the interior in Adenauer's first federal government from 1949. Left the government in October 1950, having been told by Adenauer that their views were 'so divergent that fruitful co-operation is no longer possible'. Their main disagreement was over West German rearmament, Heinemann having been a co-signatory with other Protestant leaders of an 'open letter' to Adenauer demanding that rearmament only be undertaken following approval in a popular referendum.

Advocated German neutrality first through the 'Emergency Union for European Peace' and then through the All-German People's Party, which he founded in 1952 after leaving the CDU. President of the synod of the German Evangelical Church, 1949–55.

Following the dissolution of his People's Party which had proved unsuccessful, he joined the SPD in 1957, re-entering the Bundestag in that year. Minister of justice in the grand coalition, 1966–69. Elected President of West Germany, 5 March 1969. Died West Berlin, 7 July 1976.

Henselmann, Hermann: Born Roszla (Harz), 3 February 1905. Trained in the Bauhaus, Weimar Germany's internationally famous socialist school of modernist architecture. Responsible for much of the socialist realist or Stalinist 'wedding cake' style of postwar rebuilding in East Berlin, Magdeburg and elsewhere, which, although widely derided, is in many cases wearing better than might have been expected. As chief architect of East Berlin, 1953–59, he returned for new construction to the functionalism in which he had been trained, but continued to oversee the restoration of Berlin's historic core focused on the Unter den Linden. The television tower near the Alexanderplatz, East Berlin's most conspicuous landmark, was his concept. Died 19 January 1995.

Hermlin, Stephan: Born Chemnitz, 13 April 1915, as Rudolf Leder. Of east European Jewish stock, he joined the KPD youth movement in 1931 and worked against the Nazis in Germany, 1933–36. He joined the German opposition groups in Paris in 1937 and then served with the French auxiliary forces before working on the land. Interned in 1942, he escaped to Switzerland in 1943. He returned to West Germany in 1945 but moved to East Berlin in 1947, where he joined the SED.

A substantial poet and translator, he was a stylistic modernist for whom the fight against Fascism was the essential motivation and theme. Although his apparently autobiographical writing was shown in 1996 to be less exactly rooted in his own life than had been thought, it is unlikely to diminish his long-term reputation.

Like Stefan Heym, he remained proud of East Germany's achievements and after unification joined the PDS. He was a strong critic of what he saw as the malign tendencies within the new Germany. Died 6 April 1997.

Hess, Rudolf: Born Alexandria, Egypt, 26 April 1894. Former Deputy Führer. Had flown to Scotland in 1941 in an apparent attempt to negotiate a compromise peace with Great Britain. Sentenced to life imprisonment at Nuremberg in 1946 for conspiracy to wage aggressive war and for crimes against peace. Refused to see his family for the first 28 years of his imprisonment in Spandau in the British sector of Berlin and was for 21 years its sole remaining prisoner. The Soviet Union rejected repeated appeals for his release on humanitarian grounds. Died Spandau, 17 August 1987.

Heuss, Professor Theodor: Born Brackenheim, Württemberg, 31 January 1884. An author and journalist, whose books were publicly burned by the Nazis. A member of the Reichstag for the Democratic Party until 1933. A postwar FDP chairman. Elected as West Germany's first President on 12 September 1949, despite objections from the SPD that he had voted for Hitler's Enabling Act in 1933. He enjoyed considerable popularity and served until 1959. Died Stuttgart, 12 December 1963.

Heym, Stefan: Born Chemnitz, 10 April 1913. Of Jewish origin. Real name Helmut Flieg. Left Germany, 1933, and served as an American army officer, 1943–45. He helped in the foundation of *Neue Zeitung* in the American Zone but was sent back to America because of his Communist views. He settled in East Germany in 1952. His novels include *Die Kreuzfahrer* (*The Crusaders*) (1958); *Die Papiere des Andreas Lenz* (*The Papers of Andreas Lenz*) (1963); *Lassalle* (1969); *Die Schmähschrift* (*The Libel*) (1970); *König David Bericht* (*The King David Report*) (1972); *Collin* (1979) and *Schwarzenberg* (*Black Mountain*) (1984).

A non-conforming personality who regularly criticised the East German official preference for ideological orthodoxy rather than literary merit, he won the National Prize in 1959. He was nevertheless attacked by Honecker in December 1965 over his book *Der Tag X* (*X Day*) dealing with the 1953 revolt, which Honecker would not allow to be published. His membership of the East German writers' union and his right to publish were suspended on 7 June 1979.

He became a prominent figure in the PDS after unification and a member of the Bundestag in the subsequent elections. As Father of the House, and thus entitled to give the initial Bundestag address, he annoyed Chancellor Kohl considerably by drawing attention to what he saw as the many positive features of life in East Germany before unification.

Honecker, Erich: Born Neunkirchen, Saarland, 25 August 1912. A roof tiler by trade. Joined KPD, 1929. In Moscow, 1930–31. An official of the Young Communist League of Germany from 1931. Imprisoned, 1935–45. Chairman of the Free German Youth (FDJ), 1946–55. An alternate member of the Politbüro, 1950, and full member, 1958. First Secretary of the SED, 1971–76, and General Secretary, 1976–89. Chairman of the Council of State, 1976–89. Directly involved in the erection of the Berlin Wall in 1961, he was also believed to be a key figure in the fall of Dubček in Czechoslovakia in 1968.

Although intolerant and narrow in outlook, and little loved, he was in some respects a genuinely tragic figure. Proud of his creation and blind to its deficiencies, he lived to see it disintegrate around him in the events of 1989/90. He moved initially to the Soviet Union, but with its collapse he took refuge in the Chilean embassy in Moscow in December 1991 to avoid extradition. On his returning to Germany he was charged with manslaughter in May 1992. He made just one statement to the court on 3 December 1992 denouncing the proceedings, which had opened on 12 November 1992, as a political spectacle and defending the decision to build the Berlin Wall. He accepted political responsibility for the killings at the border, although he regretted them, but felt no 'legal and moral guilt'. Following criticism of his detention by the Constitutional Court (see section 2.8 for fuller particulars), the charges against him were dropped on 13 January 1993 and he was allowed to join his wife in Chile. That decision was itself annulled by a higher court on 27 January, before the charges were definitively suspended on 7 April 1993. There was widespread suspicion that the government did not wish the trial to proceed because it feared embarassing revelations about the intimacy of earlier inter-German relations. He had claimed to be looking forward to it. Died in exile in Chile, 29 May 1994.

John, Otto: Born Marburg, 19 March 1909. Involved in the 1944 officers' plot to assassinate Hitler and in contact with the British intelligence service, MI6, through Kim Philby. Escaped, and subsequently came to England where he worked for British intelligence and the BBC. Assisted in the prosecution at Nuremberg of the Generals von Brauchitsch, von Manstein and von Runstedt, and in the defence of Ernst von Weizsäcker, former head of the German foreign office. Appointed first head of the West German security service (*Bundesamt für Verfassungsschutz*), 1950, on British initiative. Disappeared from West Berlin in July 1954 to reappear in East Berlin where he bitterly attacked Chancellor Adenauer as a neo-Nazi revanchist. Returned to West Germany on 12 December 1955, where he was immediately arrested, but claimed that he had been drugged and kidnapped. He was nevertheless sentenced to four years' imprisonment. He was granted a pension by President Richard von Weizsäcker in 1986 and died in Austria on 26 March 1997. The truth of his motivation may never be known.

Kelly, Petra: Born Günzburg/Danube, 27 November 1947, of an American father and German mother, she acquired the name Kelly from her American stepfather. Went to America in 1960, studying international politics and relations at the American University, Washington, 1966–70. A volunteer in the offices of Senators Robert Kennedy and Hubert Humphrey in their election campaigns. Studied political science and European integration at the University of Amsterdam, 1970–71. Worked for the EC in Brussels from 1971. Joined the SPD when Brandt was Chancellor, but resigned in 1979 in protest against policies on nuclear defence, health and women. She emerged in the 1970s as one of the key leaders of the embryonic Green movement, and became the best known of the leaders of the Green Party when it was founded in 1980. Appointed at that time as one of the three members of the executive committee, her formal eminence was constrained by the Green hostility to a hierarchical leadership structure. Nevertheless, she was widely perceived as the most charismatic member of the Green movement worldwide. Apparently disillusioned with factional infighting and discouraged by wider developments, she was killed by her companion, the retired army general, Gert Bastian, in what is believed to have been a suicide pact. Died Bonn, 19 October 1992.

Kiesinger, Dr Kurt: Born Ebingen, Württemberg, 6 April 1904. Studied law, history and philosophy at the Universities of Tübingen and Berlin. A lawyer in Würzburg and then Berlin. Joined the Nazi Party, 1933, and remained a member, although he subsequently claimed to have been disenchanted by the suppression of the brown shirts in 1934 and never held Party office. Seconded to the foreign ministry during the War. He was completely exonerated by Allied and West German denazification courts in 1946 and 1948 respectively, and indeed claimed to have established a resistance group in the ministry. Resumed legal practice in Tübingen after the War. Joined the CDU and entered the Bundestag, 1949. Chairman of the Bundestag foreign affairs committee, 1954. Closely associated with the cause of European unity, he represented the CDU group in the Consultative Assembly of the Council of Europe, 1950–58. *Ministerpräsident* of Baden-Württemberg, 1958–66. CDU chairman, 1967–71. Elected West German Chancellor, 1 December 1966, and served until the end of the 'grand coalition', autumn 1969. Died Tübingen, 9 March 1988.

Kinkel, Dr Klaus: Born Metzingen/Reutlingen, 17 December 1936. Educated at the Universities of Bonn, Cologne and Tübingen. A lawyer.

Head of the external intelligence service, 1983–87. Minister of justice, 1991–92, briefly as an independent but then for the FDP, and foreign minister, 1992–. A controversial chair of the FDP, 1993–95. Deputy Chancellor, 1994–.

Kohl, Dr Helmut: Born Ludwigshafen, 3 April 1930. Member of the CDU *Land* executive committee, 1955. Completed studies in history, law and politics at the University of Heidelberg with a doctoral thesis on the foundation of the political parties after the Second World War, 1958. A lawyer by profession. Entered the Rhineland-Palatinate Landtag as its youngest member, 1959, and member of the federal executive committee of the CDU, 1964. CDU *Land* chairman for the Rhineland-Palatinate, 1966, and *Ministerpräsident*, 1969. The youngest West German *Land* leader in office. Defeated by Rainer Barzel in the election for CDU federal chairman, 1971, but successful, 1973. Resigned as *Ministerpräsident*, 7 October 1976, and entered the Bundestag, where he was elected CDU/CSU Bundestag group chairman. Elected as West Germany's youngest Chancellor to date, 1982, following a constructive vote of no confidence by the Bundestag on his SPD predecessor, Helmut Schmidt.

Now Germany's longest-serving postwar Chancellor. A gifted party manager, who has triumphantly survived numerous predictions of his political demise, he has increasingly adopted a presidential style, leaving everyday politics to his ministers and advisers. If he wins in 1998, he will become Europe's longest-serving leader of government since 1945. A determined pro-European, motivated in part perhaps by the death of his elder brother at the front in the last months of the War, he took part in the breaking down of the border fences with France at Weissenburg in Alsace in 1948. He can, however, be insensitive on occasion, particularly to the sensibilities of Germany's eastern European neighbours. He compared Gorbachev with Goebbels and in 1993 supported Steffen Heitmann, the hardline justice minister in Saxony, as the CDU candidate for the 1994 presidential elections. He is already clearly one of the most significant European leaders since the War, and if EU economic and monetary union proceeds as planned and proves a success, he could even be seen in retrospect as the most significant.

Krenz, Egon: Born Kolberg, 19 March 1937. First Secretary of the Free German Youth (FDJ). Elected to the Politbüro as a candidate member, 1976, and as a full member, 1983. Member of the Council of State, 1981, and secretary of the SED central committee in charge of security, 1983. Elected a deputy chairman of the Council of State by the Volkskammer, 15 June 1984. Succeeded Erich Honecker as General Secretary of the SED on 18 October 1989 and as Chairman of the Council of State on

24 October 1989. Resigned as Chairman of the Council of State and of the National Defence Council on 6 December 1989.

Accused after unification of manslaughter in connection with the 'shoot to kill' policy, he was sentenced to six and a half years' imprisonment in Berlin on 25 August 1997, although the policy had been determined before 1983 and may never have been discussed during his Politbüro membership. An appeal is pending.

Lafontaine, Oskar: Born Saarlouis, 16 September 1943. Studied physics in Bonn and Saarbrücken, graduating in 1969. Joined the SPD, 1966. Mayor of Saabrücken, 1976. *Ministerpräsident* of the Saarland, 1985–, where he has been an exponent of red–green environmentalist politics. Unsuccessful SPD Chancellor candidate, 1990. His stabbing in the neck by Adelheid Streidel, a schizophrenic with no political motive, at an election rally in Cologne on 25 April 1990, seemed, although he was discharged from hospital on 2 May, to reduce his drive and poise for several years. Chair of the SPD, 1995–.

Lagerfeld, Karl: Born Hamburg, 10 September 1938. Internationally celebrated fashion designer. With Chloé in Paris, 1963–83. Appointed chief designer to Chanel, also in Paris, 1983. Associated with bold, flamboyant and innovative designs, and highly sensitive to street trends, he opened his own fashion house under his own name in 1984. His star model for much of the 1990s, Claudia Schiffer, is perhaps Germany's best-known face abroad.

Lübke, Dr Heinrich: Born Enkhausen (Meschede), 14 October 1894. A civil engineer and agricultural expert by profession. Centre Party member of the Prussian Landtag, 1931–33, and arrested by the Nazis on a number of occasions thereafter. Minister for food and agriculture in the postwar *Land* government of North Rhine-Westphalia. Entered the Bundestag for the CDU, 1947, and appointed to the West German cabinet, 1953. In that capacity he wrote the 'Green Plan', aimed at rationalising and improving the performance of West German agriculture.

President of West Germany, 1959–69. Shaken in the latter part of his term of office by his reported involvement in a building concern which constructed concentration camps during the War. Died Bonn, 6 April 1972.

Mann, Thomas: Born Lübeck, 6 June 1875. Germany's greatest twentieth-century novelist, his creative life stretched from 1900 to well into the postwar period. Awarded the Nobel Prize for Literature in 1929. His most political novel, *Doktor Faustus*, appeared at the end of the War and summarised the German tragedy, and is in marked contrast to his final novel, the highly humorous *Bekenntnisse des Hochstaplers Felix Krull* (*The Confessions of Felix Krull, Confidence Man*) of 1954. Died 12 August 1955 near Zürich, Switzerland.

Meinhof, Ulrike: Born Oldenburg, 7 October 1934. One of the four key members of the RAF and widely seen as its main ideologist. Active as a student in anti-nuclear demonstrations and in support of a totally neutral Germany. A journalist and television worker, she was converted to violence by the attempted assassination of Rudi Dutschke in April 1968. Arrested in 1972, she was sentenced to eight years' imprisonment in November 1974 for complicity in the freeing of Andreas Baader. The main trial, in which she was to be accused of multiple murder, attempted murder and bank robbery, opened on 19 August 1975. She committed suicide, aged 41, on 9 May 1976. Although there were immediate allegations of murder, they were not sustainable. Her death provoked widespread demonstrations and violence both in Germany and abroad. (See also section 2.9 and 'Red Army Faction' in *Glossary*.)

Niemöller, Rev. Dr Martin: Born Lippstadt, Westphalia, 14 January 1892. A U-boat commander in the First World War. A Lutheran pastor in Berlin, 1930. An outspoken critic of the Nazis, with particular reference to their anti-Semitism and restrictions on the churches' freedom to preach. Imprisoned in Sachsenhausen and Dachau concentration camps, 1937–45. A pacifist, he became a leading opponent of West German rearmament and of the Vietnam War. President of the World Council of Churches, 1961–68. Awarded the Soviet Union's Lenin Peace Prize, 1967, and the West German Grand Cross of the Order of Merit, 1972. Died Wiesbaden, 6 March 1984.

Nuschke, Otto: Born Frohburg, 23 February 1883. A newspaper editor and a Progressive People's Party member of the Prussian Landtag before 1933. Forbidden to operate as a journalist by the Nazis and twice arrested by the Gestapo. Helped to found the CDU in the Soviet Zone after the War, becoming chairman, 1948–57. A prominent member of the Evangelical Church. Unlike Lemmer and Kaiser, he was willing to co-operate with the SED, and he became a deputy prime minister on the foundation of the East German state in 1949. Died Nieder Neuendorf, 27 December 1957.

Oberländer, Professor Dr Theodor: Born Meiningen, 1 May 1905. A member of the Nazi party and a *Hauptsturmführer* in the S. A. (brown shirts). An assistant professor at the University of Königsberg (now Kaliningrad), but demoted to the University of Greifswald in 1937 following a disagreement with the *Gauleiter* of East Prussia on the treatment of non-German minorities. Forbidden to lecture, placed under house arrest, and expelled from the Nazi party, 1943, after his dissent from Nazi policy towards eastern Europe.

Officially 'denazified' in 1947, he became a member of the Bavarian *Land* government, and from 1953 of the West German government. Accused by Communist sources in the autumn of 1959 of participating in the massacre of Polish Jews and Ukrainians by the German army in Lvov in 1941. Resigned as West German minister for refugees on 4 May 1960, but denied the charges, requesting the appointment of a Bundestag committee of inquiry to allow him to clear his name. He was exonerated by an international committee of former anti-Nazi Resistance fighters in The Hague, and by a CDU court of honour during 1960, but was formally accused by the Soviet Special State Commission for Investigation of the Crimes of the German Fascist Invaders on 5 April 1960 of 'crimes against peace, war crimes, and crimes against humanity'. The Commission's report maintained that Dr Oberländer had been appointed by Rudolf Hess in 1934 to head the 'League of Germans in the East' and had served as an expert on eastern affairs in the *Abwehr*, the German counter-intelligence service. In particular, he had personally shot fifteen Soviet prisoners in their cell in October 1942. He was tried *in absentia* in East Germany on 20–29 April, found guilty, and sentenced to life imprisonment with hard labour. The East German proceedings were, however, officially ignored in West Germany and Professor Oberländer returned his court summons unopened.

West Germany's own criminal proceedings were dropped on 26 September 1960 for lack of evidence despite extensive enquiries, but Professor Oberländer was not reinstated in the cabinet.

Ollenhauer, Erich: Born Magdeburg, 27 March 1901. Chairman of the SPD, 1952–63. His leadership coincided with the long period of predominance of the CDU and in retrospect he appears an essentially transitional figure between Schumacher and the younger generation which was to be led by Brandt and Schmidt. His chairmanship nevertheless saw the adoption in 1959 of the Bad Godesberg Programme whereby the SPD unequivocally endorsed market principles, although it was Herbert Wehner, rather than Ollenhauer, who was the key architect from the older generation. Vice-president of the Socialist International from 1951 and president in 1963. Died Bonn, 14 December 1963.

Orff, Carl: Born Munich, 10 July 1895. Composer. His best-known work, *Carmina Burana*, was written in 1938, but its final sequel, *The Triumph of Aphrodite*, did not follow until 1953. His works, which are principally choral, are strongly rhythmic and use Greek and Latin texts to powerful effect. Died Munich, 29 March 1982.

Pieck, Wilhelm: Born Guben, 3 January 1876. A carpenter. Joined SPD, 1895. A Spartacist and co-founder of the KPD, 1918, of which he remained a life-long leader. A KPD member of both the Prussian Landtag, 1921–28 and 1932–33, and the Reichstag, 1928–33. Held senior positions in the executive committee of the Communist International from 1928. Went into exile in France, 1933, and elected KPD chairman by the Brussels Conference of the KPD in 1935 for the duration of Ernst Thälmann's imprisonment. (Thälmann died in Buchenwald on 28 August 1944, allegedly as the result of a US air raid.) A co-founder with Ulbricht of the 'Free Germany' National Committee (NKFD), Moscow 1943. Returned to Berlin in July 1945 with the goal of uniting the KPD and SPD, for which he was to be given the sobriquet of 'architect of unity'. Chairman of the KPD, then joint chairman of the SED, 1946–54. Elected President of East Germany, 11 October 1949. Personally jovial, he was ailing and possibly even somewhat senile as early as 1946 and spent many of his later years effectively in retirement. Died East Berlin, 7 September 1960.

Ratzinger, Cardinal Joseph: Born Marktl, Bavaria, 16 April 1927. Professor of basic theology in Bonn from 1959 and Münster from 1963. Head of the Congregation for the Doctrine of the Faith, or Holy Office (once the Inquisition), at the Vatican, 1982–. A strict opponent of what is perceived as heresy by Pope John Paul II and the Roman Catholic Church's traditionalist wing. He is feared by many in the Church and is a particular opponent of Dr Hans Küng, the radical Swiss theologian. He is widely seen as a 'kingmaker' in the conclave which will choose Pope John Paul II's successor. Cardinal Ratzinger inspired the excommunication of Father Tissa Balasuriya, a Sri Lankan theologian, in 1997, the first priest to be excommunicated since 1953.

Rau, Johannes: Born Barmen, 16 January 1931. A publishing firm manager, 1954–67. SPD member of the North Rhine-Westphalia Landtag, 1958. *Land* science and research minister, 1970–78. SPD *Land* party leader, 1977, and *Ministerpräsident,* May 1978–98. Deputy leader of the SPD at the national level, 1982–, and SPD Chancellor candidate for the 11th Bundestag elections in 1987.

Remer, Otto Ernst: Born 1912. As the major in charge of the Berlin security unit, he played a leading role in the suppression of the 1944 plot against Hitler, for which he was promoted to major-general. Despite remaining an ardent Nazi, he was untouched by postwar denazification courts and tribunals and helped to found the *Sozialistische Reichspartei* (SRP) in 1950, which sought to relaunch the Nazi movement. He repeatedly attacked the 1944 conspirators as the 'criminals of 1944', and received three months' imprisonment in March 1952 for slandering them as traitors. The SRP was banned in the October of the same year.

He nevertheless continued in his attempts to revive Nazism, to insist on the 'Auschwitz lie', and to promote anti-semitism. He was eventually sentenced to 22 months' imprisonment for 'inciting hate, violence and racism', but fled to Spain when his appeal was rejected in 1994. He was protected there by fascist sympathisers and a court ruling that the crimes of which he had been convicted in Germany had no Spanish equivalent. Died Marbella, Spain, 5 October 1997.

Scheel, Walter: Born Solingen, Ruhr, 8 July 1919. Trained as a banker. War-time fighter pilot. A member of the Nazi Party. Joined FDP, 1946. Member of the Landtag of North Rhine-Westphalia, 1948, and of the Bundestag, 1953. Minister of Economic Co-operation, 1961–66. Chairman of the FDP, 1968. Foreign minister and Vice-Chancellor in the Brandt governments of 1969 and 1972. President of West Germany, 1974–79.

Schmidt, Helmut: Born Hamburg, 23 December 1918. Served on the eastern front and in the Ardennes during the War, being awarded the Iron Cross. Joined the SPD, 1946. Studied economics at the University of Hamburg. Entered Bundestag, 1953. Senator for the interior in the Hamburg *Land* Government, 1961. Re-entered the Bundestag, 1965. Leader of the SPD Bundestag group, 1968, minister of defence, 1969–72, and minister of finance, 1972. Succeeded Brandt as Chancellor on his resignation in 1974. On appointment, he was considered an Atlanticist, particularly on economic and monetary affairs. Served until 1982 when the loss of FDP support presaged a constructive vote of no confidence in favour of Helmut Kohl of the CDU, a figure he appeared to have underestimated. He retired from politics in 1987.

Highly respected in Germany and in later years more popular than his party, his somewhat didactic manner was not always so popular with foreign leaders, particularly President Carter of America. His close working relationship with President Giscard d'Estaing of France, however, was as significant for Franco-German relations as that formed later by Chancellor Kohl with President Mitterand. Since unification in 1990, Schmidt has sought to promote greater understanding between the peoples of East and West Germany.

Schröder, Gerhard: Born Mossenberg, 7 April 1944. Initially a building labourer and commercial employee. Joined the SPD, 1963. Studied law and was admitted as a lawyer, Hannover, 1976. *Ministerpräsident,* Lower Saxony, 1990–. A rival within the SPD of first Rudolf Scharping and now Oskar Lafontaine, and generally considered a Eurosceptic, he was the choice for the Chancellor candidature in 1998.

Schumacher, Dr Kurt: Born Kulm, 13 October 1895. Educated at the Universities of Halle, Berlin and Münster. Lost his right arm on active service in the First World War. A political editor for the SPD from 1920, he was a member of the Württemberg legislature, 1924–31, and of the Reichstag, 1930–33. Arrested by the Nazis, he spent ten years in Dachau concentration camp, followed by periods of release and re-arrest. An organiser of the SPD immediately after the War, he became chairman of the western SPD in May 1946. Associated with opening the Party towards the centre, he distrusted and was distrusted by the KPD. Failing in health, he lost his left leg in 1948 and grew increasingly hostile towards his opponents. Leader of the opposition in the Bundestag from 1949, he was suspicious of Adenauer's policy of integration with the west, fearing that it would delay German unification. He was aptly described by Adenauer as 'a nationalist on a Marxist basis'. Died Bonn, 20 August 1952.

Seghers, Anna: Born Mainz, 19 November 1900, as Netty Railing. Joined the KPD in 1928, briefly arrested, 1933, and fled to France. Jewish. Returned in 1947 as probably the leading East German novelist of her generation. Most important postwar novels are *Die Toten bleiben jung* (*The Dead Stay Young*) (1949), a penetrating if weakly structured portrayal of the nihilism of the Nazi period, and *Die Entscheidung* (*The Decision*) (1959). Sometime chairman of the German Writers' Association. Died 1 June 1983.

Speer, Albert: Born Mannheim, 19 March 1905. Pursued a successful career as a writer on his experiences as Hitler's chief architect, 1933–45, and minister of armaments and war production, 1942–45, following his release from Spandau prison in 1966. He had pleaded guilty at Nuremberg and been sentenced to twenty years' imprisonment. Died London, 1 September 1981.

Speidel, Gen. Hans: Born Metzingen, Württemberg, 28 October 1897. A professional soldier serving in both World Wars. Chief of Staff to Field-Marshal Erwin Rommel, April 1944. Involved in the 1944 Officers' Plot against Hitler, but the Nazis were unable to find any incriminating evidence. Appointed as one of the two first lieutenant-generals in the new *Bundeswehr*, 1955, and the first German to be NATO C.-in-C. Allied Land Forces in Central Europe, 1957–63. Died Bad Honnef, near Bonn, 28 November 1984.

Stockhausen, Karl-Heinz: Born Mödrath, near Cologne, 28 August 1928. Composer. Studied under Milhaud and Messiaen. He is probably the most important living exponent of the atonal approach to composition pioneered by Schönberg. He has also explored electrophonic music, and some of his works have a marked element of improvisation.

Stolpe, Dr Manfred: Born Stettin (now Szczecin, Poland), 16 May 1936. Chairman of the consistory of the Evangelical Church in Berlin-Brandenburg from 1982 and a member of the Human Rights Commission of the World Council of Churches from 1976. Joined the SPD in July 1990 and elected *Ministerpräsident* of Brandenburg, 1 November 1990. He is the only SPD *Ministerpräsident* in what was East Germany to have served since 1990. Harsh accusations by his opponents that he had been too closely associated with the previous regime have never appeared to impress the electorate.

Stoph, Willi: Born Berlin, 8 July 1914. Member of the Politbüro, 1953, and Deputy Chairman of the Council of State, 1964. First Deputy Premier, July 1962, and Chairman of the Council of Ministers (prime minister), September 1964, on the death of Otto Grotewohl. He held the post until 3 October 1973, when he was elected Chairman of the Council of State. He served again as Chairman of the Council of Ministers from 1976, resigning with his whole cabinet on 7 November 1989.

Strauss, Franz-Josef: Born Munich, 6 September 1915. Studied economics at the University of Munich. Served on the Russian front in the Second World War until declared unfit for active service as a result of severe frostbite. A founder member of the CSU and one of its first Bundestag members. Appointed minister without portfolio by Adenauer, 1953, then minister of nuclear affairs, and defence minister, 1956, in which capacity he oversaw West German rearmament. Resigned over the *Spiegel* affair, 1962. (See *Glossary* for fuller particulars.) Finance minister in the grand coalition, 1966–69. Announced on 25 November 1977 that he would stand in the 1978 Bavarian Landtag elections and seek election as *Ministerpräsident.* He was duly elected on 6 November 1978. CDU/CSU Chancellor candidate in the 1980 Bundestag elections, but his poor showing, particularly in North Germany, led him to announce that he would henceforth confine himself to Bavaria and the CSU. He was nevertheless aggrieved not to replace Hans-Dietrich Genscher as foreign minister under Chancellor Kohl after 1982.

A highly intelligent man who in practice was much more flexible and readier to make contacts with the east than might have been supposed, he was compromised by his own right-wing rhetoric and lack of sensitivity to the feelings of others, particularly in the less confrontational post-Adenauer years. Temperamentally akin to the proverbial 'bull in a china shop', he was never fully trusted outside Bavaria, where he was immensely popular. The autocratic instincts which could verge on the dictatorial and betrayed him in the *Spiegel* affair undermined his ambition to be Chancellor in 1980 and later to become foreign minister. Died Regensburg, 3 October 1988.

Strauss, Richard: Born Munich, 11 June 1864. Germany's most famous twentieth-century composer, but almost all his output dates from before 1945. His *Four Last Songs* for high voice and orchestra to poems by Hermann Hesse and Joseph von Eichendorff, however, appeared in 1948. He remained active as an orchestral conductor until his death. Died Garmisch-Partenkirchen, 8 September 1949.

Ulbricht, Walter: Born Leipzig, 30 June 1893. A carpenter. Joined SPD, 1912, served in the War, 1915–18, a Spartacist, then a member of the KPD. KPD official, 1921–23. Studied in Moscow, 1924. Member of the Reichstag, 1928–33. In exile in Paris, 1933–38, and in Moscow, 1938–45. Returned to Berlin to organise the KPD, 1945. Elected SED deputy chairman, 1946. General Secretary of the SED from July 1950, a deputy chairman of the Council of Ministers, 1949–55 and First Deputy Chairman, 1955–60. First Secretary of the SED, July 1953–May 1971. Chairman of the SED, May 1971–August 1973. Chairman of the Council of State, 1960–73.

An orthodox Stalinist with a talent for organisation, but neither an orator nor a theoretician, he appears to have triumphed over his more liberal rivals in 1957 by persuading Khruschev after the 1956 Hungarian revolt that he was both totally in control of East Germany and totally committed to the interests of the Soviet Union. His fall came when he tried to discourage the rapprochement between West Germany and the Soviet Union by asserting East German interests.

A dour and seemingly humourless figure, he appears to have been increasingly deceived by his own propaganda, losing much of his contact with reality in the process. This was not perhaps totally surprising in view of his life history. Even his beard was alleged by some to be modelled on Lenin's. Little was known of the private man except for his enthusiasm for amateur sport including table tennis. Died East Berlin, 1 August 1973 and was given a muted state funeral.

Vogel, Dr Hans-Jochen: Born 3 February 1926. Educated at the Universities of Marburg and Munich. A prisoner of war. A lawyer. Governing mayor, Munich, 1960–72. Chairman of the Bavarian SPD, 1972–77. West German minister of regional planning, housing and urban development, 1972–74. Minister of justice, 1974–81. Governing mayor of West Berlin, January–June 1981. SPD Chancellor candidate in the 1983 Bundestag elections and SPD chair, 1987–91. A precise and cautious figure, he forms an interesting contrast to his more extrovert brother, Bernhard, CDU *Ministerpräsident* of Thuringia since 1992.

Wehner, Herbert: Born Dresden, 11 July 1906. Member of the SPD, 1923–27, and of the KPD, 1927–46. In exile during the Nazi period. Rejoined the SPD, 1946, and member of the Bundestag, 1949–83. One of the authors of the 1959 Bad Godesberg Programme, whereby the SPD embraced the market economy. Minister for all-German affairs in the 'grand coalition', 1966–69, and leader of the SPD Bundestag group from 1969. Considered as one of the party's three guiding spirits, with Brandt and Schmidt, in the period of SPD government 1969–82. One of the Communists and leftists referred to in the 'Generals' affair'. (See *Glossary* for fuller particulars.) Died Sweden, 19 January 1990.

Weizsäcker, Richard Freiherr von: Born Stuttgart, 15 April 1920. (Son of Ernst, state secretary in the foreign ministry, 1943–45, and ambassador to the Vatican, 1943–45. Sentenced to seven years' imprisonment in 1949 for war crimes, but released in 1950.) Initially in industry, but a lawyer in Bonn from 1967. Joined the CDU, 1950. President of the German Evangelical Church Congress, 1964–70, and from 1969 a member of the council of the German Evangelical Church and of the central and executive committees of the World Council of Churches. A deputy chairman of the CDU Bundestag group from 1973 and a member of the CDU executive committee from 1975. CDU candidate for the federal presidency in 1974. Governing mayor of Berlin, 1981–84, and president of West Germany and, with unification, Germany, 1984–94.

He proved to be one of the most admired and respected of German presidents, combining real moral stature with considerable personal charm and charisma.

Wolf, Christa: Born Landsberg (Warthe), 1929. Probably East Germany's leading novelist, her best known novels are: *Der geteilte Himmel* (*Divided Heaven*) (1963); *Nachdenken über Christa T* (*The Quest for Christa T*) (1968) and *Kindheitsmuster* (*Patterns of Childhood*) (1976). *Der geteilte Himmel* observes the canons of socialist realism, but was as highly acclaimed in West as in East Germany. *Kindheitsmuster* was, when it appeared, considered the best East German novel yet written. Her later novels include *Kassandra* (1983), *Störfall* (*Accident*) (1987), *Medea* (1996) and the controversial *Was bleibt* (*Something Remains*). Originally written in 1979 but published only in 1990, it generated the violent literary argument known as *Der Literaturstreit*. She was elected a candidate member of the Central Committee of the SED in 1963, a fact which was to be held against her by the right after unification.

Wolf, Markus: Born 1913 of Jewish origin. Brother of Konrad Wolf, a well-known East German film director (died 1982). Taken by his parents to the Soviet Union, 1934–45, where he received his education and was an officer in the Soviet army. Head of the East German military intelligence service. An urbane and sophisticated figure, he is believed to have been the model for John le Carré's famous fictional spy, Karla, and in real life is assessed as perhaps the most successful spymaster of the postwar era. He was to allege in 1997 that even Franz-Josef Strauss, the former West German defence minister and chairman of the CSU, and Herbert Wehner, leader of the SPD Bundestag group from 1969, had been amongst his informants.

He was charged with treason and espionage in September 1992 and sentenced to six years' imprisonment in Düsseldorf in December 1993, but released on appeal when the Constitutional Court in May 1995 found that agents who had operated exclusively from East German territory could not now be prosecuted in the federal courts. (See section 2.8 for fuller particulars.)

The authorities responded by charging him on 7 January 1997 with charges of abduction, coercion and causing bodily harm from 1955 onwards, but secured only the award of a two-year suspended sentence and an order to donate DM50,000 to charity.

Zaisser, Wilhelm: Born Rotthausen, 19 January 1893. Active in the Spanish Civil War as 'General Gomez'. Chief of the *Volkspolizei* (People's Police). A member of the Politbüro and East German minister of state security, 1950–53. In establishing the East German secret police (*Staatssicherheitsdienst – Stasi*), he followed the principles of his friend and mentor, Lavrenti Beria, the Soviet police chief, and his own dismissal was prompted by the arrest and summary execution of Beria in the Soviet Union, following the death of Stalin. Died East Berlin, 3 March 1958.

SECTION TWELVE

Glossary

Basic Law (*Grundgesetz*)   Effectively the West German, and now the German, constitution. (See section 2.2 for fuller particulars.)

Basic Treaty   In full, the 'Treaty on the Bases of Relations between the Federal Republic of Germany and the German Democratic Republic'.

Signed 21 December 1972 by its principal negotiators, Egon Bahr, minister without portfolio with special duties at the Federal Chancellery, for West Germany, and Dr Michael Kohl, Secretary of the Council of Ministers, for East Germany. The original intention of signature by Brandt and Stoph had been abandoned, because of 'difficulties in fixing a date'. (See section 1.2 for the provisions of the treaty.) Came into force 20–21 June 1973. The West German Federal Constitutional Court in Karlsruhe rejected on 31 July 1973 a case brought by the *Land* government of Bavaria that the treaty was contrary to the Basic Law. (See section 2.8 for further particulars.)

The Basic Treaty contained a West German note to the protocol that 'questions of nationality are not regulated by the treaty'. East Germany in a separate statement on the protocol declared that it was assuming that the treaty would ease the settlement of the nationality question. For this and related reasons, interpretation of the treaty remained contentious in the years after its signature.

Berlin blockade   The name given to the interruption of Allied land communications with West Berlin by the Soviet Union in 1948. (See section 5.2 for fuller particulars.)

Berlin: sectors of occupation   The Soviet Sector comprised the districts of Mitte (with most of Berlin's historic core focused on the Unter den Linden up to and including the Brandenburg Gate to the west), Friedrichshain, Köpenick, Lichtenberg, Pankow, Prenzlauer Berg and Weissensee. The British Sector comprised the districts of Tiergarten (with the Reichstag and some of Berlin's more fashionable quarters focused on the Kurfürstendamm), Charlottenburg, Spandau and Wilmersdorf. The American Sector consisted of Kreuzberg, Neukölln, Schöneberg, Steglitz, Tempelhof and Zehlendorf and the French sector of Reinickendorf and Wedding.

***Bezirke* of East Germany**   The *Länder* in what had become East Germany were replaced from 1952–89 by *Bezirke* (districts), comparable in many respects with the French *départements* on which they may well have been modelled. The *Bezirke* were:

1. Berlin	9. Leipzig
2. Cottbus	10. Magdeburg
3. Dresden	11 Neubrandenburg
4. Erfurt	12 Potsdam
5. Frankfurt (an der Oder)	13. Rostock
6. Gera	14 Schwerin
7. Halle	15 Suhl
8. Karl-Marx-Stadt	

Bonn The West German capital and now the seat of the German government until the move to Berlin by the year 2000. Originally a modest university city, its population had grown to some 280,000 by 1989. The reasons for its choice as the West German capital were never totally clear. It was indeed central, it was in the bizone, and the more obvious choices were mutual rivals. Some alleged that it was the one German city to which Hitler had never paid an official visit. The more cynical noted that it was highly convenient from Konrad Adenauer's private villa. He certainly opposed the alternative of Frankfurt when it was debated by the Bundestag. Be that as it may, the choice proved highly successful in political terms and the Bundestag decision of 1991 to move to Berlin was taken by a majority of just seventeen votes. One key consideration was certainly the fact that West Germany, assuming that the reunification was not a realistic possibility for the foreseeable future, had embarked on a major expansion and rebuilding programme for the whole government quarter in the late 1980s. The Bonn–Berlin law of 1994 therefore provides that some functions will remain in Bonn and that attempts will be made to direct new institutions there. One current possibility is a new UN environmental organisation.

Despite the period charm of parts of the city centre and its attractive Rhineside location, it has never acquired sophistication or vibrancy. One American journalist notoriously described it as 'half the size of a Chicago graveyard and twice as dead'. In practice, it is becoming absorbed into an ever more continuous ribbon of development along the Rhine stretching from Bad Godesberg in the south as far north as Düsseldorf.

Bundesrat The upper house of the German federal parliament, with its membership nominated by the individual *Länder*. As its approval is needed for all legislation, it is a major force for consensus politics.

Bundestag The lower house of the German federal parliament, currently in Bonn but due to move to Berlin in 1999. It is elected by direct adult suffrage.

East German sporting achievements The East German government self-consciously used sport as a means of gaining international prestige and recognition, starting when political recognition was specifically witheld outside the Communist world. It proved outstandingly successful and sport was the one field in which East Germany consistently outshone West Germany. East German participants won nine Gold Medals at the summer Olympics in Mexico City in 1968, twenty in Munich in 1972, 40 in Montreal in 1976, 47 in Moscow in 1980 and 37 in Seoul in 1988.

Extra-parliamentary opposition   See SDS.

Flick affair   The Flick affair was West Germany's largest political-financial scandal and was noteworthy for the extent to which it penetrated to the heart of all three major political parties at the highest level. At various times it appeared that it might bring down even Chancellor Kohl and Vice-Chancellor Genscher, and badly sully the reputation of former Chancellor Brandt.

It broke with an announcement in late February 1982 that Eberhard von Brauchitsch, chief executive of the Friedrich Flick holding company and deputy president of the federal employers' association (BDI), would not become association president as he was under investigation for bribing senior politicians, including Dr Otto Graf Lambsdorff, economics minister (FDP), and Hans Matthöfer, finance minister (SPD). That was followed in March by an announcement from the federal prosecutor's office that it was investigating some 700 cases of suspected tax evasion concerning all three major political groupings. Politicians concerned, besides Dr Lambsdorff and Hans Matthöfer, included: Josef Ertl, minister of food, agriculture and forestry (FDP); Rudolf Eberle (CDU); Hans Gattermann (FDP); Walter Leisler Kiep (CDU); Manfred Lahnstein, finance minister from April 1982 (SPD); and Horst Ludwig Riemer (FDP).

Eberhard von Brauchitsch maintained that Flick had given DM4.5 billion to the SPD during the 1970s in an attempt to reduce criticism of it by the left wing of the party. It was also alleged that Dr Lambsdorff had accepted bribes on four separate occasions to grant Flick tax exemptions. Dr Lambsdorff was indicted on corruption charges in December 1983, and formally committed for trial on 2 July 1984 together with Dr Hans Friderichs, his predecessor as West German finance minister (FDP). Dr Lambsdorff denied all charges of bribery, but admitted that he had broken the law as FDP treasurer in North Rhine-Westphalia in 1976 and 1977 by not declaring Flick donations. He resigned as West German economics minister on 26 June 1984.

The affair then spread to Dr Barzel, formerly CDU chairman. The press alleged that Flick had paid some DM1.7 billion between 1973 and 1979 to a Frankfurt law firm to which Dr Barzel was an adviser, and that the firm had paid him a comparable amount in the same period. Dr Barzel resigned as president of the Bundestag on 25 October 1984.

An all-party Bundestag inquiry into the affair ran from January 1984 to mid-1985. Willy Brandt denied receiving cash directly or indirectly from Flick between 1975 and 1980, but Chancellor Kohl admitted receiving DM155,000 in cash from Eberhard von Brauchitsch, whom he described as a personal friend, although he denied any purchase of influence. The Flick records appeared to show that both Chancellor Kohl and Franz-Josef Strauss had received donations substantially in excess of what they admitted.

The trial of Dr Lambsdorff, Dr Friderichs and Eberhard von Brauchitsch was delayed by the filing of tax evasion charges in addition to the original bribery charges, which led to the resignation of Dr Friderichs from the Dresdner Bank, of which he had become chief executive, with effect from 27 March 1985. It finally opened on 29 August 1985, but the bribery charges were effectively dropped on 23 July 1986. On 17 February 1987, however, all three men were found guilty of tax evasion, with Dr Lambsdorff being fined DM180,000, Dr Friderichs DM61,500 and von Brauchitsch DM550,000 with a two-year suspended prison sentence.

The case had a decidedly adverse impact on public confidence in the probity of the banks and of the political parties, particularly the FDP. It did not, however, mark the end of the political careers of either Dr Barzel or Dr Lambsdorff.

'Generals affair'   Lt.-General Walter Krupinski and Major-General Karl-Heinz Franke were dismissed by the West German minister of defence on 1 November 1976 following a reunion on 23 October of Luftwaffe and former Wehrmacht officers at which the guest of honour was Hans-Ulrich Rudel. The most decorated wartime pilot, Rudel was later associated with a number of far-right political groups such as the Socialist Reich Party, the German Reich Party and the NPD. The generals had said informally that there could be no objection to Rudel's attending a military reunion when such 'leftists and Communists' as Herbert Wehner, the leader of the SPD Bundestag group, were politically active.

Hermann Schmidt, the then Bundestag secretary of state in the ministry of defence, had reluctantly attended the reunion and his role led to calls for his resignation. He was not reappointed by Chancellor Schmidt in December 1976.

Glienicke Bridge (*Glienicker Brücke*)   The bridge on the outskirts of Potsdam, which marked the border between East Germany and West Berlin. It was the favoured spot for sensitive spy exchanges, notably that of Gary Powers, the American U2 pilot.

Hallstein Doctrine   So called after Dr Walter Hallstein, state-secretary in the West German foreign ministry in the 1950s. Promulgated after

Chancellor Adenauer's visit to Moscow in September 1955, when West Germany and the Soviet Union established full diplomatic relations. The Doctrine, as first defined by the Chancellor in the Bundestag on 22 September 1955, maintained that West Germany alone was authorised to speak for the German people as a whole and that any country which established diplomatic relations with East Germany would be deemed to have committed an 'unfriendly act'. It was strengthened by a statement on 9 December 1955 that the West German government would break off diplomatic relations in such circumstances, and that provision was applied against Yugoslavia in 1957 and Cuba in 1963.

The Doctrine was somewhat ambiguous in that it did not extend to consular or trade agreements, perhaps because the latter had been entered into by such close partners as France. Some saw a measure of philosophical inconsistency in West Germany claiming to talk for all Germans when Austria had its own recognised separate government. The Doctrine, which had complicated West Germany's relations with its eastern neighbours and with the developing world, was abandoned under Brandt's Ostpolitik.

'Hitler diaries'   *Der Stern*, the popular West German magazine, claimed on 22 April 1983 to have acquired 60 volumes of Hitler's diaries, covering the period 22 June 1932 – mid-April 1945, together with separate volumes on Rudolf Hess's flight to Britain in May 1941 and on the 20 July 1944 officers' bomb plot against Hitler's life. *Der Stern* also claimed that they had been authenticated by experts including the British Lord Dacre, more widely known as Professor Hugh Trevor-Roper. On that basis, *The Sunday Times*, the quality British newspaper, published the first of a series of excerpts on 24 April, having paid *Der Stern* $400,000 for the rights. Many other experts, however, disagreed with Lord Dacre and he claimed on 25 April that he had misunderstood the way in which they had been obtained and that he too now doubted their authenticity. *Der Stern* continued to insist they were genuine until early May, but nevertheless agreed to submit volumes to expert scrutiny. The West German Federal Archive concluded from their research that they were forgeries and denounced them as such on 6 May.

As well as refunding the royalty paid by *The Sunday Times*, *Der Stern* dismissed Gerd Heidemann, the journalist who had allegedly obtained the diaries and to whom they had paid DM8 million, accusing him of fraud. Two of the magazines three chief editors resigned on 7 May.

Allegations were made in West Germany at the time that the forgeries had been executed in East Germany for political motives, but they were denied there and were never substantiated.

The trial of Gerd Heidemann and of Konrad Kujau, the actual forger, opened in Hamburg on 21 August 1984. Heidemann claimed that he had acted in good faith, whereas Kujau alleged that Heidemann had commissioned him to forge the diaries. Heidemann was sentenced to four years eight months and Kujau to four years six months on 8 July 1985.

Kennedy speech in Berlin   Delivered at the Schöneberg Town Hall in West Berlin in the presence of Chancellor Adenauer and mayor Willy Brandt on 26 June 1963 and including the ringing declaration that '*Ich bin ein Berliner*', it instantly became one of the defining images of the postwar era. Of its public success and of the reassurance given to West Berliners as to their future security there can be no doubt, but in some respects it was rather unreal. For all its rhetorical questioning: 'And there are some who say in Europe and elsewhere that we can work with the Communists. Let them come to Berlin', there were a number of existing agreements between East and West Germany on posts and transport, not least in West Berlin where East Germany operated the suburban railway network. The number of such agreements was to grow over the years, culminating first in the Basic Treaty and then in the growing pattern of relationships charted in section 3.1. It was also to be the case that West Berlin often spearheaded such working with the Communists for primarily humanitarian reasons.

The famous '*Ich bin ein Berliner*' is a curiosity. In standard German, at least, it means 'I am a doughnut'. The correct German would have been '*Ich bin Berliner*'. Whether Kennedy delivered the whole passage impromptu and the error was his, or whether it was a drafting error, or even a slip of the tongue, is not known. It has never been felt to matter.

Kiessling affair   Lt General Günter Kiessling was appointed a Deputy Supreme Commander of the Allied Forces in Europe in 1982 but was dismissed from his post by Manfred Wörner, the West German minister of defence on 31 December 1983 because a report of 6 December had alleged that General Kiessling had contacts in two homosexual bars in Cologne. This was strenuously denied by the general, who asked for formal disciplinary proceedings to be brought against him so that any accusations could be formally discussed, and on 16 January his lawyer announced that he was bringing charges against the four anonymous witnesses 'for false accusation and slander'. The military counter-intelligence service (*Militärischer Abschirmdienst – MAD*) proved unable to substantiate the allegations, although it had first alerted the minister in mid-1983, and the formal disciplinary proceedings were dropped on 26 January 1984. The general similarly dropped his own counter-charges.

The affair was confused by further allegations that General Bernard W. Rogers, the NATO Supreme Commander in Europe, was implicated but this was never substantiated, although it was admitted that the personal relations between the two men were poor.

The minister made a statement to the Bundestag's defence committee on 18 January 1984, but failed to satisfy the SPD and the Greens, who called for his resignation. The West German press also were almost unanimously critical of the minister. Against this background, Chancellor Kohl ordered a parliamentary inquiry and the ministry a separate inquiry into the performance of MAD. He nevertheless decided on 1 February both that Manfred Wörner, who had twice offered to resign, should remain as defence minister and that the general should be reinstated with full honours. He retired in the April in accordance with an earlier agreement.

The parliamentary and ministry inquiries resulted in an announcement on 15 June 1984 that MAD would be reorganised and its staffing reduced by half.

Land (plural Länder)   Traditionally, an autonomous province. In contemporary Germany, a region with distinct political powers and responsibilities in the German federal system. (See sections 2.1, 2.2 and 6 for fuller particulars.)

Landtag   The regional parliament.

NATO   The North Atlantic Treaty Organisation (NATO) was established by a treaty signed on 4 April 1949 between the signatories of the Brussels Pact and America, and committed all members to provide mutual assistance to any member(s) under attack. West Germany joined on 8 May 1955.

The Brussels Pact had been signed in March 1948 and committed Belgium, Britain, France, Luxembourg and the Netherlands to go to war if any of them was attacked. As a successor to the Anglo-French Dunkirk Treaty of March 1947, the Pact left open the possibility of use against Germany, although by now the Soviet Union was envisaged as the more likely opponent.

Pankow   The district in the Soviet Sector of Berlin where the East German government was first located. It was used by the West German press to refer to that government partly for convenience, like Westminster or Whitehall, but also to avoid implying that it enjoyed any status.

Paris Agreements   The Agreements were signed at the NATO Conference in Paris on 23 October 1954, and embodied the decisions reached at the Nine-Power Conference held at Lancaster House, London, from 28 September–3 October the same year.

They featured a series of Four-Power, Nine-Power, and Fourteen-Power Agreements, together with a series of important protocols. The Four-Power Agreements terminated the occupation regime, restored West German sovereignty and regulated West German relations with America,

Britain and France by the conclusion of a convention on the retention of foreign forces in West Germany. The Nine-Power Agreements governed the accession of West Germany (and Italy) to the Brussels Treaty Organisation, now renamed the Western European Union (WEU). A series of protocols modified the 1948 Brussels Treaty to allow for the entry of West Germany and Italy, and to regulate armaments and arms control. Under them, West Germany undertook not to manufacture atomic, biological or chemical weapons, guided and long-distance missiles, warships of more than 3,000 tons or submarines of more than 300 tons, and strategic bombers. The Fourteen-Power Agreements were consequential to West Germany's membership of NATO and strengthened the organisation's structure.

Red Army Faction (*Rote Armee Fraktion – RAF*)   West German terrorist movement which grew out of the extreme far-left wing of the student protest movement of the 1960s. Its aim was to overthrow western capitalism, as it conceived it, and to ferment an international Marxist revolution. Its main targets were accordingly military, commercial and political, and they are listed in chronological order in section 2.9. It argued that violent attacks on American and capitalist targets were justified by the role of both in the Vietnam War. Its most important leaders, Andreas Baader and Ulrike Meinhof, who gave the RAF its more popular name of the 'Baader-Meinhof Group' were arrested in 1976 and 1972, committing suicide in prison in 1977 and 1976 respectively, but the movement remained active until the early 1990s, having diversified into a range of co-operating groups of which the 'June 2 movement' was one of the more distinct. Its last prominent victim was Detlev Rohwedder, the head of the Treuhandanstalt privatisation agency in April 1991. The movement had links with parallel movements in France and Italy, the Palestinian resistance and at least elements in the East German government. Several RAF members were arrested in East Germany after unification.

Many members of the group were well, even highly, educated and it was sustained in part by a strand of tacit sympathy in West German opinion, particularly amongst intellectuals, which in due course found more constructive expression in the Green movement.

Red–black coalition   A coalition between the CDU and the SPD, as in the 'grand coalition' under Chancellor Kiesinger between 1966 and 1969. Similar coalitions have occurred in various *Länder*, most notably in Berlin after unification when the SPD declined to co-operate with the PDS.

Red–green coalition   A coalition between the SPD and the Greens, as in the City of Frankfurt from June 1989 and West Berlin 1989–90, although in the particular circumstances of West Berlin the coalition was between the SPD and the *Alternative Liste*.

In a number of other cases, there have been informal understandings between the Greens and minority SPD administrations.

Such a coalition remains a possibility at the national level at a future date, particularly if the FDP splits or fails to clear the '5 per cent hurdle', or if there is major dissension between the CDU and the CSU.

Reichstag   The German parliament in Berlin before Hitler. Despite severe damage both under Hitler and during the War, the building survives and is being totally reconstructed for the Bundestag when it moves to Berlin.

SDS (*Sozialistischer Deutscher Studentenbund*)   Founded 1946, and at that time directed exclusively at university reform. Split in 1961 between the faction loyal to the SPD and that seeking the radical reform of West Germany and an end to western involvement in the Vietnam War. Opposed to the Communism of East Germany and the Soviet bloc, its role models were Mao Zhe Dong, Ho Chi Minh, Fidel Castro and Che Guevara. Although small in itself, with some 1,600 members, it functioned as the centre of what was dubbed the extra-parliamentary opposition, so called because the formation of the 'grand coalition' in December 1966 was perceived by many on the left, by no means just students, as fundamentally weakening the parliamentary opposition.

It was argued that the 'establishment' had concentrated exclusively since the War on rebuilding the economy and neglected its wider democratic responsibilities. More immediately, and in this respect there were close parallels with France in particular, students were highly critical of the style of university education, which was perceived as being autocratic and out of touch. Although the universities were willing to meet some of the complaints, they totally rejected the demand that professors, lecturers and students enjoy parity in university governance.

The demonstrations by the extra-parliamentary opposition increasingly alarmed the authorities, and on 11 December 1967 the ministry of the interior declared the SDS a danger to the West German constitution. By February 1968 it was considering banning it accordingly.

The tension came to a head with the attempted murder of Rudi Dutschke, the SDS leader, in West Berlin on 11 April. Violent rioting erupted there and in a number of West German cities, with the offices of the Springer newspaper group being a particular target. The group controlled some 30–40 per cent of total West German newspaper circulation and its two most influential titles, *Die Welt* and *Bild-Zeitung* had been intensely critical, and often intemperate in language, on the subject of left-wing intellectuals and militant students. The death of a press photographer on 17 April and of a student the following day, both from injuries received during the rioting in Munich, marked the end of the disturbances.

The government, clearly relieved, decided that the state had not in fact been endangered and that banning the SDS would merely engender sympathy for it. Axel Springer did, however, bow to public concern and the resulting Günther Commission on the concentration of press ownership by selling four of his magazines on 24 June.

Social market economy (*Soziale Marktwirtschaft*)   The economic basis on which West Germany was built, it was a fusion by Professor Ludwig Erhard of capitalist market principles with concepts of worker participation and worker rights more associated in many countries with the left. However, concepts of social rights go back in Germany to Bismarck in the nineteenth century, and the social market economy was conceived in part as a pre-emptive step against socialism. Its best-known and most widely praised expression has been co-determination (*Mitbestimmung*) whereby both sides of industry seek to reach a consensus on company policy.

The concept, sometimes known as the 'Rhenish model', has been compared unfavourably in the 1990s with the 'Anglo-Saxon model' of competitive capitalism focused on deregulation, and been accused of rigidity and stifling initiative. It is alleged to have generated unsustainable excess. Germany has the world's highest hourly wages and shortest average working week. Co-determination has not prevented the highest levels of unemployment since the rise of Hitler. Changes have certainly been felt necessary with takeovers becoming much more accepted and the pursuance of contentious amalgamations, such as that of Krupp and Thyssen. Co-determination has always had its German opponents. Hans-Martin Schleyer, head of the German employers' federation, and later to be assassinated by the RAF, sought unsuccessfully to have the 1976 co-determination law declared unconstitutional. Nevertheless, much of the unfavourable comment has come from Anglo-Saxon sources, and it is far from clear that an approach which served Germany well for 40 years, with its stress on common purpose, does not still have a very positive role to play.

***Spiegel* affair**   If the Flick affair was West Germany's greatest political scandal, then the *Spiegel* affair was easily its greatest political controversy. It opened apparently innocuously with an article in *Der Spiegel*, a leading West German weekly news magazine published in Hamburg, on 10 October 1962. The article purported to give an account of the NATO exercise 'Fallex 62' the previous month, and *Der Spiegel* maintained that the exercise was the first to be based on the assumption that a Third World War would start with an attack on western Europe by the forces of the Warsaw Pact, resulting in millions of dead. Moreover, the article claimed that West Germany's military and civil defence preparations were inadequate.

The affair proper broke on 26 October with the searching and sealing of the magazine's editorial offices by the criminal police on the orders of Chancellor Adenauer and Franz-Josef Strauss, defence minister. The publisher, Rudolf Augstein, and a managing editor were arrested. Other arrests followed on subsequent days and the author, Dr Conrad Ahlers, the magazine's defence expert, was detained on holiday in Spain. His detention was inspired by the personal intervention of Strauss.

The public prosecutor's office in Bonn maintained that those arrested were suspected of having committed treason and active bribery, and that key issues of national defence had been so handled that the existence of West Germany and the security and freedom of the German people had been endangered. It added that the initiative in applying for legal proceedings had been taken by private persons. This was followed by allegations on behalf of the magazine that the offending material had been cleared with the relevant authorities before publication. The status of the material found by the police in the magazine's offices was similarly contested. The prosecutor maintained that it was classified and secret, the magazine that it was old and unrelated to the case and that in any case it was not an offence to hold it.

The affair then acquired a specifically political hue when Dr Wolfgang Stammberger, FDP minister of justice, asked on 31 October to be relieved of his post, as he had not been advised of the action in advance by either the state prosecutor's office or his own CDU under-secretary of state. The four other FDP members threatened to resign likewise unless the under-secretaries of state for defence and justice were dismissed and assurances given on future co-operation between the coalition partners: demands which were met by Chancellor Adenauer on 5 November. These political developments were played out against a backdrop of growing public concern. It was noted that a similar article had appeared in another newspaper without action being taken, and that Franz-Josef Strauss, the defence minister, had been the subject of countless attacks by *Der Spiegel* over the years. The search was deemed illegal and the police action widely felt to be disagreeably reminiscent of Nazi methods. A further dimension of tension was that between the national and the Hamburg *Land* governments as to their respective prerogatives.

Pressure grew on Franz-Josef Strauss on the specific grounds that he had in the interim denied his role in the detention of Dr Ahlers in Spain. The SPD called for his resignation, singling out his description of Rudolf Augstein as a traitor before he had been tried, and the FDP members of the government resigned en bloc to facilitate a government reorganisation. Strauss had no option but to resign on 30 November.

Attempts by *Der Spiegel* to have the occupation of its premises declared unconstitutional were abortive and arrests continued into December, but the affair nevertheless petered out. The precise source of much of

Der Spiegel's information, the essential element in any successful prosecution for treason, was never established. Bribery could never be substantiated. The real loser was Strauss and the winner the press at large, including *Der Spiegel*, which was henceforth to play a much more prominent role in the democratic process. If Adenauer himself was not directly damaged, the affair nevertheless underlined the extent to which his authoritarian style was unsuited to the more confident and liberal mood of the 1960s.

Sudetenland   The border regions to the north west and south west of what is now the Czech Republic which were included within the new state of Czechoslovakia established by the Treaty of Versailles in 1919. They were included so as to give the new state defensible frontiers, but were predominantly German in population. These so-called Sudeten Germans were the subject of suspicion at best and discrimination at worst in interwar Czechoslovakia, and were highly responsive to Hitler's extreme nationalism. Powerful Nazi pressures both from Germany itself and from the Sudetenland, which the British and the French were unwilling to help the Czechoslovak government to withstand, culminated in the Munich Agreement of 1938, which transferred the regions to Germany.

They reverted to Czechoslovakia with the defeat of Germany in 1945 and the Potsdam Agreement endorsed the expulsion of the Sudeten Germans from Czechoslovakia 'in an orderly manner'. In practice, however, the passions engendered by the War made the expulsions summary and brutal. The dispossessed settled all over Germany, but particularly in Bavaria, where they in due course became influential in the CSU, reinforcing its resistance to any agreement with the Soviet bloc which would confirm the pre-1938 German–Czech border as permanent under international law.

The existence of the Munich Agreement was to make the normalisation of West German relations with Czechoslovakia under Chancellor Brandt's Ostpolitik appreciably more difficult than was the case with Poland. The Czechs, mindful that Munich had initiated the dismemberment of their country under Hitler, pressed for it to be declared invalid from the very beginning (*ab initio*). The Germans were anxious, however, that such a declaration could have exposed individual Sudetens to unforeseen legal liabilities and in particular to charges of treason for having served in the German Army. They were also concerned at possible Czech claims for reparations. The Treaty of Prague as finally agreed in 1973 avoided those pitfalls by declaring the Munich Agreement 'null and void', but nevertheless essentially reflected Czech interests.

The normalisation of West German–Czech relations did not, however, solve the Sudeten question and it resurfaced after unification in 1990.

The Sudetens urged the German government to press for a full apology for the expulsions from the Czechs and for the right of Sudetens to reclaim their lost homes or at least to settle again in their homeland. They thus pressed for the cancellation of the Beneš decrees denying property rights to ethnic Germans. In practice, the German–Czech compromise declaration, painfully reached at the end of 1996, talked merely of 'regret'. The Sudeten community was mollified neither by the terms nor by the way in which they were reached, with Franz Neubauer, the community's chairman, angrily declaring, 'The government coalition obviously did not think it necessary to inform [us] of the exact wording of the declaration. The decisions are once again being taken over the heads of those concerned.'

Traffic light coalition (*Ampelcoalition*)   A governing coalition between the SPD (red), FDP (amber) and the Greens, as established at *Land* level in Brandenburg and Bremen in 1991.

Volkskammer   The lower house of the East German parliament and, for most of East German history, the only house. For the reasons explained in section 2.3, its power, except at the very beginning and very end, was nominal.

War crimes   The definition of war crimes prior to the Nuremberg trials built in part on precedent but also broke new ground. The concept of crimes against humanity reflected established conventions such as the prohibition on the shooting of prisoners, but a completely new crime was defined: 'conspiracy to wage aggressive war'. This was initially favoured by the Americans but by neither Britain nor the Soviet Union and was attacked by defence counsel at the time as being both retrospective and a concept quite unknown to international relations. It must also be said that it is an offence of which leaders of all the Allies were to be guilty to a greater or lesser extent in the following half century. On the other hand it was an attempt to come to terms with the unleashing of a scale of violence unparalleled for some centuries, and as such was arguably a psychological necessity if Europe was to recover.

The trials at Nuremberg in 1946 and elsewhere were 'victors' justice', in the sense that only the Germans and their allies were tried and only the victors determined where an offence had been committed. This was obviously inadequate, but equally obviously, inevitable. The trials were at least fair in the narrower legal sense. Less acceptable in some respects was the failure to indict, or the premature release of, those whom the Allies thought would be useful to them in the postwar world.

The Nazi leaders accused at Nuremberg and the sentences imposed are detailed below:

Hermann Göring	Death (committed suicide before execution)
Joachim von Ribbentrop	Death
Field Marshal Wilhelm Keitel	Death
*Ernst Kaltenbrunner	Death
Alfred Rosenberg	Death
Wilhelm Frick	Death
Hans Frank	Death
Julius Streicher	Death
Fritz Sauckel	Death
Col.-Gen. Alfred Jodl	Death (subsequently exonerated by a German denazification court)
*Arthur Seyss-Inquart	Death
Rudolf Hess	Life imprisonment
Walter Funk	Life imprisonment
Grand Admiral Erich Raeder	Life imprisonment
*Baldur von Schirach	20 years' imprisonment
Albert Speer	20 years' imprisonment
Konstantin Freiherr von Neurath	15 years' imprisonment
Grand Admiral Karl Dönitz	10 years' imprisonment
Hjalmar Schacht	Acquitted
Franz von Papen	Acquitted
Hans Fritzsche	Acquitted, but subsequently rearrested by the Germans and sentenced to 9 years' imprisonment with hard labour.
Martin Bormann	Death, *in absentia*

* Austrian by birth

The drama of the Nuremberg trials has tended to draw attention from the fact that there were a number of overlapping legal processes. These were:

1. The almost immediate trial of Allied collaborators and Allied Nazi sympathisers who had operated in Germany, such as the Briton William Joyce (Lord Haw-Haw). Most were accused of treason and the majority rapidly executed.
2. The prosecution of leading German political and industrial leaders by the Allies, of which the 1946 Nuremberg trials were the initial part.
3.* The prosecution, initially by the Allies but continued by the Germans, of those accused of committing such crimes as mass murder themselves. The commandants of the annihilation camps were prominent examples.

4.* Parallel prosecutions in all the Allied countries of Germans and nationals who had committed similar offences outside Germany.

5. The exceptional case of the capture, trial and execution by Israel of Adolf Eichmann.

6. The host of denazification tribunals in which war crimes featured only to the extent to which former Nazis were deemed to be guilty by association.

* Proceedings under categories 3 and 4 were still being brought in 1998, and more than 80,000 Germans had been convicted by the end of 1964.

SECTION THIRTEEN

Bibliographical essay

Although a large number of books on Germany since 1945 have been written in, or translated into, English, the field presents certain difficulties. The early division of Germany means that the overwhelming majority of titles relate to either East or West Germany, and there are comparatively few of either which are really histories as distinct from political assessments or studies of particular phases. There is also the problem of perspective. The history of Germany more than anywhere else in Europe is the history of the Cold War and, almost inevitably, interpretations of German history reflect to a greater or lesser extent the stance of historians and commentators towards that wider conflict and the role of their country in it. Possibly for this reason, the coverage of the different aspects of German history since 1945 is very uneven, which arguably slants appreciation of the significance of specific periods and events. There is the final problem that certain developments since 1945, of which unification is only the most obvious, put Germany on a new path and made earlier approaches far less relevant. Books on Germany have tended to date very rapidly in consequence, and may well continue to do so.

The 4th edition of William Carr's well-known *A History of Germany 1815–90* (Edward Arnold, London, 1991) brings the story up to unification, but is comparatively brief on the period since 1945. Mary Fulbrook (ed.), *German History since 1800* (Edward Arnold, London, 1997) contains as its Part IV five essays on Germany since 1945, and Richard J. Evans (ed.), *Rereading German History 1800–1996. From Unification to Reunification* (Routledge, London, 1997) contains as its Part V four essays on reunification and beyond. The last two of the thirteen chapters of Martin Kitchen, *Cambridge Illustrated History Germany* (Cambridge University Press, Cambridge, 1996) which takes the story back to Roman times, cover the period since 1945. The more useful work for most students is probably Mary Fulbrook, *The Fontana History of Germany 1918–1990* (Fontana, London, 1991). A. J. Ryder, *Twentieth Century Germany: From Bismarck to Brandt* (Macmillan, Basingstoke, 1973), although now rather old, remains good on the occupation regime. Easily the most comprehensive narrative, although it remains somewhat episodic, is Dennis L. Bark and David R. Gress, *A History of West Germany, Volume 1: From Shadow to Substance 1945–63*, and *Volume 2: Democracy and its Discontents 1963–88* (Basil Blackwell, Oxford, 1989). Scrupulously fair, it is nevertheless written from an avowedly right-wing perspective. Eva Kolinsky (ed.), *The Federal Republic of Germany* (Berg, Oxford, 1991) and particularly A. J. Nicholls (ed.), *The Bonn Republic: West German Democracy 1945–1990* (Longman, Harlow, 1997) are more up to date, although similarly confined to the West.

The most comprehensive book on East Germany probably remains David Childs, *The GDR, Moscow's German Ally* (George Allen and Unwin,

London, 1983). Martin McCauley's *The German Democratic Republic since 1945* (Macmillan, London and Basingstoke, 1983) focuses more on the specifically historical and has a detailed chronology. It is usefully read in conjunction with David Childs (ed.), *Honecker's Germany* (George Allen and Unwin, London, 1985) which ranges more widely. Henry Krisch, *The German Democratic Republic, The Search for Identity* (Westview Press, Boulder, Colorado, 1985) is also valuable, as is Kurt Sontheimer and Wilhelm Bleek, *The Government and Politics of East Germany* (translated Ursula Price, Hutchinson University Library, London, 1975). Although inevitably dated, it is both thorough and fair. Norman M. Naimark, *The Russians in Germany. A History of the Soviet Zone of Occupation 1945–49* (Belknap/Harvard University Press, Cambridge, Mass., 1995) is an exhaustive study of the period in question. Lawrence L. Whetten, *Germany East and West, Conflicts, Collaboration and Confrontation* (New York University Press, New York, 1980) and A. James McAdams, *East Germany and Détente* (Cambridge University Press, Cambridge, 1985) consider the foreign policy dimension. David Childs, Thomas A. Baylis and Marilyn Rueschemeyer (eds), *East Germany in Comparative Perspective* (Routledge, London, 1989) was rather overtaken by events. Mary Fulbrook, *Anatomy of a Dictatorship. Inside the GDR 1949–89* (Oxford University Press, Oxford, 1995) contains much valuable information, but is not really a history in the narrower sense. Heinz Heitzer, *GDR An Historical Outline* (Verlag Zeit im Bild, Dresden, 1981) presents the official SED view. The definitive history of East Germany in the historical context is probably yet to be written.

The most detailed study of the SED itself is probably Peter C. Ludz, *The Changing Party Elite in East Germany* (translated by M. I. T., Cambridge, Mass., 1972). Martin McCauley, *Marxism-Leninism in the German Democratic Republic* (Macmillan, Basingstoke, 1979) is, however, more up to date and more accessible. David Childs and Richard Popplewell, *The Stasi* (Macmillan, Basingstoke, 1996) is likely to remain the definitive study of the security police. Anne McElvoy, *The Saddled Cow, East Germany's Life and Legacy* (Faber and Faber, London, 1992) is excellent as a westerner's inside view of daily life. Eva Kolinsky (ed.), *Between Hope and Fear, Everyday Life in Post-Unification East Germany* (Keele University Press, Keele, 1995) explores the human impact, with Leipzig as a case study, and Dinah Dodds and Pam Allen-Thompson (eds), *The Wall in my Backyard, East German Women in Transition* (University of Massachusets Press, Amherst, 1994) explores the same impact from a specifically feminine standpoint. For those who read German, the most comprehensive guide to East German personalities is Jochen Cerný (ed.), *Wer war wer – DDR* (Christoph Links Verlag, Berlin, 1992).

Returning to West Germany, Marion Donhöff, translated by Gabriele Annan, *The Makers of the New Germany from Konrad Adenauer to Helmut Schmidt* (Weidenfeld and Nicolson, London, 1982) and Terence Prittie,

The Velvet Chancellors. A History of Post-War Germany (Frederick Muller, London, 1979) both concentrate on the contribution of successive Chancellors. Stephen Padgett (ed.), *Adenauer to Kohl* (C. Hurst and Co., London, 1994) adopts a similar approach, but is appreciably more up to date. The highly polemical Geoffrey Stewart-Smith, MP (ed.), *Brandt and the Destruction of NATO* (Foreign Affairs Publishing, London, 1973) underlines the depth of the opposition with which Brandt had to contend.

Numerous books explore sectoral topics. The legacy of war crimes on the children of those convicted is examined in Gerald Posner, *Hitler's Children* (Heinemann, London, 1991), Peter Sichrovsky, *Born Guilty, Children of Nazi Families* (translated Jean Steinberg, I. B. Tauris, London, 1988) and Dan Bar-On, *Legacy of Silence* (Harvard University Press, Cambridge, Mass. and London, 1989). The last of these is probably the most searching. *Brown Book War and Nazi Criminals in West Germany (State, economy, administration, army, justice, science)* (Verlag Zeit im Bild, Berlin, 1965) is the East German government's indictment of alleged Nazis in prominent positions in West Germany. It self-consciously echoes the anti-Fascist Brown Book published in Paris in 1933. Ralf Dahrendorf, *Society and Democracy in Germany* (Weidenfeld and Nicolson, London, 1968) and Karl Dietrich Bracher, *The German Dilemma. The Throes of Political Emancipation* (translated Richard Barry, Weidenfeld and Nicolson, London, 1974) can both be recommended as studies of German self-perception in the established West Germany.

The interaction of society, economy and politics in twentieth-century Germany is explored in V. R. Berghahn, *Modern Germany* (Cambridge University Press, Cambridge, 2nd edition, 1987). David Childs and Jeffrey Johnson, *West German Politics and Society* (Croom Helm, London, 1981) is more limited in scope. It is usefully read in conjunction with William E. Paterson and Gordon Smith, *The West German Model. Perspectives in a Stable State* (Heinemann, London, 1981). John Ardagh, *Germany and the Germans* (Penguin Books, Harmondsworth, 3rd edition, 1995) paints a broad canvas.

More targeted in scope are Andrei S. Markovits, *The Politics of the West German Trade Unions* (Cambridge University Press, Cambridge, 1986), Alan Peacock and Hans Willgerodt (eds), *Germany's Social Market Economy: Origins and Evolution* (Macmillan, Basingstoke, 1989) and David Marsh, *The Bundesbank: The Bank that Rules Europe* (Heinemann, London, 1992). The contribution of women is discussed in Eva Kolinsky, *Women in West Germany. Life, Work and Politics* (Berg, Oxford, 1989) and Robert G. Moeller, *Protecting Motherhood. Women and the Family in the Politics of Post-war West Germany* (University of California Press, Berkeley, Los Angeles and Oxford, 1993).

Specific dimensions of West German foreign policy are considered in Lily Gardner Feldman, *The Special Relationship between West Germany and*

Israel (George Allen and Unwin, Boston, 1984), Julius W. Friend, *The Linchpin, French–German Relations 1950–90* (Praeger Publishers, New York, 1991) and Philip H. Gordon, *France, Germany and the Western Alliance* (Westview Press, Boulder, Colorado, 1995). The latter benefits from its later date of writing. Translated Susan Høivik, *The Federal Republic, Europe and the World. Perspectives on West German Foreign Policy* (Universitetsforlaget, Oslo, Bergen and Tromsø, 1980) and Avril Pittman, *From Ostpolitik to Reunification: West German–Soviet Relations since 1974* (Cambridge University Press, Cambridge, 1992) are more concerned with the Soviet Union.

Unification unleashed a flood of titles. Philip Zelikow and Condoleeza Rice give a step-by-step account in *Germany Unified and Europe Transformed, A study in statecraft* (Harvard University Press, Cambridge, Mass., 4th impression with new preface, 1997). Stephen F. Szabo, *The Diplomacy of German Unification* (St. Martins Press, New York, 1992) emphasises the extent to which East Germany's own politicians were marginalised by the whole process. Hanna Behrend (ed.), *German Unification. The Destruction of an Economy* (Pluto Press, London and East Haven, Ct, 1995) is a biting indictment of the policies adopted by the West. Most seek to predict the future of the new Germany, and may be fated to looking dated comparatively rapidly. They include: Wolfgang Heisenberg (ed.), *German Unification in European Perspective* (Brassey's (UK), London, 1991); Gregory F. Treverton, *America, Germany and the Future of Europe* (Princeton University Press, Princeton, New Jersey, 1992); Alan Watson, *The Germans. Who are They Now?* (Methuen, London, 1992); Gale A. Mattox and A. Bradley Shingleton (eds), *Germany at the Crossroads, Foreign and Domestic Policy Issues* (Westview Press, Boulder, Colorado, 1992); Peter Wallach and Ronald A. Francisco (eds), *United Germany. The Past, Politics, Prospects* (Praeger, Westport, Conn., 1992); Ernest D. Plock, *East German–West German Relations and the Fall of the GDR* (Westview Press, Boulder, Colorado, 1993); Elizabeth Pond, *Beyond the Wall, Germany's Road to Unification* (The Brookings Institute, Washington, 1993); Anulf Baring (ed.), *Germany's New Position in Europe* (Berg, Oxford, 1994); David Marsh, *Germany and Europe, The Crisis of Unity* (Heinemann, London, 1994); Manfred Görtemaker, *Unifying Germany 1989–90* (Macmillan, Basingstoke, 1994) and Derek Lewis and John R. P. McKenzie (eds), *The New Germany: Social, Political and Cultural Challenges of Unification* (University of Exeter Press, Exeter, 1995).

Politics students are well served. The standard works are David P. Conradt, *The German Polity* (Longman, White Plains, New York, 6th edition, 1996), Gordon A. Smith, William E. Paterson and Stephen Padgett (eds), *Developments in German Politics 2* (Macmillan, Basingstoke, 1996), and P. Pulzer, *German Politics 1945–95* (Oxford University Press, Oxford, 1995). Those seeking an earlier perspective are referred to Geoffrey K.

Roberts, *West German Politics* (Macmillan, Basingstoke, 1972) and Gordon Smith, *Democracy in Western Germany, Parties and Politics in the Federal Republic* (Heinemann, London, 2nd edition, 1982). Yves Mény, translated by Janet Lloyd, deals with the comparative angle in *Government and Politics in Western Europe (Britain, France, Italy, Germany)* (Oxford University Press, 2nd edition, 1993).

Further recent books on Germany, its postwar history and its place in the world include Peter H. Merkl (ed.), *The Federal Republic of Germany at Forty Five* (Macmillan, Basingstoke, 1995), Bertel Heurlin (ed.), *Germany in Europe in the Nineties* (Macmillan, Basingstoke, 1996), Jörg Brechtefeld, *Mitteleuropa and German Politics, 1848 to the Present* (Macmillan, Basingstoke, 1996), Michael Mertes, Steven Muller and Heinrich August Winkler (eds), *In Search of Germany* (Transaction Publishers, New Brunswick (USA) and London, 1996) and Stuart Parkes, *Understanding Contemporary Germany* (Routledge, London, 1997).

Tristam Carrington-Windo and Katrin Kohl, *A Dictionary of Contemporary Germany* (Hodder and Stoughton, London, 1996) is a concise guide to over 2,000 German acronyms and references.

For those who read German, the authoritative history is Karl Dietrich Bracher, Theodor Eschenburg, Joachim C. Fest and Eberhard Jäckel, *Geschichte der Bundesrepublik Deutschland* (Deutsche Verlagsanstalt, Stuttgart, F. A. Brockhaus, Wiesbaden, in five volumes from 1981).

The authoritative, regularly updated text of the *Grundgesetz* (Basic Law) with commentary appears under the names of the late Dr Theodor Maunz, and Dr Günter Dürig, and the current federal president, Dr Roman Herzog, (C. H. Beck, Munich). A comparable guide to German constitutional law is Dr Ernst Benda, Prof. Werner Maihofer and Dr Hans-Jochen Vogel, with Konrad Hesse (eds), *Handbuch des Verfassungsrechts der Bundesrepublik Deutschland* (Walter de Gruyter, Berlin, 1983).

Gerhard A. Ritter and Merith Niehuss, *Wahlen in Deutschland 1946–1991. Ein Handbuch* and *Wahlen in Deutschland 1990–1994* (C. H. Beck, Munich, 1991 and 1995) give an exhaustive analysis of German election results at all levels.

Biographies and memoirs are a valuable source of further information, although in the latter case they can conceal as much as they reveal. Biographies include Paul Weymar, *Konrad Adenauer. The Authorised Biography* (translated Peter de Mendelssohn, Andre Deutsch, London, 1957), Charles Wighton, *Adenauer – Democratic Dictator* (Frederick Muller, London, 1963), Arnold J. Heidenheimer, *Adenauer and the CDU* (Martinus Nijhoff, The Hague, 1960); Terence Prittie, *Willy Brandt* (Weidenfeld and Nicolson, London, 1974), Barbara Marshall, *Willy Brandt* (Cardinal, London, 1990); Jonathan Carr, *Helmut Schmidt, Helmsman of Germany* (Weidenfeld and Nicolson, London, 1985); Lewis J. Edinger, *Kurt Schumacher* (Oxford University Press, Oxford, 1965).

Memoirs and policy works include Konrad Adenauer, *Memoirs 1945–53* (translated Beate Ruhm von Oppen, Weidenfeld and Nicolson, London, 1966); Willy Brandt, *My Life in Politics* (translated Anthea Bell, Hamish Hamilton, London, 1992, and Penguin, Harmondsworth, 1993) and *People and Politics: The Years 1960–75* (translated J. M. Brownjohn, 1978); Ludwig Erhard, *Prosperity through Competition* (translated Edith Temple Roberts and John B. Wood, 3rd edition, Thames and Hudson, London, 1962) and *The Economics of Success* (translated J. A. Arengo-Jones and D. J. S. Thomson, Thames and Hudson, London, 1963); Erich Honecker, *From My Life* (Pergamon, Oxford, 1981); Petra Kelly, *Fighting for Hope* (translated Marianne Howarth, Chatto and Windus, London, 1984) and *Thinking Green* (published posthumously, Parallax Press, Berkeley, California, 1994); Helmut Schmidt, *Men and Powers* (translated Ruth Hein, Jonathan Cape, London, 1990) and *A Grand Strategy for the West* (Yale University Press, New Haven and London, 1985); Franz-Josef Strauss, *The Grand Design* (edited and translated Brian Connell, Weidenfeld and Nicolson, London, 1965) and *Challenge and Response: A Programme for Europe* (translated Henry Fox, Weidenfeld and Nicolson, London, 1969).

Maps

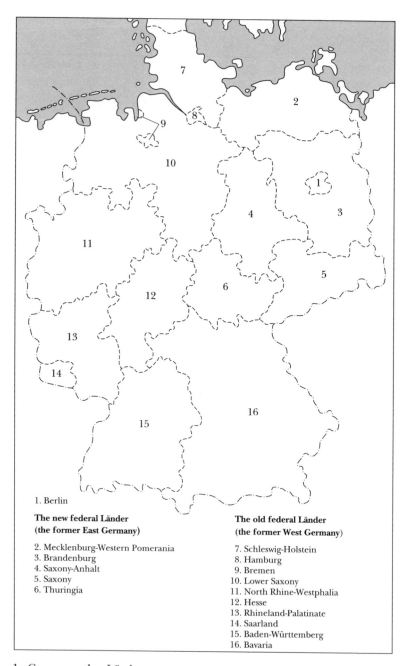

1. Berlin

**The new federal Länder
(the former East Germany)**

2. Mecklenburg-Western Pomerania
3. Brandenburg
4. Saxony-Anhalt
5. Saxony
6. Thuringia

**The old federal Länder
(the former West Germany)**

7. Schleswig-Holstein
8. Hamburg
9. Bremen
10. Lower Saxony
11. North Rhine-Westphalia
12. Hesse
13. Rhineland-Palatinate
14. Saarland
15. Baden-Württemberg
16. Bavaria

1. Germany: the *Länder*

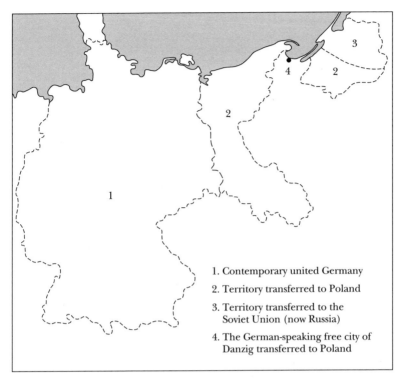

1. Contemporary united Germany

2. Territory transferred to Poland

3. Territory transferred to the
   Soviet Union (now Russia)

4. The German-speaking free city of
   Danzig transferred to Poland

2. Germany within its 1937 boundaries and the territory lost in 1945

Index

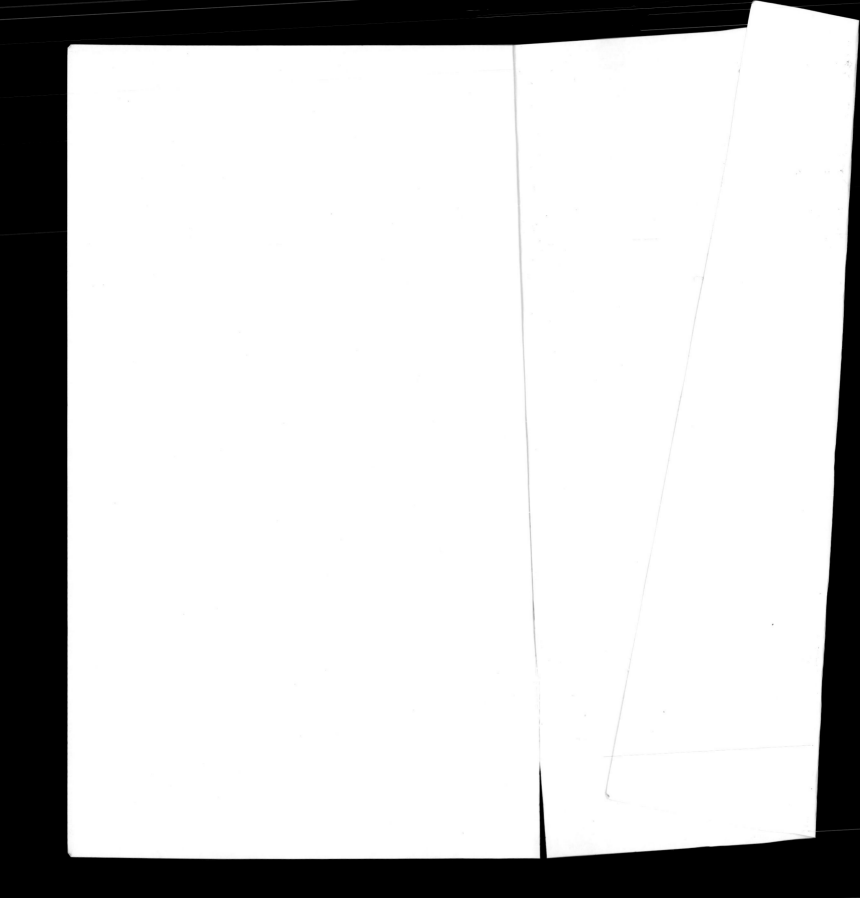